GLOBALIZATION AND
INTERNATIONAL SOCIAL WORK

Contemporary Social Work Studies

Contemporary Social Work Studies (CSWS) is a series disseminating high quality new research and scholarship in the discipline and profession of social work. The series promotes critical engagement with contemporary issues relevant across the social work community and captures the diversity of interests currently evident at national, international and local levels.

CSWS is located in the School of Social Sciences at the University of Southampton and is a development from the successful series of books published by Ashgate in association with CEDR (the Centre for Evaluative and Developmental Research) from 1991.

Globalization and International Social Work

Postmodern Change and Challenge

MALCOLM PAYNE
St Christopher's Hospice, UK

and

GURID AGA ASKELAND
Diakonhjemmet University College, Norway

ASHGATE

. Malcolm Payne and Gurid Aga Askeland have asserted their moral right under the Copyright, Designs and Patents Act, 1988, to be identified as the authors of this work.

Gurid Aga Askeland is supported by the Norwegian Non-fiction Writers and Translators Association.

Published by
Ashgate Publishing Limited
Gower House
Croft Road
Aldershot
Hampshire GU11 3HR
England

Ashgate Publishing Company
Suite 420
101 Cherry Street
Burlington, VT 05401-4405
USA

Ashgate website: http://www.ashgate.com

British Library Cataloguing in Publication Data
Payne, Malcolm, 1947-
  Globalization and international social work : postmodern
  change and challenge. - (Contemporary social work studies)
  1. Social service - International cooperation
  2. Globalization - Social aspects
  I. Title II. Askeland, Gurid Aga
  361

Library of Congress Cataloging-in-Publication Data
Payne, Malcolm, 1947-
  Globalization and international social work : postmodern change and challenge / by Malcolm Payne and Gurid Aga Askeland.
     p. cm. -- (Contemporary social work studies)
  Includes bibliographical references and indexes.
  ISBN-13: 978-0-7546-4946-5
  ISBN-10: 0-7546-4946-6
  1. Social service--International cooperation. 2. Globalization--Social aspects. I. Askeland, Gurid Aga, 1947- II. Title.

HV41.P37 2008
361.3--dc22

2008002370

ISBN-13: 9780754649465

Printed and bound in Great Britain by MPG Books Ltd, Bodmin, Cornwall.

Contents

List of Figures and Tables

Acknowledgements

We come from the UK and Norway respectively, and our interest in the subject of this book emerges from our involvement in international social work over many years. We wrote this book jointly, with some of the material based on papers delivered at various conferences and articles written together.

Acknowledgements to:

Norwegian Non-fiction Writers and Translators Association, for a grant to Gurid Aga Askeland while working on this book.

Barbara Monroe, Chief Executive, St Christopher's Hospice, London for allowing Malcolm Payne the flexibility to work on this book.

The editors of the journals for permission to adapt materials that first appeared in our articles in their pages:

Social work education's cultural hegemony, *International Social Work* 49, 731–743, mainly used in Chapter 4.

What is valid knowledge for social workers? *Social Work in Europe*, 8: 3, 13–23, mainly used in Chapter 5.

The postmodern student: piloting through uncertainty, *Journal of Teaching in Social Work* 26: 3/4, 167–179, mainly used in Chapter 7.

Broadening the mind: cross-national activities in social work, *European Journal of Social Work* 4: 3, 263–274, mainly used in Chapter 8.

Distance education and international social work education, *European Journal of Social Work* 10: 2, 161–74, mainly used in Chapter 9.

Malcolm Payne
Gurid Aga Askeland

The Words We Use

Malcolm Payne and Gurid Aga Askeland

North, South and Western

In literature about international issues, people argue about how to refer to the economic and social development of particular countries. Should we say that a country is developed, or developing, which hides an assumption that development is a desirable end result? Should we say that a country is a Western country, meaning an economically developed country whose culture originates from European and North American models? Some writers refer to the North (the northern hemisphere) and the South, implying that most countries in the North are economically developed and most in the South are not. Some countries in the Southern hemisphere, such as Australia, are 'Northern' and 'Western' in their social and economic development and culture. Some countries do not fit into any such category. Examples might be countries, such as China, experiencing rapid economic and social change and development alongside substantial poverty and inequality or Eastern European 'transition' economies, which are moving from being part of the Soviet sphere of influence to participation in European economic markets.

We have chosen to refer to economically developed countries with a largely European or North American culture as Western countries. We refer to North and South as collective terms denoting the difference between rich and economically developed nations and poorer nations with less developed economies.

'Client' and 'Service User'

There are problems with putting people into categories. Many social workers dislike giving the people they work with category names like 'client' or 'service user'. It sometimes leads to their being called 'the clients' or 'the users' in a disrespectful way. Both terms are unacceptable to some of the people to whom they are applied.

We use the word 'client' because internationally it is the most inclusive and generally understandable term. We also use the term 'service user' or 'user' where the circumstances are appropriate, for example, when we refer to people who are receiving packages of services or referring to services to people with learning disabilities where this term has the widest currency.

Glossary of Abbreviations

Abbreviation	Meaning
CCTV	Closed circuit television
CD	Compact Disk – a technology for reproduction of digitized data and sound
CIP	Cleveland International Program
DVD	Digital Video Disk – a technology for reproduction of digitized data, sound and visual material
G7, G8, G10	Group of 7, 8 or 10 nations – regular meetings of combinations of rich nations
IASSW	International Association of Schools of Social Work
ICT	Information and Communication Technology
IFSW	International Federation of Social Workers
IMF	International Monetary Fund
INGOs	International Non-governmental Organisations
MST	Multi Systemic Therapy
NASW	National Association of Social Workers, USA
NGOs	Non-governmental Organisations
OECD	Organisation for Economic Cooperation and Development – group of countries with democratic government and market economy
PR	Public Relations
UK	United Kingdom
UN	United Nations
UNDP	United Nations Development Program
UNICEF	United Nations International Children's Fund
WSF	World Social Forum

Chapter 1

International Social Work Practice and Education in a Globalized Postmodern World

Introduction

Social work has always been international. Recently it has become more so; a trend that continues. In this book, we aim to examine what is happening, some of the explanations of why it has come about, some consequences of this internationalization for social workers, their profession and their education and what we think they might do about it.

In this book we are asking, and trying to answer, a series of questions about international social work in the context of postmodern globalized societies. To what extent is there an international social work? If there is, is it any more than Western social work influencing the wider world through postcolonial cultural hegemony? Is postcolonial hegemony an outcome of economic, political and cultural globalization affecting welfare policy, social work knowledge and social work education? What could we do to create an international social work that is more open to local cultural requirements?

Social work education is an important focus in international social work. We have given it considerable attention for this reason. We have done so also because it is a significant context in which knowledge is developed for social work and because education is an important social structure in which social work becomes part of a globalized international market.

Social work is a product of modernism in Western states as industrialized economies developed in the late 19th century. That is, it emerged from an idealist belief (Offer, 2006) that the state could overcome social problems, using science and knowledge to resolve social problems. In most countries, therefore, it is part of state services and claims a rational evidence as the basis of its practice. In rich Western countries social work is substantially part of the state: it is organized public welfare provision. This is so even where services are offered by profit or not-for-profit organizations, because they are mainly funded by states. Its commitment to science means that social work as a profession and as a way of intervening in people's lives relies on the assumption that it can develop universal knowledge. Such knowledge seeks to provide explanation and understanding about human beings, their behaviour and their society. The idea is that universal knowledge will apply to everyone, in whatever culture or society they live. Therefore, it can provide firm evidence for deciding how best to act when intervening with any human beings. Relying on a claim to universal knowledge assumes, uncritically, that such knowledge may be transferred from Western societies in which most of it is developed to societies in the South with markedly different cultures and access to resources. Please refer to 'The words we use' at the beginning of the book to understand what we mean by 'the South'.

In the 21st century, globalization leads to changes that challenge social work practice and education, and the idea of postmodernism challenges the validity of a universal knowledge base. This is because where societies are built on different cultural and social assumptions postmodernism raises questions about the dominance of any particular set of ideas, both generally and in social work.

Postmodernism proposes that social phenomena such as social work vary according to the social and historical context in which they operate. An international social work, therefore, raises questions about whether Western models of social work practice and organization are universal in their application. We argue in this book that they may provide a framework for understanding social work, but that different cultural assumptions and social needs require different social works.

Among the most important consequences of the development of postmodern, globalized social works is inequality within and across societies. This is important because inequalities create social strains between different groups and psychological stresses for individuals. Social work has a commitment to social justice. Our experience as social workers dealing with individuals and small groups leads us to concern about the impact of the social on the personal. Social work that deals only with psychological problems fails to handle the consequences of unfairness and inequality and with social factors that lead to the problems. Social processes that create inequality and injustice constantly change. This means that practice and education need to be aware of inequalities created by new social trends, to understand them and how they affect individuals and communities. That is the reason for this book: globalization, postmodernism, and postcolonialism are current issues in interpersonal relations between people.

In this book, we explore how these issues affect the people that social workers work with and how social work can respond. We are concerned with ideas that affect the everyday practice of social workers, social work students and their educators, so while this is not a how-to-do-it book, ideas about a practice will have an effect on that practice. This is because social work is always a practice as well as a set of ideas. Practice always arises from the ideas that we have about what we want to accomplish and how we want to do it. So, this book aims to achieve a social work that contextualizes practice within the current changes that affect our world.

In this book, we explore, reflect on, analyse and seek to influence the conception of social work as an activity in an increasingly globalized, postmodern society. Usually, social workers see their practice and education as mainly formed by local issues and national policies. Increasingly, though, international trends and pressures influence it. We focus in this book on the implications of the interaction of the international, the national and the local for social work practice and education. We argue that this requires a concern for practice, because that is what all social work ultimately aims at: to intervene usefully in the lives of troubled people and in the current social changes that trouble them. However, we also say that this requires a concern for social work education, because this is the main instrument by which knowledge and social understanding becomes incorporated into practice. Therefore, we have to look at education, and how it responds to globalization and postmodernism, because it is a crucial element of how we may enable social work practice to respond to these ideas and explanations.

Students who read this book are in a university or college, or in practice placements aiming to prepare for practice. International currents affect their future practice and present education; they need to be understood. Educators who read this book seek to prepare students and offer educational resources in the best way to help their students. We start from the need to understand the settings that they work in and the opportunities that they have to help students pilot their way through the uncertainties that social change challenges them with. Social work practitioners who read this book are also educators because they are practice teachers, and, as part of teams providing social work services, they offer a context for education. We start from the need to understand the international currents affecting their work and to see their local practice as part of a wider picture.

International Social Work

Most social work students, educators and practitioners do not cross national borders in their work, so can we say that they work internationally? International social work refers to a number of different activities:

- *Working in development agencies in the South* – Examples of development agencies might be non-governmental organizations (NGOs) like Save the Children, Caritas, and Médicin Sans Frontiéres. Many people make careers in international agencies working in the South, or commit parts of their lives when they are young, as 'time out' or in retirement to such work. In some countries, development work in the South would not be considered social work, while elsewhere it would.
- *Working for official international agencies* – Examples of international agencies might include a range of United Nations agencies, the European Commission or aid departments of national governments. As with development agencies, there would be similar differences in how such work is viewed; in the United Kingdom of Great Britain and Northern Ireland (UK) and some other countries, work in such agencies would not be viewed as social work.
- *Working for agencies dealing with cross-national issues* – Examples might be agencies dealing with international adoption or family matters such as abduction of a child from one legal jurisdiction in family disputes. Some service user organizations, for example for disabled and mentally ill people, have staff working on international links.
- *Working for international social work organizations* – Examples might be the International Federation of Social Workers (IFSW) and the International Association of School of Social Work (IASSW) or people employed in countries on projects for or linking with such organizations.

- Participating in international conferences, educational or professional visits, exchanges and placements and research;
- Working as a social worker in a country that is foreign to them;
- Working with refugees and immigrants in their own country.

In the South, social workers will often experience directly poverty, inequalities and social and personal problems that arise from the impact of globalization in their societies. Even though the average Western practitioner does not work internationally, daily practice may lead them to experience some of the local consequences of globalization: international migration, asylum seeking, and refugees. They may also experience concern about forced marriage, cultural conflicts and terrorism that are a product of the social trends of globalization. The uncertainty about how to evaluate and respond to them emerges from the impact of postmodern ideas in Western societies.

Our analysis starts from experiences in Western countries, where social work originated and developed most strongly, and where it is most firmly established. However, it is developing fast in a diverse range of other countries – in Africa, China, Eastern European countries – that have little connection with and reliance on Western culture and social structures. Inevitably, those developments in other countries and cultures challenge dominant Western ways of thinking about social work.

We argue for seeing this interaction in these ways:

- Western social work is not necessarily relevant to non-Western countries and its relevance should always be challenged.
- Western social work should be influenced by non-Western social work, which will inevitably have different values and practices. Nevertheless, Western cultural and economic power means that we have to establish ways for it to achieve that influence.
- Non-Western countries should and do create their own social works, and may, but should not need to, compare them with or justify them against Western values and practices.

A worldwide view of social work might be richer if it included ideas from and perceptions in non-Western countries. For example, Graham's (2002) work on African worldviews suggests alternative perspectives on family and community that might lead Western social workers to value shared experience and collective spiritual, family and community engagement in resolving social and personal problems. Western cultural, economic and social power has given social work ideas from the West too much influence in other countries and cultures.

The fact that there are international social work organizations suggests that there is an international social work. This has been promoted over the years by an 'internationalist view' held by activists in the international social work organizations, particularly IFSW and IASSW. It may be seen, for example, in the successive reports about social work education across the world by Alice Salomon (1937), Eileen Younghusband, and Katherine Kendall (1978). The international view proposes that there is one diverse social work, with local variations, rather than local social works that share some common elements.

Around the millennium, the international associations began to pursue these projects by devising and promoting an international definition of social work (IFSW, 2000; IASSW, 2001), and international standards for education and training in social work (Sewpaul and Jones, 2005). Sewpaul (2005), a significant figure in the education project, accepts that postmodernism challenges such endeavours towards a 'grand narrative' of social work. Gray (2005) suggests that there is a risk that promoting global standards for social work education may lead to Western models of practice being seen as universal ideals to be reached. She notes that it may be possible to consider an international model of practice or education as a touchstone for comparisons, without trying to gain international agreement to definition or standards.

There is evidence that alternative forms of social work are available for adoption or adaptation. This questions the internationalist view, because it says that there are different forms of social work with different cultural roots, rather than variations on a common social work. Walton and el Nasr (1988) suggested that two parallel processes of interaction between international and local forms of social work may occur:

- *indigenization* of non-local social work practice, by adapting imported ideas to make them relevant to local practice;
- *authentization* of local practices to form a new locally-relevant structure of ideas.

Gray (2005) argues that indigenization is a cross-cultural practice. However, it may be an outgrowth of the history of colonialism, since it works from a largely Western conception of practice.

Gray and Fook (2004) propose that in considering international social work, we should think about four tensions, between:

- *globalization and localization* – the tendency for globalizing and localizing tendencies to occur together
- *Westernization and indigenization* – the balance between Western and alternative conceptions of practice
- *multiculturalism and universalization* – the implication and response to in-built cultural biases
- *universal-local standards* – the incorporation of both universal and localized conceptualizations of social work within our thinking.

It is important to examine the issues represented in these tensions. Some argue that they are not necessarily oppositions. Sewpaul (2005) for example, sees a universal definition of social work and a universal standard for social work education as assisting the integration of social work into countries where it is underdeveloped or insecure. In this way, universal and local standards can support each other. Similarly, Western approaches may become a touchstone against which local practices may be authentized. Nimmagadda and Cowger's (1999) study of authentization and indigenization in Indian social work agencies is an example of such a process. They look at how Western practices such as giving advice, family intervention, confrontation and reassurance are adapted by Indian social expectations and concepts of Dharma and Karma. For example, mainly female workers, who were not expected to act assertively, were not always able to confront the behaviour of mainly male alcoholics, as Western social workers would. Advice-giving, which was contrary to Western social work values of self-determination and non-directiveness, was accepted because Indian values acknowledge the duty of workers to take authority in particular situations.

In summary, we argue that social workers need an understanding of international social work as part of their profession. Even if they are not international social workers themselves, their daily practice and the needs and problems that users of their services face will be affected by international social trends. Students and educators will also be aware that the international element in the literature and practice that they study questions universal validity of knowledge and practice.

Conclusion: The Plan of this Book

From such accounts, we can see the vital importance of detailed analysis of how Western and local ideas adapt to one another. Generalized assumptions of an increasingly universal and international social work do not represent the complexities of the interaction of globalization, postmodernism and postcolonialism. As we commented in this Chapter, few people are actively involved in international social work practice. Globalization is affecting the organization of the social work profession and its knowledge base, however. Globalization is also a way of understanding social change that is sweeping the world and affecting the issues and particularly the inequalities that social workers deal with, even if they do not step across a national border. 'Post' ideas, particularly postmodernism and postcolonialism, provide helpful analyses of the insecurity, alienation and loss of identity that many people, and the social work profession, feel facing the social consequences of globalization.

What can social workers do? Is social work and its education out of control under globalization and in a postmodern era?

In this book, we argue for ways of using knowledge in social work to understand these complex issues, incorporate them into our practice and develop strategies to begin to tackle them. These are major social changes: practitioners who claim to help people struggle with personal difficulties and social injustices affecting their lives must respond to them.

In Chapter 2, our focus is globalization, postmodernism and related concepts. Globalization and postmodernism are theories and ideas that seek to explain social changes in societies across the world around the beginning of the new millennium. However, these general social changes and explanations have personal causes and consequences, which affect and are affected by the people social workers work with and social workers themselves. We ask: how should social agencies be organized and social workers act to serve their clients best in the midst of these changes?

In Chapter 3 we examine how knowledge and skills may be created through critical reflection in the local contexts in which it is practised. Thus, postmodern flexibility may enable us to respond to local context. In Chapter 4, we explore some of the consequences for social work of migration, discrimination and ethnic and cultural factors made more significant in many societies by the impact of globalizing trends. We argue for a practice that incorporates structures for cultural translation within social work organizations and practice. Therefore in Chapter 5, we examine the extent to which knowledge and evidence about social work may be seen as universally valid for use in practice in all cultures and with all ethnic groups. We suggest that social workers and educators need to set out explicitly to translate knowledge and skill between different cultures. Chapter 6 explores empowerment responses to the managerialist changes of new public management ideas on social work and its education. Chapter 7 looks at how postmodern ideas on practitioners, students and educators may enable them to respond to the challenges of globalization, by 'piloting through chaos'. Chapter 8 examines how we may manage international activities such as exchanges in practice and education in developing an international social work. Chapter 9 looks particularly at the impact of new technologies on our capacity to develop an international social work practice and education. Chapter 10 draws these more detailed analyses together.

Chapter 2

Globalization, Postcolonialism
and Postmodernism:
Conflicts and Connections

This book focuses on three main ideas, which offer explanations of present social trends that are current in social work debates. We also explore a number of related concepts, such as civil society and social capital. This Chapter introduces these ideas and discusses some debates about their meaning, and we emphasize some of the ways in which they are relevant to social work.

Globalization refers to trends in social change in the economic, political and cultural relationships between people across the world. Postcolonialism refers to power relationships in which Western cultural influences dominate other cultures as globalization increases. Postmodernism refers to changes in knowledge and understanding about people and societies. All these social changes may be evaluated differently, and the various views often reflect social values. Holton (2005) claims that people see an image of 'saints and sinners' from different points of view. Some views regard economic growth as fundamental to securing the resources for people's security and happiness. Such views are often associated with neo-liberal or conservative political values. Opposing views, often associated with socialist, left-wing or green political values, argue that giving priority to economic growth leads to insecurity of social and cultural identity, social inequality and a poor environment. Debate rages around these values.

Globalization, postcolonialism and postmodernism offer both conflicting and connected understandings of current social trends. They conflict because an important focus of globalization is the dominance of economic power achieved through industrial, scientific and cultural influence by the West partly through postcolonialism. Postmodernism, on the other hand, rejects the dominance of rational, technical knowledge in understanding the world, which underlies industrial societies. Therefore, it questions the influence of economics as a technical form of explanation. Instead, it emphasizes how the local, social and historical context influences or creates our understanding of the world. We exist in these contexts and, within them, we interact with the natural world as we try to understand and deal with it.

The most important connection between globalization, postcolonialism and postmodernism is that they all represent interlocking social trends in the same direction. As we look at one, we raise another. For example, globalization means that powerful Western countries dominate the global economic system. This strengthens postcolonialism, because former colonial powers continue their dominance of former colonies through hegemony, that is economic and cultural power. One country's dominance is another country's disadvantage, so our concerns stem from and lead to inequality. That is, some parts of each community, some parts of each region and of the world as a whole do not achieve the speed of development or the economies and social success of other parts. People, their lives and the environment in which they live are impoverished as a result.

The aspect of life that connects all three ideas is culture, which is important to social workers because it is central to how human beings respond to their surroundings. Culture is an important link between apparently disparate people. Huntingdon's (1996) influential book on globalization: *The Clash of Civilizations and the Remaking of the World Order*, for example, emphasizes that economic changes bring different civilizations and cultures into conflict with each other. He argues that after the fall of communism as a political force with the collapse of the Soviet regime in the early 1990s, different cultural approaches to organizing civilization replaced political ideology as the major focus of international conflict. Another important aspect that connects these three concepts is the way in which identity is being eroded by social trends, so that people are more insecure and uncertain of themselves.

Globalization

Globalization comprises interconnected economic, political and cultural trends. These reduce the strength of national boundaries and national identity. In a comprehensive study, the United Nations Development Programme (UNDP, 1999) identified four structural changes affecting human institutions in the later 1990s and early 2000s:

- *New global markets* in services such as banking, insurance and transport, in particular new deregulated financial markets, and global consumer markets.
- *New actors*, such as multinational corporations integrating production and marketing, the WTO, an international criminal court, international NGOs, regional economic blocs and policy coordination through groups of countries with particular interests, such as the OECD and the G7, G8 or G10.
- *New rules and norms*, such as market economic policies, democratic regimes, human rights conventions, global environment conventions and multilateral trade agreements.
- *New communication tools* such as the Internet and email linking many people simultaneously, cellular (mobile) phones, fax machines, fast, cheap air transport and computer-aided design.

One explanation of this focuses on capitalism, and therefore emphasizes the economic basis of globalization. This argues that as capitalism has developed – commentators often talk about 'late' or 'advanced' capitalism – business organizations have become increasingly efficient at accumulating capital to finance more complex and extensive activities, particularly through transnational organizations. Political and social structures have adapted to support this process.

Writers such as Wolf (2005) argue that this is an inevitable consequence of natural human development. People's social and economic networks always have a tendency to widen. Moreover, he argues that eventual integration in a world market is the only way for all economies to prosper and for poverty and inequality to be defeated. Shipman (2005) argues that globalization is a political creation, that economic markets cannot and do not impose cultural uniformity. Instead, he argues that there are many contrary pressures in tension with each other. The independence of transnational corporations and supra-national bodies are the best means of overcoming oppressive governments and the excessive power of the state, which reliance on state welfare tends to encourage.

However, even writers who accept the natural progression towards economic globalization question the way in which this has taken place or how it has been managed. Stiglitz (2002: 268), a former chief economist at the World Bank, argues that: 'globalization is a powerful force that has brought enormous gains to some. Because of the way it has been mismanaged, however, millions have not enjoyed its benefits, and millions more have been made worse off'. He suggests that poorer nations have little choice in economic decision-making, and that international economic agencies have imposed policies through them that favour Western political and financial interests and cripple emerging economies. He argues that instead globalizing policies should be developed to respond to social need and to benefit the welfare of the populations of the South. Weak or over-intrusive governments have served poor countries badly, and a crucial requirement is transparent policy-making in international organizations and open democratic government in individual nations. Sen (1999), another leading economist, argues similarly that poverty comes from deprivation of the political and social freedoms that offer people the capability to achieve a satisfactory life. Accepting a political commitment to democratic freedom allows people to achieve beneficial social change and thus to avoid poverty and famine. This is crucial to successful economic development. An aspect of this is to see individual freedom as a social commitment, so that women, for example can attain active agency in changing local social circumstances for the benefit of their families.

Other writers, in particular Giddens (1990) and Robertson (1992), argue that a range of factors are involved in and operate to some extent independently within the process of globalization. Giddens refers to capitalism, the inter-state system, militarism and industrialism. Robertson refers to the interaction of economic, political and cultural changes. Thus, although economic changes are central to understanding globalization, and therefore we start with them, many other factors are changing independently and adding their own elements to the process.

Economic Changes

Economic globalization starts from policies that favour and enforce free trade. Mechanisms such as the World Trade Organization promote the idea and negotiate and regulate treaties to remove economic barriers, such as tariffs, to the free movement of goods and services. Tariffs are charges or taxes made by the government of a country on the price of goods that are imported from elsewhere. When tariffs are charged, the cost of goods rises, and this discourages consumers from buying goods from outside the country because they become more expensive than locally-produced equivalents. This protects local producers. However, such protection can prevent local producers from becoming more efficient to produce their goods more cheaply, so prices to consumers may eventually rise higher than they would if local producers were forced to be competitive. Free trade allows direct price competition from across the globe, which forces everyone to be as efficient as possible, and brings down prices to consumers to the lowest possible level. This may benefit the poorest people, and it encourages economic growth, which increases employment, also benefiting unemployed people. The problem with such policies is that local producers and employers in countries in the South may be at a disadvantage compared with large international companies, who can produce things very cheaply in large quantities because they have such large markets. This in turn allows them to drive down the prices of raw materials and technology, giving them an advantage over smaller producers. This impoverishes local producers, who have to reduce costs to compete. It also impoverishes workers, who are often the biggest cost. They lose their jobs or have their wages reduced to enable producers to compete. Ideas such as 'fair-trade' goods, in which Western consumers pay a higher price, which is returned as a direct benefit to producer countries in the South, aim to combat this problem.

Economic globalization presents social work and welfare services with the basic quandary of globalization. This is because helping societies to respond to unemployment and poverty from low wages means increasing costs and ultimately throwing more people out of work. Protecting local economies from competition increases the cost of goods to poor people. Thus, economic policy prefers to see social work and welfare as easing the social consequences of economic changes. However, economic globalization may mean permanent inequality and poverty for people in weak economies. Social work organized to 'ease' economic transition may be inappropriate; economic and social change is needed instead.

Large companies trying to produce goods efficiently leads to 'Fordism', named after the motor manufacturer, Henry Ford. He devised the idea of 'production lines' to produce manufactured goods such as cars very efficiently. Industrialized production uses machines and work that requires human beings is simplified into sequences of tasks that low-skilled workers can perform. The cost of labour is thereby reduced, since less-skilled workers receive lower wages, and are easily replaced. Therefore, they have less power in the employment market than skilled people.

Globalizing processes have generalized from industry to social work. Recent changes in Western social care emphasize coordination and efficient delivery of services, conformity with government regulation and structured forms of practice. All this tends to reduce the discretion and independence of social workers, and emphasizes managerial control of decisions. This tends to deprofessionalize social work, seeing it as a more routine, less-skilled activity (Harris, 2003; Jordan, 2000) that can employ cheaper labour.

To make the international economic system work, there are global flows of finance for industry. These benefit developed economies most, and make it difficult for less-developed countries to expand their industries. Therefore, global systems of economic support for weaker economies have been established, such as the

World Bank and International Monetary Fund (IMF). These often enforce free trade and Western forms of democratic government, sometimes claimed mainly to benefit companies and countries in the North. 'Structural adjustment' is a policy of reorganizing economies to reduce or eliminate tariffs that protect local and national industries from competition. During the 1980s and '90s the World Bank and IMF used it in many African countries. Mainly, it was a response to uncontrollable debt built up by poor countries that were adversely affected by the rapid rise of the oil price in the 1970s (Perrons, 2004: 57–8). However, this added to economic underdevelopment of the former colonies caused by the way colonial powers gave priority to their own economic interests rather than the interests of the colonies. By forcing rapid economic improvement, it created serious difficulties for poor people in the countries affected (Adepoju, 1993) and demands on social work and welfare services.

These changes in flows of finance also lead to global flows in work and labour. Economic efficiency shifts work from high-wage to low-wage economies. For example, telephone call centres, answering customer enquiries to a company in one country, can be answered anywhere in the world. Another example is the shift of jobs in manufacturing to places where workers are cheaper to employ. This helps low-wage economies develop, but means that routine jobs shift away from high-wage economies. High-wage economies then become 'knowledge economies', concentrating on work that requires high levels of education, such as research and innovation, and cultural and social understanding, such as design, fashion, literature, other arts and, indeed, social work. Employment and wages decline in more routine or practical work. On the other hand, education becomes more important in Western countries, because higher levels of innovation and creativity require more complex and sophisticated education. Even in routine work, people have to master more complex technology. All these processes further impoverish the poorest, and people with disabilities, and exclude them from economic participation in generally rich Western societies.

Competition encourages companies to eliminate or take over competitors and this leads to the formation of transnational corporations, large companies that dominate markets in many different countries. Thus, local influence over economic decisions is lost.

Perrons (2004) shows how particular industries tend to cluster in parts of countries, groups of countries and in regions of the world. Oil, for example, is only found in certain parts of the world. Manufacturing relies on the availability of specific raw materials, and countries with those raw materials generate related industries, then seek to import them to maintain their industries as they run out. Climate affects what crops may grow. Related industries therefore cluster together. Eventually 'superstar' clusters emerge, such as 'silicon valley' in the United States, where computer development accumulated in the 1980s. There are 'value chains' in which goods are produced, then collected, refined, manufactured, packed and sold, gaining value at each stage. Thus, coffee is produced in relatively poor countries, refined, transported to rich countries, where it is traded, blended and eventually sold at a higher cost. 'Global commodity chains' build up, and in recent years 'cool chains' have grown up to transport delicate food or goods such as cut flowers rapidly in cooled containers from poor countries in the South, where they are produced, to rich countries in the West so that commodities may be consumed out of season. These trends have increased the feminization of labour, since cheap, and usually female, employees are needed to care for and produce the goods, and to sell them in the rich countries.

Because knowledge-based employees are often rich in money and poor in time, there are also 'care chains', in which low-paid women undertake caring tasks for richer women. This includes care of children and elders. Social care services become a part of such chains where people are unable to care for members of their own families themselves, or pay for care directly. Increasingly, these care chains are also international, since migrants do much of this work in rich countries, while middle class women follow careers, or rich people migrate to countries with cheap labour. Such care chains also extend to the trafficking of women for prostitution and routine labourers for farm work.

Political Changes

Political changes arise from these economic changes; nation states become less important. They are less in control of their own economies and transnational companies often have larger economies than states. Decisions are made where the transnational company is based, rather than in affected countries. Nations cannot manage their economies to protect local producers. Developed nations get richer, while less-developed nations are less able to compete and lose employment.

Countries in the South may require greater social work and welfare help to respond to this, but poverty means that their taxes are less able to pay for it. Moreover, in seeking a sustainable end to poverty, they may focus on social provision that helps them increase employment, and education to improve employability rather than direct help for poor people. Consequently, welfare and social work may be provided mainly by international agencies, controlled by professional priorities in rich countries. Thus, poor countries lose control of their own welfare systems by being offered crisis intervention and short term development aid, rather than being helped to extend indigenous welfare provision. Poor or rural people may be excluded from education or help because their work does not benefit the country in international competition. All these factors link to economic migration from poorer regions and countries to richer regions and countries as rural economies fail to produce sufficient income for a satisfactory life. Poorer regions then have to deal with the political consequences of loss of population, and richer regions have to deal with the social problems that attend rapidly rising populations.

Political changes respond to cultural change; see 'cultural changes' below. Transnational media and Internet companies make people aware of lifestyles, fashions and attitudes in the West. They have access to sources of information other than their own government, religious leadership or culture. Their identity may focus on 'celebrities' or international sports and fashion, they may aspire to become international business people. Public discourse may exclude people with more local or traditional interests. This adds to economic migration as some people move to the towns to gain the benefits of connection with a more attractive lifestyle based on Western culture.

Due to economic and social changes, many countries share similar problems, and policy. On the other hand, social movements may also easily become world wide; examples are feminism and environmental concern. These draw commitment from a wide range of people and can be a powerful counterbalance to transnational organizations and nation states. Policy formation in nations may be less local, and therefore less susceptible to influence by people in poor communities or politicians representing them. They may be excluded because they have little economic power. Since social work mainly helps excluded people, it becomes less important because those people's issues are not important to politics. States with less economic power focus on the traditional roles of the state, such as foreign affairs. Lack of economic power means that nation states are less able to work independently for their interests. Consequently, global and regional alliances, such as the European Union, become more important.

For social work, the most important feature of the 'management' focus of disempowered government is the need to be able to manage social issues that appear to be out of control. Concern about drug misuse and consequential crime and cultural changes is a good example, because the complexity of the issue and its interaction with global trends and problems makes it hard for governments to manage either alone or collectively. Thus, the Afghanistan government is powerless to prevent growing and refining illegal drugs, and Western governments are unable to prevent their importation and distribution. Professions, such as social work, that only deal with one aspect of it can equally seem inadequate to the task. It is important not to claim too much, or accept unrealistic responsibility for such global issues. The time when social work thought that casework was the answer to all social problems has long gone. However, it has a part to play in responding to individual distress, and so should not be dismissed. In the same way, it is important to argue that local treatment facilities or community projects have a part to play, but cannot be the whole solution. Again, international police action against drug cartels or military action against countries growing drug crops may have a part to play, but cannot simplistically resolve such complex issues in one swoop either.

Cultural Changes

Because of the decline of the political power of the nation state, localization, ethnicity and culture become more important than nationality in defining and defending people's social identities. A global economy makes a wide range of cultural possibilities available to more people, and local cultures may have opportunities to have influence elsewhere. A social work example is the impact of family group conferences (Marsh and Crow, 1997; NCFGD, 2006) to involve children in public care in decisions affecting their lives. This idea originally came from a Maori tradition in New Zealand, and has been adopted in many countries, including Western countries, to meet local needs.

Important cultural changes arise from migration, since people who migrate usually form somewhat separate communities in the new country, retaining many of their cultural and social traditions. This then leads to diverse social traditions from different cultures being present in countries that have been more homogeneous.

Some, often conservative, groups may try to preserve a homogeneous culture; others may value the interest and stimulation of the diversity. Social workers often face this starkly. How far should child care services expect conformity with the expectations of the new country? How far should they respect or promote the child care values of the new ethnic group? Is behaviour that is to us unusual to be assessed as mental illness or a behaviour that is accepted in the culture of a particular minority ethnic group? Should elderly Asians who have lived on curry all their lives be expected to eat conventional Western food in an old people's home?

Hybridity (Kraidy, 2005) may arise. Religious and social ideas and beliefs form constantly changing systems of culture, influenced by other cultures. Thus, cultures may become hybrids, or there may be social pressures towards hybridity, which some people and groups try to resist. All sorts of questions arise from hybridity; see Chapter 4. For example, is it traditional or conservative to try to maintain a commitment to a faith such as Islam or another aspect of culture in a Western society?

An important cultural aspect of globalization is consumerism (Sklair, 2002: Chapter 5). In the West, people come to expect increasing material wealth, possessions and better services, and enjoy a lifestyle of increasing consumption, which in turn generates continuing economic development. People in the South may aspire to such expectations as advertisements have persuaded them to believe that they have to have it. New mass media generate these expectations, by emphasizing fashion, novelty and advertising new products, services and social expectations. These are all framed to entice consumers, so that shopping becomes a symbolic event, an important social activity. Image and fashion become increasingly important, and thus maintaining a suitable lifestyle and image becomes a more important aspect of people's identity.

Consequently, cultural industries also become important to Western economies. Because, as we saw when discussing economic globalization, manufacturing and routine work is transferred to low-wage economies, high-wage economies have to generate income by concentrating on work that produces ideas. Design and fashion become important to consumerism, and constant change in ideas becomes important, because being current stimulates more sales. These ideas then have to become economically powerful, so that entertainment and communication media, such as television, the Internet communicate new ideas and fashions at an ever-increasing rate. Education has to provide for understanding constantly changing cultural understandings, and respond to new cultural identities. It also has to compete with the expectations raised by sophisticated communication technologies. As we see in Chapters 7 and 9, education processes are increasingly influenced by demands to use such technologies to mimic the style and presentation of entertainment, rather than focus on academic debate and analysis. While such changes may sometimes make appropriate use of new technology, the focus on 'edutainment' as a role of education is also partly a product of the cultural change attendant on the demands of global economies to use expensive technologies that countries in the South are less able to afford.

Religion is an important aspect of globalization because religion is an important basis of national difference, and of the organization of the state (Hopkins, et al., 2001). In some Nordic countries, ministers of religion are paid by the state. In the UK, the Church of England is 'established' as part of the government of the state, while several eastern countries base the law on sharia or Islamic law. However, religion is also the origin of important inequalities, including, race, gender and class oppression. We argue that, to be empowering, concern about spirituality should be part of social structures that seek to remove inequalities. One of these may be social work.

Postcolonialism

Colonialism is associated with a historical period from the 1600s to the mid-1900s and is connected to cultural globalization. During the period of the height of modernity, globalization developed by European nations dominating other countries through military conquest and government. Postcolonialism is a post idea particularly relevant to international social work. It emerged during the late 20th century (see Table 1.2, Said) when Western nations dominated others through emphasizing cultural superiority. Western writers and social workers often assumed that this superiority was demonstrated in Western economic and technological success, and Western cultural domination was, in turn, justified because of that success. Said (1978, quoted in Ashcroft et al. 1995) believed that: 'Orientalism is more particularly valuable as a sign of European-Atlantic power over the Orient than it is a veridic [about reality] discourse about the Orient'. Some writers, famously Franz Fanon (1967), argued that there were competing national cultures and non-Western nations should fight to maintain their cultures. Similarly, a number of social work writers have sought to stress the importance of social workers understanding indigenous cultures where they are working with people from such cultures. Graham (2002) for example, discusses the influence of African-centred world-views in people from the Caribbean and Africa, and argues for the importance to social workers of understanding how such world views may lead to alternative ideas about what is important in life.

Postcolonialism, therefore, is an analysis of power relationships in which Western people claim cultural superiority over people from former colonies. This may be done in subtle and surprising ways. Larson (1973) strikingly describes teaching English literature to students in Nigeria and discovering, when discussing a novel by Jane Austin, that kissing was not a cultural custom among his students. The significance of a kiss between characters in the book they were reading was not only misunderstood, but completely irrelevant to the students' experience. Anyone who teaches abroad has such experiences, even in Western countries. Postcolonialism particularly arises where it is assumed that Western knowledge bases are more advanced. Linked to this may be an assumption that the Western knowledge is capable of universal application; these issues are dealt with more fully in Chapters 5, 7 and 8.

Attempts at cultural and social influence affect other historical relationships between countries that were not involved in the period of European colonialism. For example, the Soviet Union influenced a large political bloc of countries in Eastern Europe and Asia with a communist regime between 1945 and 1990, and seeks to maintain its influence in this area partly through cultural means. Similarly, the USA seeks to preserve cultural and social influence in Central and South America. However, Russian power over the former Soviet bloc and American power in the Americas is partly achieved by cultural means. Its main aim is political security and economic influence. Both sets of influence are, therefore, more colonial than postcolonial, and is more a sign of globalizing relationships than postcolonial influences.

Effects of Globalization

To summarize this discussion of the effects of globalization, arguments that it is a natural or desirable economic, political and social development are disputed by claims that it causes a variety of adverse social effects (George and Page, 2004). We have already seen that globalization is likely to have effects on the environment, because transnational companies have no local loyalties and may ignore the global environmental consequences of economic development, such as global warming and degradation of natural resources through overuse. Globalization also has consequences for poverty through impoverishment of countries in the South, reduction of resources for social provision and social consequences of migration such as loss of traditional support mechanisms. Other health and social consequences are less income in poor countries to combat global pandemics, such as HIV/AIDS, or the risk of influenza carried by migrating birds affecting human beings as 'avian flu'. Countries in the South may be prevented from using available drug and other treatments, because international intellectual property laws favour the transnational pharmaceutical companies.

Poverty also has consequences for crime. The only economic crop to earn adequate income in some countries is drugs. Smuggling and gang warfare over drugs can lead to high levels of crime in many countries, some of them a long way from the growing area. Poverty means that social and psychological pressures to exploit women and children in the workforce and towards domestic violence and child abuse are commonplace in developing countries (Pahl et al., 2004). Moreover there are conflicts between ethnic and religious groups that may lead to terrorism and inter-communal violence.

In addition to these general effects of globalization, there are also effects on social welfare, as the consequences of globalization for poverty, employment and health and education suggest. Page (2004) focuses on the consequences for:

- *The welfare state* – Globalization raises questions about whether states can provide comprehensive welfare services for their citizens.
- *Developing nations* in the South – Globalization presses developing nations to focus on economic rather than social development.

However, there are various ways of responding to these effects according to Page:

- Protection of citizens' and workers' rights.
- Control of global capital movements.
- Management of transnational companies.
- Creation of non-governmental organizations (NGOs), so that they have the capacity to respond to problems and campaign against damaging movements in global capital and transnational companies, independent of the kinds of pressures that affect government. NGOs can form a counterbalance to transnational companies and their globalizing tendencies.

Similarly, it is possible to combat many globalizing trends. However, effective international co-operation and commitment to a continuing effort, balancing the many political and social conflicts, is needed to achieve this. In an extensive statement about possible alternatives to globalization, the World Social Forum (WSF; Fisher and Ponniah, 2003) suggested a range of areas of action, set out in Table 2.1. Such approaches seek to reduce inequalities within countries, and between countries and regions of the world. They emphasize democratic participation in decision-making about development as a right, since simple opposition to development may disadvantage poor people by preventing them from gaining its benefits. Cohesion and cooperation rather than competition, and openness and shared ownership rather than corporate structures are necessary. The WSF report argues that democratic mechanisms are needed to develop cooperation and cohesion. People should have rights to the basic resources of living, including food, knowledge, medicine and water; these should not be treated as commodities. These ideas may be dreams in present international conditions, but they illustrate that alternative visions are possible and offer directions for a strategy when opportunities arise. Many of them might contribute to setting objectives that social work could achieve in response to globalization, and could be part of social work's advocacy for a better response to globalization.

Both natural and human disasters always affect the poorest most. For example climate change will affect people in the poorest regions where coastal defences against inundation are least good. This happened when Hurricane Katrina breached the coastal defences at New Orleans; the poorest people were most affected. This happens in the richest countries, therefore, as well as the poorest.

Postmodernism

We now turn to the conceptualization of a second major concept. Postmodernism is one of a number of 'post' ideas, among which there are many connections, but also some discontinuities. Table 2.2 briefly explains some of these, column 3 'social consequences' shows many connections between them and also between postmodernism and some of the social outcomes of globalization. The following account relies on the same sources as Table 2.2.

To refer to an idea as 'post- something' inevitably implies that something that previously existed is being replaced. Therefore, it is clear that these ideas are about trends in thinking, and to understand them, we need to understand what they are reacting to. However, although 'post' ideas identify social reactions to previously existing trends, the pattern is complex. 'Post' ideas coexist with the previous thinking, creating a discourse between the original trend and reactions to it. Indeed, the 'post' idea in reacting to the original trend often clarifies, stimulates and redirects the pre-existing trends

Modernity and Modernism

To understand postmodernism, therefore, we need to ask about trends and debates about 'modernity' and 'modernism'. A useful way of thinking about this is to start

Table 2.1   Actions for alternatives to globalization

Area of globalization	Critical issues	Alternative actions
Wealth production, social reproduction	External debt	Abolish external debt Regulate financial markets
	Financial capital	Control capital flows Tax foreign investment Eliminate tax havens
	Transnational corporations	Reinforce democratic controls Promote dialogue on socio-economic needs Transparent relationship between corporations and states
	Labour	Promote bias to poor in socio-economic policy Concern for global inequalities Structures for global wage bargaining
	Solidarity	Economies to promote cohesion, not competition
Access to wealth and sustainability	Environment and sustainability	Rights to participation in economic decisions Multinational environmental agreements to have priority over development Financial system to support sustainability
	Water	Seen as a common shared good, not commodity
	Knowledge	Knowledge, especially public knowledge, to be open
	HIV/AIDS	Access to needed medicines
	Food	Human right to adequate food, not a commodity Local, national and regional sovereignty over rights to produce food
	Cities	Urbanization promotes loss of access to community welfare Act on the way city life weakens public management of safety, illegality, poor environments
	Indigenous peoples	Rights to form a new relationships with states Right to maintain way of life

Affirmation of civil society and public space	Media	Right to communicate; right of reply Limits on monopoly ownership of media Reduce commodification of information
	Education	Education given as a right, not a commodity or form of assistance Education of poor and excluded people
	Culture	Promote cultural diversity Right to determine identity through culture Cultural products should not be commodified as entertainment
	Violence	Eliminate violence against poor, women, children, trafficking in people Reduce militarization of responses to issues
	Discrimination and intolerance	All peoples should have full access to human rights Awareness, education, communication, research and knowledge development
	Migration	Right to deal with the way migration has become international, been feminized, leads to more intense exclusion
	Global civil society movement	Young people, women and workers major players – most affected by disadvantages of globalization People need to participate in open, democratic social structures
Political power and ethics	International architecture of power	Develop plural economic governance structures as alternatives to IMF and World Bank
	Militarism	End use of military aid Welfare for victims of war
	Human rights	Ensure primacy of human rights over economic and military objectives
	Sovereignty	Colonialism and post-colonialism associated with globalization Create new divisions and spheres of influence to give rights to pursue interests globally
	Democracy	Participation requires decentralization and devolution of powers Conscious programmes of education
	Values	Plural values, liberty, equality, fraternity, solidarity, democracy, concern for the environment

Source: Fisher and Ponniah (2003)

Table 2.2   'Post' ideas

Idea	*Meaning*	*Social consequences*
Postcolonialism	Domination of colonies by military and political control is replaced by economic and cultural domination by transnational companies and the cultures of developed countries	Transnational products such as Hollywood, BBC television, Pizza Hut or McDonalds replace locally produced and culturally relevant products and ideas World languages, e.g. English, and products using them, e.g. books, DVDs, replace local languages and oral traditions
Post-feminism	Social movements aiming to free women from social domination by men and male assumptions are replaced by assumptions that equality is a false goal and that feminism has spoiled many female advantages and preferences e.g. being able to flirt, mothering rather than working	A reduced emphasis on responding to inequalities that affect women, such as women's poverty or domestic violence
Post-Fordism	Industrialized processes are replaced by teamwork in groups of highly educated people doing knowledge- and culture-based work such as education and television	Devaluation of practical and physical labour Emphasis on rapid changes in cultural trends, fashion and design
Post-industrialism	Developed economies reduce their emphasis on industrial production of consumer goods, such as cars, washing machines and computers, instead focusing on work that uses knowledge, such as design, services and software, leading to 'hollowing-out' of industry in Western countries, which designs and markets goods produced in less-developed countries	Greater economic globalization – pre-industrial or industrial societies supply goods and depend upon knowledge from developed societies; Unemployment and low wages among less-skilled, less-intellectually-able people.

Postmodernism	An emphasis on rational, technical knowledge used to achieve social progress through designing products and goods and understanding the world and societies through science is replaced by an view that understanding and knowledge is provisional and arises and applies only in its social and historical context	Moral and political relativism – nothing can be finally agreed; Rise in uncertainty and risk leads to social and personal insecurity; Rejection of social order and social structure; Possibility of social change.
Post-structuralism	Philosophical approach rejecting the ideas of French structuralism, which claimed that all social phenomena displayed evidence of 'deep structures' formed into interlocking systems that could be identified and classified, allowing us to know society through rational analysis	People are free-floating individuals and groups, pursuing selfish social aims; Social structures, if their effects are understood by deconstruction through examining power relations, discipline and regulate people.

Sources: Boyne and Rattansi (1990), Docherty (1993), Hall et al. (1992), Rose (1991), Sim (1998).

by how we understand and know about the world around us. The study and analysis of understanding and knowledge is called epistemology. Many important questions turn on 'representation', how we write about what we understand and believe. The world is so complex, that we cannot describe it completely. Therefore, we select and organize data according to our focus, so knowledge is a representation of aspects of the world that are important for our present focus; they are never complete or absolute. To use knowledge, we have to appreciate how it connects with the reality that it only partially represents.

Until the 1600s, people accepted as true what they were told by powerful social structures, the church and the monarch. These important authorities held a monopoly of access to knowledge contained in books, and they had power to organize the world so that for most people their experiences fitted with what they were told by such authorities. During the 1600s, this view of knowledge began to be displaced in a social revolution called the 'Enlightenment' (Hamilton, 1992; Porter, 2000). Enlightenment ideas emphasize that knowledge is available to anyone, not just people with power and authority, by investigating the real world through observation of it. Thus, ultimately a more democratic political system and the idea of human rights and education emerged as knowledge came to be seen as everyone's right, not just that of the political elite. Rules of scientific method provide an organized form of observation, increasing objectivity and reducing the impact of the individuals on the development of their knowledge and understanding. This approach to knowledge developed science and technology, enabling Western societies to manage the natural environment, industrialize and achieve economic expansion with high standards of living. *Modernity* thus emphasizes progress and development as constant, a product of the growth of knowledge through science.

Modernism is an artistic and cultural expression of modernity, starting in architecture and design during the 1920s. It emphasizes the way technology can use modern components such as concrete, steel and glass to design buildings and furniture to express the functions it serves. This led in the 1920s to a shift in fashion away from decorated buildings in traditional materials popular in the 1800s, to plain buildings with concrete curving faces, with metal window frames, and plain furniture. The plainer, less ornate decoration and brighter lighting of buildings and homes from the 1930s onwards reflects this increasing use of technological innovation, and is perhaps typical of the architecture we associate with Nordic countries, the Finnish architect Alvar Aalto and of design companies such as Ikea. A later expression of these ideas came in the 1960s with office buildings covered in glass, in which there was little external decoration and designed to use space as efficiently as possible, different functions being grouped together. Many people found buildings such as these uninspiring, and it has been argued that using this architecture in large public housing projects built with prefabricated building systems was an oppressive imposition of an elite preference on poor people with few choices in housing. Modernist architecture led to buildings such as the Pompidou Centre in Paris or the stock exchange in London. In these, the framework of the building and many of its technical services, such as pipe work, are exposed on outside, as part of the design, instead of the traditional approach of hiding these within the structure.

Modernity is expressed in most areas of human activity, and modernism is expressed in modernity's systems of knowledge. In medicine, scientific investigation of bodily mechanisms and the effects of medications gained priority over the practical human skills of communication and observation of and interaction with patients, even though, of course, both are necessary. In management, 'scientific management' emphasizes observing and measuring work activities and outputs through techniques such as work study, planning them meticulously and setting targets to motivate workers to achieve more. Human relations management thinking, on the other hand, emphasizes that people want to achieve successes and helping them, by encouraging initiative and teamwork, is likely to achieve successful outcomes in a different way than measurement and targets.

Social work also presents this ambivalence. Many people are motivated to become social workers by their religious and social commitment or human feelings and experience. They experience their practice as being mainly about concern for other human beings. However, social work also emerged in the late 1800s from the idea of 'scientific charity', in which objective evidence about society and psychology would enable social improvements to be achieved (Payne, 2005). Idealist philosophy was also influential: it argues that it is possible and right to intervene in people's lives and to develop social structures, particularly through the state, to improve general social conditions (Offer, 2006).

Modernity generates strains and difficulties (Lyon, 1994):

- Complexity, differentiation and consequently discipline, uniformity and bureaucratization
- Rationalization and social control
- Urbanization, loss of rural community identity and loss of social cohesion commonplace in small communities
- Secularization, anomie (loss of agreed norms and values) and loss of moral influence
- Alienation, exploitation and the creation of a society of strangers, competing with each other.

The process by which all these problems arise is complex. Human diversity and irrationality comes up against modernist rational preferences for certainty and clarity. This also connects with the nation state's loss of power over social management. Government attempts to simplify the complexity of social interactions and claims to manage them through rationalist means. So, the British probation service becomes part of a National Offender Management Service, using cognitive behavioural techniques rather than representing through social work the complexities of the social reasons for criminality. It concentrates on offending behaviour, rather than looking at the whole social situation of the offender and the family, cultural and social pressures towards offending. This enables government to deny the relevance to offending of social factors such as poverty and unemployment, which in the economic straitjacket of a globalizing world they feel unable to resolve by economic management. We can see this in the debate about evidence-based practice in social work. Proponents of evidence-based practice argue for constructing social work practices through the rationality of accumulating evidence and argument based on it. Then, practitioners specify the problems to be dealt with and use the methods that would best deal with those problems. As with medicine discussed briefly above, this emphasizes the manageability of the specific as against the uncertainty of dealing holistically the person in their social context. This is modernist in the sense that it believes that structuring knowledge enables us to understand and manage a reality that we can understand without requiring interpretation.

Postmodernist and Postmodernism

Building on understanding of modernity and modernism, we can move on to understand 'postmodernism'. Table 2.3 lists important writers who have influenced this perspective and some of their ideas. We can take from this the following points, which we take up again in Chapter 7:

- Postmodernism avoids grand or meta-narratives, so it does not seek one overall explanation of social trends.
- Postmodernism accepts instability and complexity in social relationships; it does not try to simplify.
- Language and signs or symbols are important carriers of the meaning we give to social phenomena.

Table 2.3　　Important authors on postmodernism

Author	Example work	Important ideas
Lyotard	*The Postmodern Condition* (1979)	Argues that 'grand narratives' or metanarratives explaining society have collapsed, and knowledge is legitimated by 'language games', systems of rules by which language is understood and within social bonds and relationships.
Hassan	*The Postmodern Turn* (1987)	Focus on literature. Argues for instability and complexity in the relationship between modernity and postmodernity: they are not periods, but there are continuities and discontinuities between them. Produced a well-known list comparing modernist and postmodernist words/ideas. Postmodern terms tend towards indeterminacies and immanences relying on symbols rather than certainties and clarities.
Baudrillard	*Symbolic Exchange and Death* (1976)	Initially a Marxist, writes as a language game, with a provocative irony about the 'death' of capitalism in present-day societies. A sense of origins and history is lost, and societies are simulation, represented by technology creating images on screens through network which endlessly reproduce sign systems, as in celebrity culture and the glossy surface attractions of fashion, with societies becoming mobile and losing firm reference points.
Rorty	*Contingency, Irony and Solidarity* (1988)	Emphasized that all understanding and meaning is contingent on the social environment and literature and social theory, interpreted ironically, are better guides to understanding the human condition than rational debate and linguistic philosophy.
Derrida	*On Grammatology* (1998)	Emphasized deconstruction of texts, including behaviour and social experiences, as representations of multiple meanings, which may therefore be extracted from them by close examination; all text contains a network of unfinished meanings. All interpretation and knowledge is provisional
Said	*Orientalism* (1978)	The West represents the 'Orient', that is, Africa and Asia, as 'other', thus asserting (particularly through its literature and writing) cultural dominance over other cultures and justifying economic, religious and social superiority.

- How we understand the world depends on how our social group gives meaning to language and signs. Our understanding comes from our social context, not some absolute knowledge that we can observe outside ourselves.
- Detailed examination or deconstruction of behaviour and uses of language, signs and symbols in our social environment is important for understanding social and power relations.

These ideas are very relevant for social work practitioners. They emphasize individuality and personal agency, the possibility of influencing our social surroundings. Postmodernism also shows the complexity of relationships and social networks. Language and the signs and symbols we use are important aspects of how we operate in the world, how we understand it and interpret the behaviour of the people around us. Social work mainly uses language and an understanding of how people interpret the world. Our understanding is gained through examining in detail how people's behaviour and thinking about their social environment, expressed in and interpreted by language, affects what they do and the people around them. Because social work focuses on injustice, it also focuses on understanding power relationships, both obvious and hidden.

Postmodernism also has consequences for the thinking about history, which have led to considerable debate among historians (Jenkins, 1997). History studies the past, using written documents and texts, such as art, films and photographs. According to postmodernism, evidence such as this is always the product of people's use of language at the time, and when historians analyse materials to find evidence of what took place in the past they interpret them according to the context of their own time and culture. This has led some historians to argue that it is impossible to create a 'true' picture of the past.

Social workers connect with this apparently abstruse historical debate. This is because we also deal with historical events in the lives and social context of our clients, families and communities and try to understand how different people involved have interpreted them. Then, we use this understanding to decide how to help people with difficulties in these relationships, or communities with desired developments. We often have the responsibility of explaining them through such media as assessments for services, advocacy for clients or communities in official decision-making, reports to courts and social histories for other professions. Thus, our professional thinking represents a 'filtering' of social information in one situation, and the use of this filtered and interpreted data in representations or narratives for audiences (Askeland and Payne, 1999). Therefore, in the same way as historians, social workers have to be careful of how the range of possible alternative views interact, how groups of people, such as families, clans, tribes, communities, have often constructed narratives about their affairs over time which will be only a partial representation of the possible ways of viewing and understanding the situation. We have to look at different kinds of evidence about what happened and interpret it appropriately for our audiences. Those audiences include ourselves, because we have to act and try to help in the situation, and if we have not understood its complexities, we may be unsuccessful, or we may be unfair to one or several participants in the situation. This points to the importance of reflexivity, placing ourselves and our interpretation in the action, which is dealt with particularly in Chapter 3.

Communitarianism, Civil Society, Social Capital, Risk

Three important social and political ideas are relevant to the connections between globalization and postmodernism and their consequences for social work. *Communitarian* ideas argue that individuals should accept personal moral responsibility for contributing to the health and well-being of the community in which they live in return for the rights that they enjoy, as citizens, to safety, protection and support (Etzioni, 1995). An example is Hesselbein et al's (1998) book, *The Community of the Future*, which argues that global economic development can only be achieved in societies that have a strong social fabric. Capitalism and business does not provide for education, infrastructure and social development of societies (Thurow, 1998). This means that communities need a strong identity and clear rules of inclusion, must share information openly, create reciprocity among their members over time, not just in the present. They must create and sustain values using myths, symbols and stories and generate similarities that make people feel secure (Ulrich, 1998). Thus, people would have a 'life course interdependence' (Twine, 1994) with others in their communities, rather than just responding to current needs.

Civil society is an ideal that societies should be regulated by democracy, liberty and solidarity rather than solely by economic and political power. Therefore, organizational structures outside political and economic systems are a focus for social development and an important counterbalance to the adverse effects of globalization. This is often taken to refer to voluntary or charitable organizations, and aspects of society that are concerned with meeting social needs, for example education, housing, health and social care. Organizations that focus on such issues form civil society. It includes social work agencies and voluntary or third sector organizations, outside the conventional structures of economic and political power. Creating civil society was considered important in transition societies, where former communist regimes in Soviet Russia and Eastern Europe were converting their economies and political systems towards more democratic regimes, where welfare and public health and safety did not depend on the institutionalization of particular political and economic philosophies (Alexander, 1998).

Social capital follows from these two ideas. It proposes that active participation in communities and societies is essential to maintain the social fabric. Putnam's (2000) book *Bowling Alone* became influential by showing how formal political, civic and religious participation was declining in American society, and was being replaced by informal links and relationships. This, Putnam claimed, came from the same pressures that generated globalization. He refers to economic pressures on people's time and money, suburbanization and urban sprawl, which reduced local social identity and interconnections, the way in which electronic mass media have made leisure more private and individual and generational change in which socially involved older people are being replaced by less involved younger generations. Commitment to social movements and the growth of a wide range of social networks, particularly through the Internet, are among the factors that combat and mitigate these trends. Developing social capital might be seen as a strategy for drawing on the human resources in the South both to contribute to social movements and to redirect and re-energize global social movements to respond to issues in the South.

One of the uncertainties experienced for individuals in postmodernity is the insecure feeling that their world is out of human control. Society seems to be increasingly difficult to understand, increasingly complex, like a large lorry whose brakes have failed (Giddens refers to a juggernaut – Craib, 1992, 179). This makes people feel at risk, and another important theorist, Beck (1992), has argued that people and social institutions increasingly see the world as risky to live in, and seek out safety and security. This is so, even though there has been a remarkable increase in good health and security in most societies (Slovic, 1999). We can see this trend in the criticism of social workers and social care services where they are unable to protect children from abuse by their parents, or elderly people from falling and injuring themselves. Craib (1992: 179) argues that this comes from a common experience of fragmentation. Psychoanalysts such as Melanie Klein argued that people responded to difficult experiences in their lives by fragmenting their personality, so that they have one set of behaviours in one situation, but appear completely different in other circumstances. Goffman (1968) analysed this process as a form of role theory, in which people behaved according to varying social expectations in different situations. If they were poor or disabled, they might be stigmatized, and might try to 'pass' as 'normal', rather than proclaim the validity of their alternative lifestyle.

Adams (1995) argues that people deal with risk by balancing different factors that are affecting them. Human beings have a propensity to take risks, which is increased if there are rewards for doing so. A disabled person might risk injury, for example, by trying a new treatment to increase their mobility, only if they thought the improvement might be significant. However, people judge the risk they will take according to their perceptions of the extent of the danger and the likelihood of accidents. Their judgements are affected by social trust: if they are broadly trusting of the institutions that they deal with and their society, they are more likely to take risks (Cvetkovich and Löfstedt, 1999). Reviewing relevant studies, Cvetkovich (1999) suggests that people are more likely to trust institutions whose social values they share, which they see as having similar objectives as themselves and where the order and history of events that affect them seem to indicate that the institution is seeking similar objectives as themselves. Looking at cultural experiences, therefore, people such as migrants will take risks in relationships and personal development if they trust the culture in which they exist, if it has treated them well, and have aims and values that fit with theirs. People will take the risk of trusting a social worker and social work agency if they appear similar in values and aims as themselves and where the history of their treatment suggests they have the same aims.

Conclusion

In this Chapter, we have presented three major concepts – globalization, postmodernism and postcolonialism – that may be adduced to explain the social issues discussed in this book that affect social workers, their practice with clients and their education. In the following chapters, we explore these explanations of social trends in greater detail to examine some of the tensions and difficulties that social workers face in doing their work. We also identify ways of thinking and reflecting on social work practice and education that can help to manage the effects of these social trends upon social work and its education. While we cannot expect social work to achieve major social change by itself, understanding and participating in social development and other responses to these social trends can contribute to and participate in wider reactions to social change that builds inequalities and oppresses the lives of the poorest people that social workers work with.

Chapter 3

Critical Reflection to Promote Contextual Social Work Practice and Education

Introduction

Seated at the far end of a classroom of a Mongolian university listening to a lecture in social work, Gurid could not understand a word. However, from the drawings on the blackboard she realized that the subject was casework and the source was an American textbook (Shulman, 1999). When she talked to the students afterwards without their lecturer present, they proclaimed that it was difficult for them to understand what social work is. In their society it was more important to understand and solve a social problem from the family and local community perspectives than from an individual perspective which the lecture had focused on.

Listening to the Mongolian experience Gurid recalled a session in a Norwegian classroom. A student who gave an input from the same book criticized how badly the book, which is used in many Norwegian social work programmes, fitted the Norwegian context. His concern was not so much the individual perspective as that the suggested solutions would be very different in a welfare state. Other American books generate similar student comments.

Most students and social workers around the world do not have the opportunity to gain first-hand knowledge about the society from which their textbooks originate. Social work students and social workers have to deal with the consequences of the mobility of people, are faced with ideas, theories and knowledge created in different contexts from their own; and are introduced to and expected to practice social work methods that are developed far away from their own locality. To fit their context social workers are therefore forced to take on the process of transforming what may be presented as universal social work and to draw on their local experiences to create relevant general knowledge. In this process critical reflection might become useful.

The Mongolian and Norwegian experiences illustrate how important it is to reflect critically on issues like:

- What literature is chosen for the students' curriculum? What is its theoretical and ideological basis?
- How is the literature used in the course? Is it transferred as universal knowledge in social work or are the students expected to reflect critically on it to transform it to their own context?
- In what historical, political, economical, social, cultural and religious context is the knowledge/literature created in relation to where it is used?

- How do theories, models and methods taught fit or alienate social work from local cultures?
- Who are the stakeholders in the knowledge production, in what positions and with what interests in social work?
- What purpose is the knowledge serving: oppression or empowerment?
- How applicable is the theory/literature in practice in the local context?
- What new knowledge could be drawn from local practice on an individual and collective level?
- How are practice and education linked? Is it a one-way or circular relationship?
- What changes should follow from the new knowledge created through critical reflection?

Postmodernists claim that social work is contextual and socially constructed (Mäntysaari, 2005; Payne, 2005; 2006). Taking this seriously would have implications for how we regard the worldwide dissemination of social work literature, models and methods that has already taken place and how we handle it in the future. The Mongolian and Norwegian examples show that what is taken for granted as basic social work in one context may not be recognizable in other contexts.

The global community is a concept used to indicate how we live in a small world, primarily due to easy access to communication and travel. However, using fast communication does not take into consideration that people, ideas and practice are all formed in their own contexts. Transferring them to another setting does not necessarily mean that they are immediately transformed or transformable to fit new contexts. As discussed in Chapter 2, social work used to be modernist. Commitment to 'grand theories' and universal knowledge made social work predictable to some degree. However, postmodernism has put an end to this belief. Instead there is an urgent demand for relevant and adequate, rather than universal, knowledge.

To be able to perform critical social work, we have to be conscious of the knowledge on which we base our practice, and how this knowledge is created, see Chapter 5. Then we need to be reflective and to be critical; however is that the same as to be critically reflective? In this Chapter, we clarify what we mean by critical reflection, why it is important and where the critical in critical reflection and critical practice comes from. We then introduce an approach to critical reflection, the critical incident method, which shows why and how critical reflection may be used for professional growth in social work education and practice to promote contextual knowledge creation. One of the reasons for introducing critical reflection is that we see it as means of combating the undesirable effect of globalization, postcolonialism and postmodernism.

What are Critical Reflection and Critical Practice?

Critical reflection and reflective practice are widely used concepts in fields like education, nursing, medicine, business and law as well as social work. However, the concepts are often used interchangeably without a common definition or understanding of what they mean and imply (Fook et al., 2006). For example this is true of the IASSW/IFSW Global Standard for Social Work Education as well as in curricula for social work programmes in the Nordic countries (Askeland, 2006).

In this book we do not discuss the diverse meanings of these concepts, and refer you to Fook et al., (2006) a comprehensive literature study which reveals the complexity and various understandings and use of these concepts. It covers a range of disciplines, traditions and theoretical frameworks.

Critical reflection as we use it in this book is an educational and supervision method that combines practice, research and education in a circular process. The aim is twofold. The first aim is to develop professional growth and competence by critical reflection on own practice. The second aim is to create a general professional contextual knowledge base by practice research, which combines the outcome of critical reflection on several individual experiences. Knowledge creation through critical reflection is a different way of knowing from empirical studies. It includes sources like creative wisdom, intuition and emotions. It focuses particularly on what people take for granted in social, cultural and political contexts as well as focusing on power relations.

Critical reflection may serve various purposes, separately or simultaneously. The extent to which it does so depend on the time and effort put into it and how deeply the material is explored. Fook et al. (2006: 2) mention four focuses and emphasize the importance of being clear about the purpose of the reflection:

- learning about and improving practice;
- learning to develop practice based theory;
- learning to connect theory and practice;
- improving and changing practice.

While the idea of critical reflection is knowledge creation in order to contribute to emancipation and change, critical practice is different. Critical practice is a model of social work practice using critical social theory extended from 1970s radical social work (Healy, 2000). Critical practice focuses on how to solve specific situations in their socio-political context in an empowering, non-oppressive and anti-discriminatory way. According to Ford et al., (2005), critical practitioners are professionals who are aware of their own choices when mediating in a social, educational, disciplinary and political context. Critical practitioners should be able to link three domains: formal knowledge, the self and practice, and reflect and act across them. We argue that critical reflection may benefit any kind of social work practice; critical social work, however, depends on critical reflection.

Why Critical Reflection?

Chapter 2 contends that the changes and challenges explored in this book are closely linked to global movements in a broad sense, which means more than economic transactions. It includes also the mobility of people, transfer of ideas, theories, knowledge and relocation of practice methods from one part of the world to others. Globalization in a postmodern era has contributed to making social work a complex, uncertain and risky enterprise.

As social work has become more academic around the world, particularly in Europe (Labonté-Roset, 2004; Lorenz, 2005), the contribution of more and better research to knowledge has been emphasized. At the same time education needs to highlight the aim of training students to become competent practitioners, using that knowledge. Research methods that are close to practice, like critical reflection, help to link research and education. Another method is evidence based practice which we discuss in Chapter 5.

In Chapter 4, we explore the impact of postcolonialism and imperialism in the academic field. This is a political issue as much as a professional and ethical one. Critical reflection might therefore be a useful and necessary instrument in becoming aware of and responding to the mainly one-way direction of knowledge and research dissemination in teaching, distribution of literature and research resources from North to South.

As social work programmes expand, for example in China, Africa and Eastern Europe, it helps to be mindful through critical reflection of what can be transferred, and what has to be created locally and yet be recognized as social work. In Ghana for example, a group of social work researchers and a 'Mother Queen', a bearer of traditional authority, met over a period of 10 months to build understanding of similarities and differences in their roles and lay the basis for collaboration and thus develop indigenous social work. Although social work training has been offered in Ghana since 1946, and both 'Mother Queens' and social workers are concerned with community development and the welfare of women and children, little had been done to develop mutual understanding and cooperation between the two (Kretzer, 2005). Without such links social work might introduce something that does not fit into people's daily life.

Social work practitioners are increasingly mobile. While formerly social workers from the North would go South, often involved in developmental aid work, this trend is changing. This is not only because development aid organizations have changed their policies to employ more local people. Western countries are actively recruiting particularly newly trained social workers from the South. This is so in the United Kingdom, where there are not enough social workers. Areas for recruitment are former colonies and Commonwealth (Firth, 2007). This is more thoroughly discussed in Chapter 6 and 7. It has three consequences open to critical reflection. First, social workers might be badly needed in countries that have paid for their education. Second, they may be recruited to lower status jobs where it is less easy to attract indigenous British social workers. Third, they will be trained for social work in a totally different context.

Paralleling the growth in educational programmes, social work is an expanding profession around the world. Social work is not a neutral activity: it depends upon and is exposed to what is happening in other sectors in society. Thus it could also be seen as a political activity. It may be used to support oppressed people or sustain the suppressing institutions or hegemonic systems, see Chapter 6. Critical reflection might be used both to increase accountability and to emancipate social workers (Fook et al., 2006) and clients.

During the communist regimes in the Soviet Union and Central or Eastern Europe social work barely existed (Szmagalski, 2004), also mentioned in Chapter 6. It was demolished during the Maoist period in China, the Marxist period in Ethiopia and lost its university status during the Pinochet regime in Chile. Radical social work was well fitted to the radical political climate in the Western democracies in the 1960–70s (Healy, 2000). However, a similar social work ideology as expressed in IASSW and IFSW ethics and global standards documents, may become more demanding in today's Western neo-liberal societies. Critical reflection raises consciousness of such issues, questioning 'whose side are we on?'

Recent trends emphasize evidence-based research or research-mindedness as the best basis for social work education and practice (Karvinen-Niinikoski, 2005). Lifelong learning, learning on the job (Eraut, 1998; Boud et al., 2006) and organizational learning (Mezirow, 2000; Gould, 2000) are connected to each other as modes of informal learning. Critical reflection lays the groundwork for this kind of informal learning, and also helps to combine it with knowledge from empirical research.

Reflection and Criticality

Reflection is not all critical; neither is all social work practice. Here we will briefly introduce reflection and criticality as a basis for considering critical reflection and critical practice.

Reflection

Argyris and Schön (1976) first introduced the concept *reflective practitioner*, and Schön (1987; 1991) developed reflection on professional practice. His idea was that by reflecting on their own practice professionals would obtain new knowledge bridging gaps between theory and practice, between theories in use versus espoused theories. This bottom-up method of learning from experience has gained recognition in several professions, including social work. Schön distinguished between *reflection-on-action*, which takes place after the actual event, and *reflection-in-action*, which means to act and reflect simultaneously, then without interruption immediately put the new insight into action. He considers reflection-in-action a characteristic of a competent professional practitioner.

Reflection is a cognitive process; nevertheless reflection is influenced by emotions and bodily reactions, which are considered important sources of knowledge. Reflection is a process that takes place when people are faced with something unusual, unexpected or surprising and need to create new meanings or change their understanding. It is a conscious process where people relive and assess their experiences.

Reflection as a tool for professional development often focuses only on individual practitioners' practice, primarily on their working processes and how they handle the situation and relationships with people. Its relevance to knowledge is above all about how theory is applied to practice (Taylor and White, 2000; Hunt, 2006). Reflective learning is similar to the circular experiential learning cycle: action, reflection, conceptualization and experimentation (Kolb, 1984; Moxnes, 2000).

Habermas (1995) distinguished between three types of knowledge:

- technical, produced through empirical studies
- practical, through a focus on language and its hermeneutic interpretation
- emancipatory, through reflection based on critical theory.

The diverse knowledges are related to different areas of work. This distinction is widely referred to in professional literature (Lauvås and Handal, 2000; Taylor, 2000; Karvinen, 2001; Askeland, 2006). Reflection on the technical or instrumental aspects of practice might contribute to quality insurance by particularly focusing on procedures, decision-making and problem-solving. Critical thinking, as a cognitive process, and technical reflection seem to cover the same thing. Reflection on practical or communicative aspects may result in deeper understanding of human interaction, while the emancipatory knowledge will appear through reflection on what is taken for granted and the oppressive powers in people's lives, organizations and society. Only the latter kind of reflection that results in emancipatory knowledge is appropriately called critical reflection.

Criticality

'Critical' is used in combination with several other concepts, with no unified meaning whatever the combination. There is a variety of understandings. Ford et al. (2005) refer to Barnett's (1997) framework, distinguishing between three forms of criticality: critical reason in the domain of knowledge, critical self-reflection and critical action in the domain of the world. Similarly, Jensen (1993) proposes that critical reflection links three different types of knowledge for professional people: life historical knowledge, professional knowledge and scientific knowledge. See Chapter 5 for further discussion. Brookfield (2005) discusses four traditions to explain how criticality has influenced critical theory in adult learning. These traditions are also relevant to critical reflection in social work.

Ideological critique – The most prominent tradition is ideological critique from a critical theory perspective, scrutinizing power relations and hegemony (Brookfield, 2005).

There are several contributors to this critique. The first generation of Marxists analysed economic and political structures such as capitalism, the Enlightenment, and how standardization, bureaucratization and commodification oppressed and alienated people. Brookfield argues that Marxist influence has been almost forgotten in critical theory today, particularly in the American literature, to avoid associations with communism. Even if Marxist ideas are 'intellectually discredited', they 'refuse to disappear' (Brookfield, 1995: 21). Brookfield claims that ignoring the Marxist contribution to social thought restricts critical reflection to an individual level (Brookfield, 1995: 18–19). In a global world with a strong market orientation, where a few get richer on the sacrifice of the majority, and slum areas are growing at a fast rate, a Marxist analysis is not outdated. In critical reflection in social work it is important to include such an ideological critique.

The Frankfurt school was a multiprofessional society and comprises the second generation of critical theorists. It develops an extensive critique of influential social science theories. Habermas, in particular, is often referred to in relation to critical reflection (Fook et al., 2006). He criticized how science was used to promote established power structures in the society. He maintained that social science's most important task was to promote emancipation. However, he was criticized for the lack of a practical way to transform his theory into practice. In response to the critique, he developed his theory on communicative action, seeking to combine social science with political theory, Marxist theory and analytic philosophy, which is related to language (Skjervheim, 1979; Tranøy, 1988).

The third generation of critical theorists includes postmodernism and feminism (How, 2003). Agger (1998), an American representative of the third generation, conveys an optimistic belief in change. He maintains that social change must start from people's everyday life, in the family and at work, even if structural conditions have a determining influence. By emphasizing the individual perspective, he plays down structural issues. This is in accordance with what Brookfield (1995) suggests is characteristic of American critical theorists.

Psychoanalytical and psychotherapeutic traditions – The second tradition of criticality is influenced by psychoanalysis and psychotherapy (Brookfield, 2005).

Postmodernism permits valuing the personal within the professional. In this aspect of postmodernism, critical elements emphasize how gaining personal insight and learning to know oneself is a never-ending task (Bauman/Tester, 2000), important for professional improvement. Without adhering to traditional psychoanalysis, it is nevertheless necessary to focus on deep-seated assumptions that consciously and unconsciously influence people's minds and rule their actions.

Nelson Mandela illustrates how hegemonic values in a society influence people against their will and cause a gap between what people deeply believe in and how they behave. While in 1962 living underground in South Africa, he was on his way to attend an African conference in Ethiopia and changed to Ethiopian Airlines in Khartoum. Mandela (1995: 348-49) panicked when he realized that the pilot was black, never having seen a black pilot before. For a moment, a leader in the fight for equal rights and social justice for black people fell into an apartheid mindset telling him that a black man was unable to fly a plane.

Analytic philosophy and logic – The third tradition of criticality, according to Brookfield (2005), is analytic philosophy and logic. This refers to ability to analyse arguments and recognize logical fallacies. Critical thinking is a cognitive process that refers to a rational analytic process, without any specific ideological critique embedded. Critique has a Greek origin and means to be able to distinguish between truth and falseness, bias and fact, opinion and evidence, valid and invalid arguments and inference in ethical, political and legal issues. In a scholarly connection, it refers to judging between arguments that are well-founded and those that are not (Skjervheim, 1979).

Critical thinking and critical reflection is often used interchangeably. In problem-solving and decision-making, critical thinking may ensure that various arguments and alternatives have been considered before taking action. Critical thinking is highly esteemed in all Western professional work. This is also true of social work research and critical practice. It is secured through analytical procedures and structures, and is similar to Habermas' technological reflection.

Pragmatist constructivism – How people construct and deconstruct their experiences and opinions is an issue in the fourth tradition (Brookfield, 2005). It becomes important to find out how different people create and interpret their experiences as constructivism denies that universal truths exist.

Pragmatism focuses on practice and emphasizes constant experimentation in order to improve society continually. A democracy that exercises openness, inclusiveness and tolerance is an essential basis for such experimentation and change.

Deconstruction, originally developed by Derrida, is a concept from literature. It is a tool for textual analysis. An experience, or a critical incident, could be seen as a text. Deconstructing a text splits it up to assess critically the various aspects of it. To grasp meaning, it is important to understand how the text was created and composed as well as its content. This implies a search for underlying assumptions, contradictions and concealed power relations (Burr, 2003).

Practice and language create each other mutually. In Chapter 5, we deal with how majority languages can be used to oppress people. Words, jargon and professional language may have a similar effect. Thus, language becomes a political tool and therefore an issue for critical reflection.

Reflexivity – In addition to Brookfield's four traditions, reflexivity is an important aspect of critical reflection. Reflexivity and reflection have the same linguistic origin (Taylor and White, 2000). Although also these two concepts are sometimes used interchangeably, they have different meanings in research and knowledge production depending on the theoretical basis of the discussion. Reflexivity is specifically treated in research literature (Fook, 1999a; Jørgensen, 2002), and developed further into an issue of concern in professional practice and education.

While reflection is an intellectual and affective exploration of an experience or a situation, reflexivity in critical reflection is concerned with the positioning of the self. Reflexivity requires a focus on social workers or researchers as subjects that influence the situations they are involved in at every stage. Therefore, they also influence the outcome that is being dealt with or analysed, whether they accept that they are a participant or claim to be merely an observer. How power is experienced and exercised is a core issue in critical reflection. Reflexivity, focusing on the influence of our own position, becomes imperative in critical reflection because doing research on our own practice from the position of a neutral outside observer is impossible.

Critical Incident Analysis

A variety of models, tools and techniques exist for how to conduct critical reflection. The distinction is partly related to the diverse theoretical frameworks on which they build, but more importantly how many levels of reflection the models contain, as mentioned above, and how deeply the material is scrutinized (Fook et al., 2006: 5).

Fook (1996, 1999) has developed critical incident analysis as a method of critical reflection in social work, which aims to combine practice, theory and research. Critical incident analysis was developed by Flanagan (1954) as a research technique. Trained researchers would observe how professionals who were deemed competent handled a large number of cases, on the basis of which a professional knowledge base could be created. Flanagan defined an incident as critical if it made a 'significant' contribution, either positively or negatively, to the general aim of the activity observed (Flanagan, 1954: 338). Thus 'critical' in Flanagan's concept has no relation to critical theory or thinking. Critical incident analysis represents only raw data, and it does not automatically provide practical solutions to problems (Flanagan, 1954: 355).

The critical incident method may be used individually and in group settings. In groups, the participants take turns presenting and reflecting on their critical incidents working from critically reflective questions posed by other group members. It is a cognitive, emotional and experiential process, proceeding from lower to higher levels of reflection; from analysing the experiences to conceptualizing new knowledge and suggesting alternatives for experimentation (Fook et al., 2006, 12, 13–14). The aim on the first level is to promote professional growth and knowledge to improve practice. On a second level, which may take more time as critical reflection is a process; the goal is to obtain a collective knowledge base that may promote professional, organizational and structural changes (Mezirow, 2000; Gould and Baldwin, 2004).

The procedure is as follows:

- Describe the critical incident, making and restructuring meaning of it by analysing and understanding the situation.
- Reveal deep-seated assumptions that are taken for granted.
- Explore the individual experience in light of historical, social, political, economic, cultural and religious contexts.
- Create emancipatory knowledge resulting in professional growth and development.
- Create a collective professional knowledge base to be followed by transformative change (Fook and Askeland, 2006).

Individual and Professional Growth

The following two examples of critical incidents show some of what the participants got out of their critical reflection at the first level.

One Sunday, I went to visit my mother who is living 125 km away from the capital. There, I visited many of my relatives and acquaintances who were sick or had lost their family members. In our tradition, if someone is too ill or bereaved due to loss of beloved ones, providing financial assistance is customary. I did that in four or five cases. I didn't know exactly how much money I had in my pocket before I left home. But I was sure that I had enough money to cover the transportation and other unexpected expenses during my trip.

In the afternoon, I left for a nearby town by taxi to take a bus back to the capital. In the taxi, when I was asked for the fare, I put my hands in my pockets and found out I had only 13.50 (local currency). I made a quick calculation in my mind and realized I needed all the 13 to reach the capital and that I would have only 0.50 left which was not enough even to cover a taxi fare home from the centre of the capital. I felt angry for my own carelessness, for not checking my pocket. I could do nothing but tried to feel at ease and planned how to manage my trip. I had an earlier plan to visit a friend who lost his mother and was living in the town where I was to catch the bus. Deciding to keep the 0.50 for a bus fare when I reached the capital, I just walked to my friend's home. Near the bus station is my favourite hotel, where I used to take a beer or two before leaving the town. Besides the habit, I was very thirsty for a cold drink due to the heat. I totally forgot that I was penniless, went to the hotel and sat down on the veranda. I ordered a bottle of beer as usual. Just at that moment, my mind reminded me that I had no money to cover my order. I slowly stood up and left the area before the waiter returned. Very embarrassed, I went directly to the station, got on a bus and left for the capital. When I reached the capital, I was caught by torrential rain, worse than I had ever seen before. I had to stay near a building until it stopped. Then checking my 0.50 in my pocket, I took a bus for 0.25 and changed into another bus for 0.25. While waiting for the second bus, I was praying not to meet someone whom I know because it is customary to pay the transport cost for persons you know very well. Fortunately, there was no one at that particular moment. Thus, I felt relieved and got on the bus.

When this critical incident was presented in an African country, classmates received it with laughter, as this was a recognizable situation. Critical reflection on the incident started with questions like why was this critical for the student, where did his assumptions about why to share and how to handle the situation come from, and ended up with what he could learn about social work from critically reflecting on this incident, particularly in his local setting. The student maintained that 'poor and other segments of the population could encounter similar incidents'. He became aware of the 'false pride' that prevented him from asking his friend for help. This might be a contradiction in a culture where sharing would be part of social work thinking. The critical incident shows how important it is to contextualize social work. It shows the psychological influence of hegemonic values in a society. In Western cultures, it is taken for granted that individuals are responsible for themselves. For other people in other places, to share what one has and take responsibility for the extended family and the community overrule individual satisfaction.

When Western practice and literature emphasizing individualized solutions are introduced in a collectively oriented society it seems anomalous and alienating. It might violate the sharing and mutual responsibility embedded in the tradition where there is neither a welfare state, nor an individual and family insurance, and where people are totally dependent on the community.

A local project officer working in an NGO presented a critical incident about being sent to do some work with women in a remote area in an African country. Having grown up in the capital, she spoke the official language. She took it for granted that the women too would be able to speak the official language. She neither took into account the many ethnic groups in the country speaking their own languages, nor the fact that a proportion of the population is illiterate. When she found out that they were unable to communicate with her, she got very annoyed with them. Not until later when she got an English-speaking friend that she could barely understand, did she realize what it is like to feel inferior because of communication difficulties.

Critical reflection on her incident made her connect her own experience with what it might have been like for the women. She became conscious of the impact of using language to oppress people, and how she in her position had contributed to disempower the women. Several of the other group members belonged to various minority language groups. They might personally have experienced the connection between language and power, which could be used as a basis in developing a collective local knowledge about the subject in social work. In Chapter 4 we discuss the connection between language and power.

Collective Knowledge

The following examples show how experiences from critical reflection on individual critical incidents can be summarized as collective knowledge. A group of experienced Norwegian social workers at a social service department used a critical reflection method for group supervision for two semesters. They all presented work-related critical incidents on which they reflected, assisted by critically reflective questions from their colleagues. The issues presented varied. Nevertheless, a common topic that stood out was the ethical dilemmas and frustrations related to having to follow the rules and regulations of a bureaucratic welfare regime, influenced by New Public Management (NPM), see Chapter 6, that did not meet people's needs.

At the same time a class of about 40 master students in an African country without extensive welfare services was introduced to critical reflection. Several of them had extensive social work experience, particularly from non-governmental organizations. In groups, they all presented their critical incidents. Several of them reflected on the experience of having no money in a cultural setting where people are expected to share and take responsibility for each other, others on being in life threatening situations caused by natural disasters and accidents or for political reasons. A third issue was related to being humiliated in school or university. In plenary, the students summarized what they had learned about social work by critically reflecting on their own critical incidents. Firstly, they highlighted the importance of contextualizing social work, secondly, acknowledging the cultural aspect of social work. This was noticeable as most of the books in the social work library, from which they had learned about social work, were American. Thirdly, appreciating diversity as they, by listening to each others' presentations, realized with surprise that what their co-students found critical and how they chose to handle it, was different from their own reactions and actions, a parallel to what they would experience with the people they were to work with. These three aspects were the same ones that another class a year earlier had summarized as their new knowledge as a result of critical reflection (Askeland and Bradley, 2007).

These two situations are not comparable as the circumstances are different. Nevertheless, they show that social work may be diverse, whether there are extensive welfare services or not. They also give an idea of that critical reflection on various critical incidents may challenge group thinking and result in collective consciousness raising and sharing new knowledge. It would be the first step for the Norwegian group in changing practice and influence policy, and in creating social work knowledge, relevant for the local context for the African group. If critical reflection takes place in an agency setting, it tends to focus on implementation of structures and policies

(Høyrup and Elkjær, 2006), as it did in the Norwegian case. However, it also revealed power relations and emotions related to them (Vince, 2002 in Høyrup and Elkjær, 2006). If the consciousness raising and sharing of new knowledge amongst the African students of contextualization, cultural appropriateness and diversity would make them test the written and oral social work material to which they are introduced, the critical reflection might have started them on a journey towards a locally appropriate basis for social work.

Discussion

How does criticality manifest itself in the critical incident method? The critical incidents people present mean significant happenings in their lives, on which they critically reflect. The critical reflection is based on critical theory, including a prominent ideological critique, particularly of power relations in social work at all levels. It also focuses on the relationship between knowledge and power, including hegemonic assumptions that are taken for granted by most people and may be used to disempower, oppress, discriminate and dominate. In a critical incident method, the presenter scrutinizes her own taken-for-granted assumptions from a reflexive position to make explicit how they are expressed in values, attitudes and practice. The critical incident and the revealed assumptions are tested in historical, economic, political, social and professional contexts. Critical thinking and pragmatic constructivist perspectives allow the critical incident, as a text, to be deconstructed and the language becomes important. From a constructivist point of view, a universal and general knowledge base would be rejected. In this way, critical reflection on a critical incident may help to show how important it is to create local knowledge to make social work relevant and adequate. Without change, critical reflection has not fulfilled its utmost goal, and pragmatism accentuates experimentation as a forerunner for change. The critical incident method includes an experiential phase.

Critical reflection might serve differing interests depending on its theoretical traditions and frameworks. As we discuss in Chapter 5 and 8, several stakeholders and ringmasters with various interests create social work on both a local and an international level. Critical theory as a frame of reference, however, gives the exercise a basis and a direction that makes reflection more complex and comprehensive (Fook et al., 2006; Askeland, 2006).

Social work serves different interests around the world. In the Nordic countries a demand for social workers grew out of a need for a profession to serve the welfare state. Social workers are mainly employed by public agencies and institutions. Some clients consider them their counterparts and threaten them. In welfare regimes that provide benefits and services as part of social work, social work has been accused of contributing to silencing and keeping people in oppressed positions through the way it rations resources according to dominant cultural expectations. In other societies, social workers side with people against the ruling powers and have been imprisoned for their stands (IFSW, 2007).

Social work creates a fine balance between professional responsibilities and political issues. A collective approach is necessary to promote changes to meet the political ideals of social work. Flanagan's original critical incident research technique opens up the opportunity of using critical reflection to develop collective knowledge production as a basis for more extensive influence (Askeland and Bradley, 2007). Knowledge has an empowering effect when it is produced under non-oppressive conditions and when it contributes to reduce social inequality (Fisher, 2005). Social workers exposing their practice for scrutiny may become vulnerable (Preston-Shoot, 2000; Høyrup and Elkjær, 2006; Fook and Askeland, 2007). Critical reflection may therefore not be appropriate to every practice situation. Many social workers' conditions of service do not allow space and time for reflection, let alone critical reflection. To critically reflect on our own performance and agency role may be provocative to social workers in itself, not in the least as it may threaten an agency's and political interests. It may therefore be neither encouraged, nor expected, rather unwanted. It is thus a professional challenge to secure an open, non-judgemental and safe culture and atmosphere within which the critical reflection can take place (Mezirow, 2000; Fook et al., 2000; Fook and Askeland, 2007).

If the ultimate goal of critical reflection is to create knowledge to emancipate and promote professional growth and social change, it is important to understand how power is constructed and exercised (cf. Fook et al., 2006). Reflection, as a tool in developing professional practice as it is described in Schön's model, has been criticized for being a-theoretical and not specifically concerned with power. However, empowerment has become fundamental to social work both theoretically and in practice. Practising empowerment individually, collectively and internationally would be almost impossible without scrutinizing how power is exercised. Empowerment and oppression have to be seen in relation to each other both in academic studies and practice. In Chapter 2, we focus on postcolonialism in relation to international social work and social work education. We have to critically reflect on how power relations also influence what is accepted as social work in the international community.

In countries where social work is a new field, or with little locally developed literature as for example in the Caribbean (Maxwell et al., 2003), the profession has to build relevant practice from the ground up. Critical reflection by practitioners on their personal experiences and work is a useful starting point, in turn reducing dependence on importing literature that alienates social work from the local people and culture. When literature is imported, critical reflection may helpfully contextualize knowledge and fit practice approaches better to local needs. Incorporating local traditions in ways of responding to local needs (cf. Kretzer, 2005) is likely to make social work more effective for those it serves.

Cross-border teaching and practice demand critical reflection for both provider and receiver of knowledge, to avoid oppressing and becoming oppressed by others' inappropriate constructions of social understanding. Reflection only is insufficient; the critical perspective secures the empowering and emancipatory impact of reflection.

Critical reflection demands a self-critical stance. Knowledge-building self-evidently requires a critical perspective on the theory that is created and the creators' influence. We have to be cautious not to treat either critical reflection or new knowledge created through a critically reflective process, as if it is universal (Brookfield, 2005).

In cultures influenced by Confucianism, Taoism, Buddhism, Hinduism and Islam there is no sharp distinction between the self or individual identity and others, and stability and harmony are more prominent than change (Yip, 2004; for further discussion see also Chapter 6). Even with a holistic method, Western views tend to distinguish between spiritual and materialistic aspects of life. We are therefore unwise to assume that critical theory, reflexivity and critical reflection will have the same meaning and implication in Asian as in Western cultures. Culture, including religion and values, influences the focus of critical reflective processes and how, when and where they may be pursued.

Knowledge creation solely through reflection and critical reflection might become descriptive more than prescriptive (Mäntysaari, 2005). With over-emphasizing contextual knowledge there may be a danger of cultural relativism, accepting all ideas as equally valuable. However, social workers must nevertheless act, and therefore must make decisions between different ideas. The international trend towards evidence-based social work practice commends decision-making methods that can be specified, quantified, measured and thus become more predictable. Evidence-based practice tends to conceal the political and cultural aspect of social work (Lindén, 2004). On the contrary, we would emphasize the political and cultural aspects, uncertainty and complexity in selecting, developing and adapting knowledge for use in practice. This continually grounds research, education and practice contextually, test taken-for-granted knowledge and creates new and relevant knowledge to meet the requirements in a constantly changing society.

Until now, there is little empirical research on outcomes of critical reflection. Fook et al. (2006) argue that it is difficult to conduct research projects without a consistent theoretical framework and agreed tools and methods. To research the result of critical reflection may be even more difficult when it builds on critical theory. Brookfield (2005:9) claims that to verify that the visions critical theory inspires have been realized implies social change.

So far, critical reflection has mainly been used to develop individual professional competence, and, to some degree, a shared workplace knowledge base. Several descriptive studies are available of individual results of critical reflection (Fook et al., 2006). However, it is a future challenge to develop critical reflection, using critical incident method, to create collective, contextual knowledge bases. This is a challenge anywhere, but more so where social work is newly-established. New professions have resources for developing professional knowledge and practice models independently of the dominant international understandings of the nature of social work, which would serve as useful reference points.

Conclusion

Critical reflection combines criticality and reflection. Critical incident analysis is a method to aid critical reflection. Developed for supervision and education, it combines practice, education and research in a circular process. The aim is twofold: to promote professional growth and competence by critically reflect on personal practice and to create a professional contextual knowledge base.

Critical incident method is useful for contextualizing knowledge. Reflecting critically on personal practice may promote changes to enable social workers to respond better to local circumstances. In a postmodern, postcolonial era with growing globalization, it is sound policy to be sceptical about indiscriminate transfer of knowledge and practice approaches around the world. Critical reflection including critical incident analysis may help contribute to:

- a conscious perspective on the consequences of the global movements for social work, being specifically concerned about power, dominance and oppression;
- preventing postcolonialism in education and practice;
- creating local and contextual social work knowledges where the profession has been dependent on dominant western literature;
- establishing professional and collective knowledge that have an emancipatory and empowering effect.

Chapter 4

Racism, Social Exclusion and Cultural Translation

Introduction

Globalization draws attention to inequality: the inequalities between peoples, nations, regions of the world and different social groups. Social inequalities create power relations in which some groups in societies are disadvantaged, discriminated against and excluded from social participation. Social workers often work particularly with such groups and are therefore concerned with how to deal with exclusion in a practical way. As professionals and as government officials they are also part of the social structures that contribute to inequality. Inequalities between Northern and Southern hemispheres are mirrored in richer countries, where the urban south of Norway is richer than the arctic, rural north, the rich south-east of the UK is richer than Scotland and the north. Also, there are inequalities across regions such as Europe, where countries to the east are poorer than countries in the West, or North America, where countries in the north are richer than Mexico and many of the Caribbean islands. Social work values, concerned with creating social cohesion, seek social justice between countries and regions.

However, the position is complex, as postmodern analysis leads us to expect. Economic and social development is variable. During the late twentieth century, countries in East Asia, Japan, Korea, and Malaysia expanded rapidly and in the twenty-first century, India and China began to develop fast, too. Countries in South America have developed rich economies, although there continues to be gross inequality and considerable poverty. However, particularly in Africa, economies in the South generally remain very underdeveloped. Poor people migrate from the poorer to the richer economies and a global economy, benefits larger and richer economies. Social work has to deal with the dissatisfaction, despair and distress caused by these inequalities. Globalization means that everyone has greater knowledge and understanding of how inequality affects attitudes and understanding across the world.

Inequality is not only economic, but economic inequality leads to other social inequalities, which are expressed in culture and language. In this Chapter, we explore, in the next section, racism as an issue that has been a widespread concern in social work. It is an example of how inequalities are played out in social conflicts that affect social work through postcolonial hegemony. Then, we build on the introduction in Chapter 2 to explore how postcolonialism leads to cultural oppression particularly through language. Subsequently, we discuss how social work education demonstrates similar postcolonial oppression. We argue that social workers from dominant Western, English-speaking cultures in social work, and elsewhere, should facilitate cultural translation in addition to and as part of language translation. This would enable social work and other cultural ideas to be indigenized and authentized in minority cultures. Minority forms of social work might then be reintroduced into dominant cultures and gain cultural and eventually economic power.

There are a number of responses in various societies about these issues, which fall into three categories:

- Citizenship approaches, which emphasize social structures that support rights to equality and social inclusion.
- Interpersonal and intercultural approaches, which emphasize developing interactions between different peoples and cultures to reduce social exclusion.
- Social movement and protest approaches, which emphasize being aware of, valuing and seeking to respond to difference collectively.

These approaches are not separate from or inconsistent with each other; rather they are elements that may be observed in different interventions. For example, many aspects of international social work as we have described in Chapter 1, form a social movement approach. This is because it promotes a particular role for social work in poor countries and regions. It offers a response that criticizes a globalized approach to inequalities by asserting and demonstrating the importance of intervening on social issues as well as the economic development that globalization gives priority to. Social development focuses on an alliance with economic development in poorer countries (Midgley, 1997). It seeks to correct inequalities by incorporating social objectives into the purely economic imperatives generated by globalization. It also helps to promote local and community solidarity by encouraging cooperation to provide important social facilities, which will then enable people to contribute to wider development in poorer countries.

Cox and Pawar (2006), for example, identify the issues of poverty, conflict and post-conflict reconstruction, displacement and forced migration as the main focuses of social development and international social work. All these issues connect to globalizing forces. Thus, the social work response to globalization calls particularly on ways of supporting community, locality and family through empowerment, capacity-building, promoting self-help and self-reliance, enhancing social integration, income-generation and community development, which are elements of how many societies respond to inequalities. Social work often focuses on strengthening individuals and groups to take control of their own economic interests, using improved social relationships in families, localities and communities that share common interests to do so. Examples of social groups where this has worked well are street children, child labourers, migrant workers and their families, AIDS orphans in Africa and women as workers and as contributors to good relationships in family and community.

These personal and local social networks are important in maintaining solidarity and order in societies, and social work is one of the ways in which societies intervene in these issues. Husband (1996) argues that ideas of community, ethnicity and citizenship define and contain potential diversity in British community care. 'Community', particularly in communitarian ideas, represents a value of solidarity, participation and citizenship. The following section examines race and discrimination as an area in which social work has been active. These issues particularly connect with postcolonialism and its cultural and linguistic oppression and allow us to see the processes that social work needs to combat in Western countries and as part of international social work.

'Race' and Discrimination

Social Movements around Racism

During the last half of the 20th century, conflicts around several major issues raised concern internationally about race and ethnicity as a source of inequality and potential social disorder. Among important drivers of this concern were:

- International campaigns about the policy of apartheid (separate development of states for black and white population groups) in South Africa from the 1960s onwards.
- Discrimination against migrants from India, the Caribbean and other parts of the 'New Commonwealth' to the UK, which eventually led to civil disorder.
- American civil rights movements seeking equal treatment of black people.
- Discrimination against Turkish 'guest workers' in Germany.
- Discrimination against migrants from North Africa, particularly Algeria, in France.
- Concern about oppression of indigenous peoples such as Aboriginal people in Australia through policies criticized as being concerned primarily with creating a 'white Australia', native Americans in Canada and the USA and Maoris in New Zealand.

All such social concerns focused around a political campaign about the oppression of an ethnic group within the societies because of their 'race'. Some of these campaigns, such as the campaign against apartheid, became international, even global. Some, such as the American civil rights movement and legal developments in the US, achieved international influence. While social workers were sometimes as individuals engaged in such movements and their professional organizations contributed, these were social movements of concerned and politically committed people much wider than social work. Although 'race' does not have a biological basis, it attains a social 'truth' because there is a history of people being categorized in societies by assumed 'racial' characteristics derived from visible aspects of their ethnicity. Generally, white people of Western European or American origins categorized and treated unequally non-white people. The particular circumstances of each of these social movements varied, but seen on a global scale have these similar characteristics of oppression of non-white by white people because of 'racial' categorizations that have no basis in biological differences. This oppression and the social inequalities that result therefore are considered unjustified and unjust. Consequently, people concerned about these issues sought to rectify the injustice, either for ideological reasons, that the inequality is unjust and injustices should be rectified, or for a variety of practical reasons, such as the civil disorder or waste of human resources that might result from unfair discrimination.

Globalization may contribute to racism and cultural postcolonialism because of the impact of transnational corporations. These then influence government and social organizations to promote a powerful culture that leaves little space for maintaining separate cultures. Two aspects of globalization relevant to cultural imperialism are the tendency to make economies more interdependent and the use of information and communication technology (ICT) forcing formerly separated cultures into closer contact; see Chapter 9. People working in or studying international social work and its education can raise awareness of these issues, and adapt their approaches to respond to oppressions that arise from them. In doing so, it is important not to assume a universal knowledge that may usefully be applied in or adapted to all cultures; see Chapters 2 and 5.

Social Work and Anti-racism Movements

Citizenship is a crucial concept raised by these social changes deriving from globalization. It involves a number of interdependent rights (Castles and Davidson, 2000: Ch. 5). These include various human rights such as freedom of expression and religion, political rights such as the right to vote and stand for election and various social rights such as rights to employment, social security payments and equality of access to education or services.

The history of social change in many countries arising from migration increasingly makes it more complex to understand people's identity, because national, religious and cultural identity are not the clear markers of individual identity that many people assume. Globalization and postcolonialism have an oppressive impact on local cultures in three ways: through the economic power of globalization discussed in Chapter 2, through cultural oppression and through language and linguistic oppression, discussed in this chapter.

Globalization ideas focus on the economic, and also affect culture and language. Identities are no longer clearly associated with a particular national culture or with a particular language. Many countries have multiple languages, or border on countries that speak other languages and all countries interact through globalization with dominant cultures and languages. There may be loyalties to or interest in two or more cultures. For example, at the time of writing, a twelve-year-old girl chose to leave her mother, the legal guardian, in Scotland to travel to be with her Muslim Pakistani father and other family members, changing her name from an English to an Islamic form. Thus, everyone, including social workers, has to deal with complex identities in a globalized world. We must all translate understanding of the culture in which we live into a cultural framework that is relevant for others. Anti-racist practice must deal with that complexity, seeing where potential oppression connects with complex identities and relationships.

Social work incorporates three broad approaches to these issues, which are examples of the three general social responses to inequalities, referred to above:

- *Anti-discriminatory, anti-oppressive and anti-racist practice is a citizenship, structural approach* – Drawing particularly on left-wing political philosophies and characteristic of the UK, this practice argues that the main issue is inequality between social groups and racism focusing on non-white groups. Practice should challenge examples of discriminatory, oppressive or racist behaviour. Discrimination, oppression and racism that are integral to the organization of society and agencies should be identified and eliminated.

- *Empowerment practice is an interpersonal, intercultural approach* – Characteristic of the US and Canada, but also used elsewhere, it draws on systems theories and social democratic political philosophies. It sees discrimination, oppression and racism as creating barriers in society, which people affected can learn to overcome. It primarily sees intervention as interpersonal, although personal empowerment may also be extended to achieve social change.

- *Cultural pluralism, diversity and multicultural ideas and social movement approaches* – leading to cultural competence practice. They focus on cultural and social differences between ethnic groups, rather than inequalities. Societies and social institutions should accept and value cultural difference as a resource to the community. In a rather cognitive-behavioural approach to the problems, education about and experience of the range of ethnicities present in a community or society is promoted, and practitioners should become knowledgeable about and competent to respond to issues that emerge from difference among the cultures they deal with.

To which we would add a fourth, which we argue for in this chapter:

- *Cultural translation which draws together structural, interpersonal and social movement approaches* – Our approach accepts the crucial relevance of understanding that the structural issue of inequality is the major issue for resolution, and argues for both empowerment and cultural competence. However, omnicompetence in practitioners is impractical and disempowering; since it implies that they are able to interpret their own dominant culture and understanding to people with less power. They may be able to do something, but it should not be assumed and people from the dominant cultures should not be solely in control of the processes. Instead, practice and education should be organized in such a way that it enables adaptation of cultural ideas, and users and students should be enabled to create their own formulations of ideas and actions, through critical reflection. Thus, the users have control of how the idea is translated, not the dominant culture, and are enabled also to re-offer their translation as a renewed cultural understanding to the dominant culture.

Cultural Translation

Figure 4.1 shows the concept of cultural translation in a diagram. An initial requirement, which we draw from the ideas of anti-oppressive practice, is a realistic acceptance by people and agencies with power that their cultures dominate other cultures. While we refer here to dominant and minority cultures, their power is exercised through social structures such as governments, corporations, NGOs and organizations of all kinds, including social work agencies. Thus, people in an organization of social work agency must develop awareness of its institutional racism, using processes such as critical reflection. Consequently, they accept their responsibility for making available their ideas and practices in a way that others may redirect, and they make available resources to help less powerful people indigenize the ideas and authentize them with their own approach. An exchange process goes on, wholly controlled by the less powerful group. The dominant culture's resources then make available culturally acceptable ideas from the minority culture to the dominant culture.

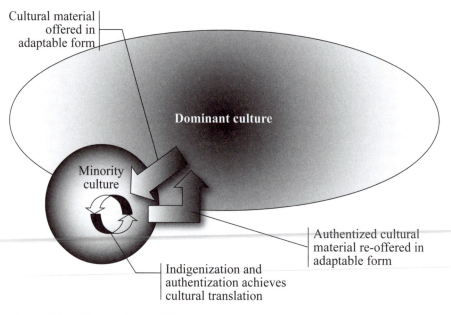

Cultural material offered in adaptable form

Dominant culture

Minority culture

Authentized cultural material re-offered in adaptable form

Indigenization and authentization achieves cultural translation

Figure 4.1   Cultural translation

An example is the way in which palliative care agencies caring for dying people, their families and carers respond to different cultural expectations at the end of life. Guides are available about cultural expectations (Neuberger, 2004) and the hospice where Malcolm works has guidance available for staff on appropriate ways of responding to common problems. However, he recently discussed with a Muslim daughter details of the death of her mother. She walked with him back to the main entrance, and caught sight of the Christian chapel on the way. She saw candles burning and asked to go in. The Chapel can be adapted within moment from its Christian iconography. He offered her a prayer mat, pointed out the direction of Mecca, both conventional recognitions of Muslim prayer, and offered to remove the Christian symbols. But no, she asked simply to light a candle for her mother and spent some private time facing the Christian pictures. Then, she left a written prayer for her mother as part of a Christian device for leaving memorials. She said that the respect shown for her difference made her feel happy to meet her own spiritual needs, even in this environment that might be seen as inappropriate. These kinds of flexibilities are part of any life in a multicultural environment, but the whole range of possible responses must be catered for to allow her to make her own translation of the Christian environment for her own use. Malcolm's responsibility and that of the agency was to be open to both this flexibility and the possibility of a more orthodox need.

One of the concerns about multicultural or diversity approaches is the fear of or resistance to homogenization or hybridization of cultures (Kraidy, 2005). People do not want to see everything mixed together, and may seek to retain their cultural heritage and resist its dilution by other cultures. For example, groups of migrants may seek to live in the same area, so that they can maintain their religion, establish churches, mosques or temples with a large enough population to support them, and can get food and entertainment that maintains their cultural separateness. Often, as with many traditional communities, people may seek marriage partners within the community. Multicultural approaches question this separateness, since as the new cultures become influential they may dilute the power of the majority culture. Black perspectives approaches to social work, for example, argue that it is important to identify and work within the view of situations that minorities themselves hold rather than within culturally dominant assumptions (Graham, 2004; Ahmad, 1990). American research proposes the importance of using cultural history and black experience to appreciate the ways in which black people have responded to the oppression they have experienced (Martin and Martin, 1995). French debate on these issues explores the importance of nigrescence (Robinson, 1995, 1999), the development of black identity particularly in young people. The related idea of negritude (Kraidy, 2005: 67–71) refers to the specificity of black culture. These ideas contest the dominance of postcolonial hegemony, pointing to evidence that national and ethnic cultures explore and develop their own conceptualizations of their ethnic and social identities.

Social Movements, Social Inclusion and Social Capital

The paradox that globalization and postmodern societies seek both to homogenize cultures and to offer variety raises the question of what social workers, among others, should do about these issues. Racism leads to political action and social protest, which in turn connects it to policy about urban living and regeneration, civil unrest, and policing (Solomos, 2003). Thus, racial inequality and discrimination connects with other inequalities and the social response to them. In the same way that there were worldwide social movements around racial inequalities, from 1970 onwards there were also several other social movements concerned with inequalities, which swept the world and gained wide support, including many social workers. The most important of these interpreted in different ways in different countries, are:

- The women's movement.
- Environmental movements, including concerns about food, pollution and, more recently, climate change.

- Movements for effective healthcare, particularly to prevent conditions that have a wide impact such as malaria and tuberculosis, around HIV/AIDS and around physical disabilities.

All such movements are connected with the impact of globalization on social and economic inequalities, and particularly on poverty. For example, women are the main generators of income for their families in many poor countries as well as being the main organizer of care for family members. Help to them is often one of the best ways of reducing poverty, ill-health and childhood mortality. Environmental concerns often affect the poorest nations, communities and families the most quickly and strongly. Better preventive healthcare and treatment for common disabling conditions such as malaria, HIV/AIDS and tuberculosis can lead to rapid improvements in economic and social strength in poor countries. One of the weaknesses of social work in responding to such issues is that its professional role has focused on individualized help too much to make a contribution to such vigorous social movements.

In all societies, however, poor people tend to be clustered together in poor environments and share similar problems. It is unclear whether this is because people with shared characteristics tend to lose income and resources in their families and accumulate in areas with poor resources (Wilkinson, 1996). It may be instead that their poverty leads to greater ill-health and social difficulties. Probably it is a combination. The clustering of populations with social difficulties has led to concern that in the same way that globalization may lead to whole countries being excluded from participation in international economy, the cultural and social consequences of globalization leads to neighbourhoods or communities being excluded from participation in political and social life and in opportunities for healthy lifestyles.

Consequently, social work in Western societies should also emulate development work in addressing the needs of social groups and communities collectively. Loizos (2000) in a historical study of a variety of refugee situations, points out that refugee agencies have found it 'politically hazardous' (p. 140) to target aid at destitute refugees if populations where they end up are also poor and receive no help. Instead, 'refugee-affected populations' should be jointly assisted alongside migrants. Similarly, more broadly, Washington and Paylor (1999) argue that European Union (EU) poverty policy developed new practices designed to reduce social exclusion of groups suffering from economic inequality, and increase social solidarity across the EU. They argue that this might offer a new identity for social work.

In the same way that refugees bring with them social capital by their energy and commitment to finding a new life, excluded communities need to be helped to find the social capital in their networks and relationships. Although sometimes destitute, refugees may bring some wealth or possessions from their previous life, they bring relationships and contacts in their community, they bring their family supports and may bring skills, knowledge, resilience and motivation to re-establish themselves (Loizos, 2000). There is international evidence, for example, that young people from migrant families often do better in education than people from local ethnic groups. This is because, compared with other local people, they use stronger social ties from their community to provide opportunities, when their competition in the open job market is restricted by discrimination (Lauglo, 2000). Munn (2000) argues that we can use findings such as these to help people within educationally deprived areas to strengthen their social networks to achieve better work and school experiences, through mentoring and other schemes.

The Truth and Reconciliation Commission in South Africa reviewed from all points of view human rights crimes during the period that apartheid policies led to serious social conflict. It allowed people to admit their crimes and others to tell their stories. The Chairperson argued that this process of revealing truth led to greater stability than criminal trials:

> … we have seen how unsuccessful prosecutions lead to bitterness and frustration in the community. Amnesty applicants often confessed to more gruesome crimes than were the subject of the Basson trial, yet their assumption of responsibility, and the sense that at least people were getting some measure of truth from the process, resulted in much less anger (Tutu, 2003).

A similar cultural approach in social work has emerged from a group of workers in the Balkans. This focuses on the exploration of cultural memory within a supportive setting, using the welfare organization as a support in developing alternative understandings of damaging cultural memories and to strengthen resilience. Stubbs (2002) suggests that this work shows that one of the contributions of welfare organizations to civil society is to contribute to an alternative culture of understanding difficulties and stresses. A parallel occurred in Afghanistan where social workers from an INGO also used damaged cultural memories to strengthen resilience (Løfsnæs, 2006). Zaviršek (1999), in a Balkan case study, points out that memories, perceptions and understandings of people with disabilities or mental illnesses are marginalized in many societies. Stubbs (2002) argues that memories and narratives of users' and workers' everyday experiences in such societies undergoing stressful change are important resources for understanding how social work and welfare regimes work in detail. Možina (2002) illustrates this analysis with a further Balkan case study showing how spending time working through a mentally ill person's experiences of relationships in her life enabled the service users to analyse and remember her experiences differently through the experience of support and caring by workers in a voluntary organization. The important aspect of this work is how experiences of relationships in organizations in the present connected with traumatic experiences from the past. For example battles over the management of finances, now allowed the user to reconstruct, rethink and ultimately deal with past experiences, which were inhibiting the ability to develop appropriate relationships with others.

Culture as a Determinant of Social Intervention and Education

Working on such social reconstruction crucially involves our view of culture. The postmodern view is that different historical and social environments form both our attempts at social development and also how we see and understand social issues. We argue in Chapter 5 that the idea of universal knowledge conflicts with the idea that different cultures have different ways of understanding the world. Cultures are shared world views about three elements of a society:

- Systems of values and behaviour that are widely acknowledged as characteristic of a society.
- Aesthetic, artistic and intellectual achievements of that society, again acknowledged as characteristic of it.
- The way in which that society achieves change in and development of values and behaviours and their expression, which then affects the cultural assumptions that individuals develop.

Colonialism and postcolonialism imposes cultures through power relations, limiting the available cultural resources. But, cultural diversity is needed just as much as biodiversity. An ecosystem is more viable in the long term if it has a large gene pool, because this may offer a wider range of possibilities for dealing with unexpected changes in the environment. Similarly, a larger pool of cultures and knowledges may make it possible to deal with a wider range of human situations. Moreover, it produces a more interesting and varied environment, which offers more stimulation and creativity, both generally and also in education and social relations. Colonialism means that local and minority cultures are discounted in favour of the dominant culture, in the same way that globalization overvalues the economically powerful cultures.

The colonizer rules the colonized partly through cultural hegemony. Hegemony is the use of cultural and social relations to impose or maintain power. It is:

> ... the process whereby ideas, structures and actions come to be seen by the majority of people as wholly natural, preordained, and working for their own good, when in fact they are constructed and transmitted by powerful minority interests to protect the status quo that serves those interests (Brookfield, 1995: 5).

Internationalizing social work and its education creates a Western hegemony in the valuing of certain kinds of internationally credible knowledge and control of the dissemination of knowledge. Bringing skills and knowledge of practice or education to countries or regions where it would otherwise be inaccessible appears to be a valuable gift. However, it is also a cultural hegemony that tightens the dependency of the receiving on the giving countries. Globalized economic and technological superiority makes it clear that colonialism and racism continues postcolonialism (Owolabi, 2001).

Therefore, education and social work practice needs to develop processes for cultural translation as well as language translation. In social work education, we understand cultural translation to mean identifying and assessing ways in which and the degree to which understanding from learning materials created in one cultural setting can be adapted to be used in another setting. The creator of learning materials may do this prospectively, so that they can be more open to use in other cultures than the one in which they are created. The educators using materials can also do it retrospectively. They need to understand factors that affect the validity of the materials for use in the new setting.

Language as a Factor in Social Construction

Language is an important factor in social construction, because it is an important aspect of personal and cultural identity, as well as being the carrier of knowledge.

Which languages are used in social development? Which are used to convey knowledge through education? These questions are connected with cultural hegemony. Linguistic diversity is important because it allows us to describe our country, feelings, and experiences related to our specific environment, which is essential in social work, rather than using language related to another environment. As language is lost, traditional environmental knowledge also disappears (Skutnabb-Kangas, 1999). For example, people from Greenland have many different concepts in their language for describing snow, a variety unnecessary in most languages, which have linguistic diversity in other ways. This shows how language is a resource in particular environments, not a problem to be erased by less complexity and greater universality (Phillipson, 1999).

However, language has not been treated as a human rights issue. In the original United Nations' Charter (Art. 13) language was one of the four basic human rights together with race, sex, and religion (Skutnabb-Kangas, 1999: 177), but was later deleted. Today there are about 6,700 oral languages. Only 600 of these are considered safe for survival to the end of the present century. The top ten languages in the world, which have at least 100 million speakers each, are spoken by 50% of people altogether. There are about 200 states in the world, and 141 have one of the top languages as its official one in administration and education. In most of these countries, the official language has its position even if the majority of the people in the country has other mother tongues. All inhabitants are not required to have command of the official language, particularly if people have little formal education (Skutnabb-Kangas, 1999: 72), the case for many people that social workers are dealing with. The top languages kill others, and English is by far the most important, used in 75 countries.

What makes this possible is that 'the speakers of these languages have allocated to themselves more structural power and material resources, than their numbers would justify, at the cost of speakers of other languages' (Skutnabb-Kangas, 1999: 70). The dominance of English is not an accident, but a well-planned policy. An adviser to the British Council wrote in 1941:

> a new career service is needed, to lay the foundation of a world language and culture based on our own... an army of linguistic missionaries ... a central office in London, from which teachers radiate all over the world (Routh, 1941: 2–13).

English teaching has become the second biggest business in the British economy (Phillipson, 1999: 204). English as a global language is an extension of colonialism; the same is true for other European top languages. Of 173 countries that have gained independence from a colonial power, 62 have gained independence from UK, 28 from France and 17 from Spain (Globastat, 2001). The acceptance and extension of languages depend on political and economic interests. People belonging to a small language group are made powerless and inferior.

Nuances in linguistic power differences may affect understanding and attitudes. Africans as well as people in small language groups in Europe are led to think that foreign languages are synonymous with knowledge and privileges (Bgoya, 1999: 223). African languages are then considered only a medium for transfer of culture and folklore (Bgoya, 1999: 226), while European languages are needed for development (Phillipson, 1999: 199). Depending on European and American support and consultancy for their economic success makes it difficult to claim their own interests and beliefs in their own language. In negotiations and discussion, participants have to translate between dominant and local languages, with meaning often compromised. Education, publications and interactions in a foreign language alienate educators, students, social workers and clients, and often give concepts a slightly different meaning.

These issues do not only affect poor or previously colonized countries, but have wider importance. Rich countries where the language is not one of the top languages are also affected. When a new Higher Education Act was implemented in 2005, the paragraph that established Norwegian as the common teaching language in Norwegian universities and colleges was deleted. Debate on changing it led the University of Oslo to form its own language policy. Nevertheless, some courses formerly offered in Norwegian are now in English to meet the requirements for international student exchanges. This is also true of social work education. This might be considered a step toward the decline of Norwegian as a teaching language. Publishing internationally, primarily in English, is more highly valued and gains educational institutions more governmental financial support than publishing in Norwegian (Broch-Utne, 2006).

In a globalized world, resistance to using English or another world language may cause difficulties for linguistic minorities and disaster for economies dependent on improving education. There is a close relation between poverty and lack of competence in a dominant language (Skutnabb-Kangas, 1999: 188). Chapter 9 further explores how technology uses dominant languages, again supporting their hegemony in oral languages (Lund, 2000). Everything important has to be written or, to go further, made available on the Internet. To become accessible for others to quote and copy, it has to be documented and disseminated in powerful and technological language. What is said or written locally or in a minority language becomes unimportant and loses influence. Aggression towards Western Women's Liberation from women from Asian and African countries, according to Susan Rakhsh (2003), reporting the award of the Nobel Peace Price to Shirin Ebadi:

> Western women look upon Eastern women as helpless in need of Western assistance. It may be that Western women are ignorant about the liberation and development work eastern women have done because there might be little published about it, since men do not write about it. Alternatively, they are ignorant about what is written because they cannot read it. Nevertheless, Western ignorance about it does not mean that it does not happen.

Postcolonialism in Social Work Education

We now move to discussing how social work becomes part of postcolonialism through pressures on its education. This discussion raises general issues within social work education; the personal effects on students, educators and practitioners are picked up again in Chapter 7.

By deepening economic inequalities and creating economic dependency, globalization emphasizes the affluence of the rich and the poverty of the poor. As people are more accessible to each other, this is more visible (Owolabi, 2001: 5). Globalization therefore draws attention to, confirms and increases postcolonial inequalities. As globalization increases the gap between rich and poor, it widens the gap between people with and without education. Providing aid for economies in the South requires systems of knowledge dissemination to recognize the needs of developing knowledge systems.

Social work education is in a global market. Those who have the resources to produce and market social work literature and academic courses are able to disseminate their social work theory and practice throughout the world as preferred or unique professional ways of handling social issues. In doing so, they ignore the differences between local contexts in which their knowledge is produced and those where it is used.

Social practices such as social work and institutions such as education are part of homogenizing processes allowing culture to be used in a postcolonial environment to dominate. As Ashcroft et al. (1995: 425) say: 'Education...is a massive cannon in the artillery of empire'. The problems that globalization brings for education are connected with postcolonialism because '[e]ducation is perhaps the most insidious and in some ways the most cryptic of colonial survivals, older systems, now passing, sometimes imperceptibly, into neo-colonialist configurations' (Ashcroft et al., 1995; 425).

Colonialism often involves constructing the colonized nation incompletely, representing it in terms that the colonizer can understand, and evaluating its culture and civilization according to the colonizer's values and attitudes. Colonizers use education and cultural experiences to shift the colonized people's culture and values towards that of the colonial power. In the postcolonial period, education and cultural development continues the same process. To respond to colonial and postcolonial experience, countries need to develop or recover both their own, and recognize and value other, cultural identities. Each has to gain self-sufficiency and confidence in their own cultural identity. Each has to establish a fair valuation of the identity of the other, which does not rely on a continuation of the cultural power relationship. This is an important reason for social workers responding to racism to focus on how their participation in a dominating culture contributes to their racism in the way they disseminate research, writing and education in the international market. It is not enough to respond to racism only in practice with minorities in their own practice and education settings.

Like globalization, both colonialism and postcolonial behaviour imply a universal, unitary and homogeneous human nature. Educational colonialism claims that the colonizer's universal knowledge is superior, devaluing and marginalizing the characteristics of the colonized civilization. Again, postcolonial education maintains these relationships. Social work education is an example of these processes. As it attempts to become an international, universal profession, social work's education takes on a postcolonial character, in which its assumptions about culture and its use of language allow economically powerful dominant Anglo-American cultures to oppress local cultures. Examples of potential cultural hegemony in social work education are:

- attempts to create global or regional standards in education and qualification.
- use of the same learning materials in different countries to meet different learning aims imposing learning aims and assessment methods.
- lack of flexibility for local adaptation in many learning programmes.
- use of world languages, particularly English, as a medium of education.

We will pick up some of the practical implications for these issues as they apply to educators and students in Chapters 7, 8 and 9.

Social Work Education's Cultural Hegemony

Global Standards and Definition

The recent initiatives to create international definitions of social work and standards in social work education, mentioned in Chapter 1, are thus examples of postcolonial cultural hegemony. IASSW's (2004) global standards for social work education working party established jointly with IFSW defines core purposes of social work education and lists proposed standards on the organization of schools and curriculum contents. However, what is valued academically, epistemologically and ontologically varies between countries and cultures (Yip, 2004; Hamäläinen and Vornanen, 1996). Joint work might achieve open agreement about local and regional definitions and relevant objectives. Standards are often set in countries where resources are plentiful, and this devalues schools in different traditions and at different stages of development that have made real achievements.

Work on standardization contains a hidden implication that resisting 'standard' points of view is a question of poor quality in local education systems, rather than alternative perspectives. Since modes and traditions of practice, educational approaches, and cultures and national policy objectives vary so widely, we argue standards should be defined as processes to meet local traditions and policies rather than some hegemonic international perspective.

Language in Social Work Education

If education is not given in indigenous languages, it kills mother tongues, for all the reasons given above. However, efforts to develop social work education internationally are primarily written and carried out in English, and to a significantly lesser extent one of the other world languages. The official languages of IASSW, for example, are English, French, Spanish, and Japanese, all powerful colonial languages. Education in a foreign language always makes people feel inferior, less fluent and competent. Uncertain about language competence, educators and students, social workers and clients might be inactive or unresponsive, which might be wrongly perceived as lack of ability (Levin and Trost, 1996). Writing and reading in a foreign language both makes it difficult to understand and to convey ideas. So, people from a less powerful language group cannot gain influence for their work, and cultures based in minor languages have less influence in developing professional knowledge base.

Also, language is important in creating valid knowledge. Knowledge expressed in a minority language may be ignored or devalued, even though it is particularly relevant to the environment that provides the context for that language and its knowledge. Language thus oppressively excludes people and their knowledge from full participation where it is most relevant. Without full participation, people will be unable to define valid knowledge in their own context. The consequences might be that also few cultural backgrounds are represented. Thus, social work education becomes not international, but between English speakers, who appear to be trendsetters, when their trends simply displace valid understanding expressed in different languages and cultures.

Cultural Translation in Social Work Education

Therefore, educational programmes influenced by global 'standards' and postcolonial 'universal' knowledge may alienate social work from the local challenges in social life and policy. Social work would be richer if it uses its cultural diversity creatively through cultural translation. We argue for two aspects of this. First we should create educational materials to make them accessible to cultural translation, so that less powerful cultures and experiences can easily pick up material in a way that does not dominate their culture. In the process of doing this, education reproducing dominant cultures and knowledge would also be shifted. Ways of doing this include:

- Enabling local values, research and skill-development to influence the dominant literature by co-writing or editing materials that interpret minority cultural and professional experience to the dominant literature;
- Searching out, translating and publishing materials from minority cultures and interests;
- Being explicit in curricula and course organization about requirements to apply knowledge in and from different cultural settings;
- Developing funding to allow material from minority cultures to be published in world languages;
- Providing training, supervision and support to social work educators to become cultural translators between dominant and local cultures and vice versa;
- Writing learning materials and teaching in such a way that are open to cultural translation by students and colleagues from minority cultures;
- Formulating literature as inspiration to enable people to develop their ideas instead of writing as though it provides universal prescriptions and guidelines for practice;
- Describing the local contexts that have particularly influenced the form in which ideas have developed, so that people can understand what may be irrelevant and what may be adaptable to their culture.

The second aspect of cultural translation should be to educate using resources from diverse cultures by:

- Being open to minority cultures and approaches in their choice and use of educational materials in their teaching;

- Transferring openness to the practice of the students;
- Making cultural translations so that material is relevant to local concerns and local material has an impact on global concerns;
- Acknowledging and encouraging proactive attempts to deal with the difficulties in adapting materials where they are produced in a different culture from that in which they will be used.

Conclusion

We have argued in this Chapter that globalization and postcolonialism interact so that Western cultures continue to dominate former colonies through economic oppression and cultural and linguistic hegemony. Social work has worked on racism and discrimination in everyday practice through various interpersonal professional practices. These also interconnected with wider political campaigns and attempts at social construction.

We have argued that education and social work are instruments of discrimination through postcolonialism, particularly in the oppressive way language is used. International projects on standardisation of social work illustrate that. Therefore, it is important to avoid cultural hegemony and respond to pressures towards it in international social work. Practitioners and educators may, in their everyday practice, also make a contribution. In attempting cultural translation, they need to be aware of and prepared to tackle the structural inequalities that always affect an agency, or an educational process. Cultural translation can make available their decisions and understandings in a way that can be reinterpreted and indigenized in a minority culture. In practice they can do so by offering transparent opportunities for participation and, in education, by creating educational materials that actively advantage less powerful cultures so that they may gain more influence on culturally dominant knowledge and decision-making.

Once ideas are indigenized and authentized, practitioners can also learn from the ideas developed in the minority culture for changing their practice. For example, they might pick up user perspectives. There is a strong history of black perspectives, and, more widely, user perspectives from disabilities groups, child advocacy and advocacy from mental health service users, which have questioned and changed the dominant culture in social work practice. In education, educational materials from diverse cultures might help to avoid the tendency for globalization to emphasize universality in favour of emphasizing difference and locality. Practice may use perspectives drawing on the social capital of local communities, responding to user perspectives, and educational materials can facilitate cultural translation to enable minority cultural materials to influence dominant, Western, English-speaking cultures.

Chapter 5

Knowledge Production: What is Valid Knowledge?

Introduction

Relevant Knowledge and Research

Social workers in some Western countries claim that what they learn during their studies cannot be applied to what they are expected to do when they start working (Marsh and Triseliotis, 1996). Useful knowledge for social workers in the field might be different from what is considered valid for academics, who rarely see clients. In some countries, academics might not have practised social work, or only at the beginning of their careers, and in all countries academic jobs are not primarily about or validated by practice. Thus educators are often distant from contexts in which social work is practised, and it therefore becomes difficult if not impossible, to teach *how to* do social work in a convincing way. Educators often focus on competences and service delivery, not usually on practices. Students are taught, based on this research, about *who* and *what* instead of *how.* Consequently, students may not gain practical help in professional relationships with people. A social worker complained to Gurid about the irrelevance of role-plays during her studies. Most of her clients are single men who live on social security benefits. Some threaten her, some have abused their wives, some have been in prison, all provoked her feelings and attitudes in various ways. Her role-plays had been about interviewing families who were asked to come to the office for a meeting. They had not been as complicated or conflictual as the work she experiences. However, even if educators are familiar with social workers' working conditions, it is difficult to construct a complex 'real world' learning environment in the classroom.

In earlier chapters, we argued that a postmodern international social work also raises questions about a scientific research- or evidence-based practice. A scientific social work has been an ambition of social workers since the idea of 'scientific charity' sought to help people on the basis of understanding their behaviour and patterns of relationships. Germain (1970) saw the development of social work as a search for greater scientific precision in understanding and working with human beings. The first rigorous research in social casework during the 1950s and 1960s led to consternation when it failed to demonstrate that it achieved the results it set out to achieve (Fischer, 1973, 1976; Mullen et al., 1972). An important argument for the value of behavioural and cognitive-behavioural practice techniques since the 1960s has been their demonstrable success in achieving small-scale behavioural change. Subsequently, research into well-designed agency programmes in the US and elsewhere demonstrated success in achieving outcomes (Reid and Hanrahan, 1982; MacDonald and Sheldon, 1992).

This has led in the 1990s to an accelerating trend to encourage social workers to be aware of research that might bear on their practice (Everitt et al., 1992) or to base their interventions on reviews of the evidence in particular situations (Thyer and Kazi, 2004). The International Definition of Social Work reflects this trend in its text: 'Social work bases its methodology on a systematic body of evidence-based knowledge derived from research and practice evaluation, including local and indigenous knowledge specific to its content ...' (IFSW, 2000). Trinder (2000) suggests that this concern has arisen because:

- a gap between research and practice means that people do not know how to implement research in practice;
- poor research means that it is not relevant or worthwhile to use;
- information overload means that there is too much information to assimilate in a busy practice setting;
- and, therefore, people continue to use practices that they have developed from training and convention that are not evidence-based.

Enthusiasm for evidence-based practice has been so great that it has become something of a professional movement, with enthusiasts and detractors (Gibbs and Gambrill, 2002; Webb, 2001). In the same way, a previous generation argued about the possibility of an 'empirical' practice, in Fischer's (1978) terms, seeing the opposing concept as 'social construction' (Thyer, 1994). Brechin and Sidell (2000) point out that this has been a continuing philosophical debate over the centuries between positivists, who believe the world is orderly and follows natural rules that we can investigate and understand, and interpretivists, who believe that independent human beings can change the world around them according to their own aims and interpretations. Thus, this debate is in part about how knowledge is produced and in part about how we see the world.

However, as postmodernist ideas suggest, a range of approaches to a scientific social work, as to everything else, is possible. Orcutt (1990) for example, sees science as a number of forms of inquiry, and Kirk and Reid (2002) show that there are a number of different approaches to incorporating research into practice. If we accept this point, practitioners and educators need to discover what kinds of knowledge and understanding are useful and valid for particular kinds of practice. Schön (1991) claims that a gap between research and practice arises when the research is not relevant for practice, and not necessarily, as Tinder (2000) proposes, that practitioners do not know how to use research. Critical reflection, see Chapter 3, is one way of validating knowledge in and for the context to which it is relevant.

Variation in Social Works and Transfer Between Them

Chapter 1 raised the possibility that globalization leads people to expect that social work's knowledge base should be increasingly universal, shared across the world. Globalization emphasizes bringing societies, and therefore their knowledges, closer together in culture and understanding, and social work would be part of that. In this view, an international social work would have a strong element of agreed, universal knowledge; otherwise, it would not be recognizable as the same thing in different countries. Postmodernism, on the other hand, suggests that any knowledge base varies according to social and historical situations in which it arises and is used. In this view, international social work is a complex of interlocking ideas, knowledge and practices useful and valid for different purposes and in different places, rather than one set of knowledge. A postmodern global world would permit many different social works emerging from many different cultures to exist alongside each other. Both these trends interact: ideas and cultures that attain global significance gain greater power, but many different ideas and cultures exist that are less powerful but valid in their context. Chapter 4 examined how globalization and postcolonialism allows Western cultures to dominate others, creating discrimination and oppression through inequalities in people's access to knowledge that might be relevant to their culture and social environment.

Globalization, therefore, raises the possibility that assuming knowledge and social work to be universal will lead to social inequalities because a universal social work will not deal with the issues faced locally. Chapter 3 offered critical reflection as a model to deal with this issue, Chapter 4 cultural translation. In this Chapter, we propose that social workers need to be aware of the possibility that claimed universal social work knowledge might not be appropriate to their situation and that of their clients. First we explore how they can examine what might be valid knowledge for their cultural and social situation within the knowledge for social work that might be available internationally. We then explore ways of transferring learning from one type of knowledge to another to make it valid for practice in different contexts. This not only involves transfer from different national or regional social works, but also between different priorities and purposes. The priorities of care managers in social care services might be different to the priorities and purposes of social work in other situations. The priorities of educators to devise valid research and of governments or other funders to finance it in ways that achieve policy or political objectives might be different from the priorities of practitioners to learn how to practice.

Purposes of Different Social Work Knowledges

We question, first, validity for what purpose? Different purposes of social work imply different kinds of knowledge. For example, if social work is mainly about social change it will require different knowledge from social work that is about personal change or maintaining people's stability or providing care services. It will be different where it requires helping families to develop interdependence and mutual support within a tribal culture from helping children grow away from their parents, accepting and developing independence in a Western culture.

Related to this, different stakeholders in social work make differing assessments of the validity of particular aspects of knowledge. Practitioners, for example, might value different knowledge from managers, clients, educators, researchers and professionals from related disciplines. Thus, in palliative care, a social worker focuses on strengthening family relationships during the dying process and in bereavement, while a nurse might focus on symptom management, and a social care manager on the effective delivery of services to support members of the family at home.

Moreover, the processes of knowledge creation and transmission that we discussed in Chapter 3 affect its validity. Critical reflection, reflexivity and models of education and research all influence how social work is constructed and used. This means that such processes affect how practitioners practice, how policy is developed and how education develops people's knowledge, skills and values. Exploring how the local, national, and international interact to affect social work and users of social work services directs us to the knowledge that social work uses and that clients, agencies and societies contribute to the world. Knowledge creation and transmission are universal human processes; they go on everywhere and at all times and because they are human, they are also social.

We argue that the creation and use of knowledge within a profession is a social process, taking place in a variety of arenas. The people who are involved and their role and stake in the process construct how knowledges come to have differing validities in different times and places. Comparative international experiences can help us explore the way in which different validities arise. We can identify different approaches to using knowledge, different ways of participating and different ways of learning, teaching and using knowledge in different cultures. There are also imbalances of power between national participants in the international arenas in which knowledge is shared and debated.

Validity, Knowledge and Social Work

Social work, like any profession, requires knowledge to be validated. Validity is an end-state, the point at which knowledge is accepted; that this state exists implies a social process to get there. Some views of professions and professionalization propose an identifiable knowledge base as an essential characteristic of a profession (Greenwood, 1957). A modern example is the opening statement of Reamer's authoritative text:

> From its roots in the charity organization society and settlement house movements, social work has evolved into a full-fledged profession with a distinctive value base, *body of knowledge*, and method of training (Reamer, 1994: 2; our emphasis).

If we take this view, knowledge validated within a profession, being distinctive, characterizes that specific profession, and characterizes others less. Therefore, being partly characterized by its validated knowledge, a profession's validation processes are crucial in understanding its character and achievement.

This has consequences for social work because a particular characteristic of it, which influences the validation process, is that it operates at the crossroads of management and treatment, of professional work and politics, and of multidisciplinary theories and approaches. Social workers therefore need to have broad, rather than in-depth knowledge. Consequently, others may easily deny or underestimate social workers' knowledge. However, in postmodern times multi- and interdisciplinary knowledge is increasingly useful. Yet, sometimes, doctoral students find it difficult to get interdisciplinary theses accepted, and the British research assessment exercise has a record of devaluing interdisciplinary studies in assessing universities. These examples, point to problems that social workers may have in claiming the validity of their knowledge base.

The crossroads position also means that many stakeholders may claim a say in the validation process, including researchers, educators, practitioners, administrators, politicians, clients, carers, and the media. Each occupies different positions in arenas of discourse about a profession, and might potentially interact in constructing valid knowledge for social workers. However, often politicians interact with other politicians, academics with academics, practitioners talk to other professionals, and clients and carers talk among themselves, in their interest groups or to media. Therefore, adequate arrangements have to be established for exchanges to take place across the barriers.

Stakeholders influence validation through their roles in creating knowledge, its transfer between different people and its use. If we take empowerment seriously, clients' perspectives would be important. Empowerment may be needed both for practitioners and clients, since both are likely to have the least status and power to influence validation processes.

To understand how to practise social work, therefore, we must understand how knowledge is validated within the profession. While social work is similar to other professions in some validation processes, it also has distinctive characteristics within its validation processes. In the following sections, we discuss briefly some basic ideas about validity, knowledge and social work as a preliminary to considering social work's validation of professional knowledge.

Validity

Validity has two related but different senses. It implies that something is approved formally, for example documents or contracts gain validity when signed and officially stamped or sealed. Validity also implies worth and usefulness, for example, saying that a question is valid, means accepting that it is reasonable to ask it. Knowledge becomes valid only when people find it meaningful to them and want to use it. The international definition of social work and the document on global standards of education discussed in Chapters 1 and 4 may offer validation in the first sense, but not in the second sense, because they may not be relevant for social workers and educators everywhere.

Validity implies power and authority: either the power of formal approval or the power of use and value. However, formally approved knowledge might not be equally valid for use to people from different cultures and countries. People from minority or gender groups may not be able to use and value knowledge, where it does not respect their context. Knowledge taken for granted in some cultures may be unacceptable elsewhere due to ideology, value and political systems. Therefore, the power of validity is bound up in existing social relationships and structures and the influence of different stakeholders in those relationships and structures. It is therefore important to reflect critically upon who are the stakeholders in the validation process – see Chapter 8 on this issue.

Validity implies a process. Validation processes change something neutral into something that has the power to influence others. When someone accepts something as valid, they have been through some process of recognizing it and assessing its worth, and they claim the authority or power to validate it. In social work practice, that validation is part of a social interaction between clients, their networks including social workers and social assumptions. The process also includes the social structure of agencies and their stakeholders and the social worker and the knowledge and skill that they incorporate within themselves.

Knowledge

Knowledge implies human thoughts and ideas about the world and about human beings. However, if we categorize thoughts and ideas as 'knowledge', we mean that they are 'true', that in some way they reflect the world accurately. If knowledge includes human thoughts and ideas, it is internal to us and the controversy arises because our knowledge may be only internal, unconnected with any external world. It only becomes 'valid' knowledge when it is expressed and tested through a validation process in the social interactions discussed above. Knowledge is closely bound up with language, because, as we saw in Chapter 4, it only becomes socially relevant if it is expressed and the way it is expressed in language derives from cultural expectations and assumptions. Action is also important to knowledge, because actions, as well as language, express our knowledge. Also, we accept ideas and thoughts as knowledge when they allow us to act in the world and gain predictable results. Evidence-based practice assumes that knowledge is only true when tests devised according to a particular structure, tradition and culture of thought reveal that action based on it consistently produces the same results. However, contrary to this view, we argue that knowledge is always adapted by human thoughts and interpretations from a range of points of view. For example, helping a parent to manage their anger and aggression with their children may reduce the risk of child abuse. Some stakeholders, though, may see it as an unacceptable risk to allow parents they assess as unsuitable to remain caring for children. The parents might have another point of view: that it as unacceptable interference in their family life. So evidence-based knowledge that people may be trained to manage aggression caused by anger may be interpreted from a number of points of view. Looked at internationally, some of these points of view might be more or less acceptable or valid in particular cultures or societies. For example, some might regard sustaining parental rights and responsibilities as more important than intervening in family relationships to reduce a low risk of violence to children. Since psychological and social evidence leads to professional, agency and public policy made on the basis of likelihood and risk identified statistically, there is always the possibility that a reasonable overall policy may bear unreasonably on individual families. Therefore, evidence can never be an absolute driver of practice policies: there must always be interpretation in individual cases.

Knowledge is, therefore, closely connected to validity and validation. This is because integral to the idea of knowledge is acceptance that it will be useful in action affecting the world. Leonard (1983) shows that, throughout social work's history, ideological trends of the time influence social work knowledge and methods. He also suggests that social workers are ideologically blind in relation to our present time, by which he means that everyone takes for granted the current ideology of their time and context. In Western societies of today, individualism is a ruling ideology. A social work method that has achieved growing influence in Western countries is the solution-focused approach, which is highly individualistic. It avoids analysis of structural problem-creating forces. Therefore, it fails to offer an understanding of such areas of knowledge as political systems, poverty, class, race and gender oppression, which are often taken for granted as a natural part of the world, rather than questioned from the point of view of oppressed peoples. For something to be useful, the knowledge that underlies it needs to be accepted both by people who use it and by people with whom the knowledge is used. Therefore, it must respond to the contexts that form both realities. Knowledge is only partial if it refers just to 'problems' defined by the cultural assumptions or ideas of an agency or social worker. Clients may resist a social worker's actions unless they understand the validity of the knowledge assessments are based on, or the credibility of the social worker or the social worker's profession.

Similarly, a student might not accept the validity of knowledge unless it meets certain criteria. For example, they may think it should be part of a system of knowledge that seems fit for the purposes of social work as they understand them, rejecting knowledge that fits with purposes they do not understand or accept. Alternatively, the educator's personal or academic credibility may be important, or the relevance of the knowledge to potential actions may need to be clear. In addition knowledge may be validated for students through based education being clearly research-based.

Validation in the sense of formalization is, therefore, also relevant. To be used, knowledge must be expressed at least in conscious ideas or consistent actions, and more probably in language. Also, in education or in professional social work actions, a structured validation around knowledge enhances its credibility. Publication in peer-reviewed journal articles or books is a formal expression of knowledge; the process of publication is a validation process, implying acceptance by others. However, as we have seen already in Chapter 4, for international social work, such formal expressions of knowledge may be culturally limited and oppressive.

Social Work

Social work may be seen either as an activity, something that is done, or as a profession, a social institution or formally-organized occupational group. In either case, its validation is bound up with knowledge. Since knowledge relates closely to action, social work as an activity requires knowledge to permit action. In turn, to act with purpose requires knowledge, of the situation in which action takes place, of the purpose and of the options for action. Understanding social work as a profession involves considering its distinctive knowledge and its knowledge validation processes.

Validity in Social Work Knowledge

A classic distinction in sociology questions the extent to which social structure conditions people's actions, or to which people's actions are capable of forming social structures. In international social work, this distinction raises two connected postmodernist questions:

- To what extent do the social structures of the profession and agencies in each country constrain the possibilities of practice offered by the international knowledge base?
- To what extent do social work practices construct the profession, agency and political policies and social change in each country?

Attempts to justify validity of knowledge only in professional and educational structures do not necessarily make it apply in practice, and acceptance in practice requires validation for acceptance in research and education. International social work makes this more complex, since validation in practice, research or education in one place may not validate it in similar or different settings in another.

It is therefore impossible to take the position that there must be only one knowledge or type of knowledge for practice, and one process that validates it. Instead, we suggest that there may be a range of knowledges used in different contexts for different purposes. If this is so, rather than demand only one means of universal validation, social workers need to understand validation processes as an interaction between different kinds and sources of knowledge. Validation is the way in which knowledge is transferred between one practice, educational or research situation and another.

Discourse about social work takes place in particular arenas. Payne (1999, 2005a: Ch. 1) identifies:

- political-social-ideological arenas of policy and philosophical debate, often in the media;
- agency-professional arenas, where social workers and service managers interact to define how social work is applied in practice;
- interpersonal arenas where social workers interact with clients, carers and the community within which they operate.

These are nexuses within a wide range of social and interpersonal arenas. Social work interacts with social structures and institutions in these arenas and social workers with various stakeholders in their practice. In the political-social arena, knowledge for social work is validated by policy debate, political power and social discourse about what kinds of knowledge are valid for use in social work. In the agency-professional arena, knowledge is validated by such processes as the creation of agency policy and professionally derived standards of practice. Agency policy may emerge from political or managerial policies, such as NPM, see Chapter 6. Professionally validated practice may emerge from such processes as team discussion, professional debate and journals. All might be influenced by research. In the client-social worker arena, the process of validation is interpersonal: validation occurs when clients accept the social worker's knowledge, and social workers accept clients' knowledge.

Clients may have an impact on the validity of knowledge used by social workers in interpersonal actions and more widely. In interpersonal work, for example, a mother may reject the child-care advice of a social worker who does not have her own children, if the mother values experience rather than academic understanding of child development. Gurid was invited to introduce some communication skills to a group of deprived single parents while visiting another country. One of the participants confided to the group leader afterwards that she wanted to find out if Gurid would accept her using corporal punishment in socializing her children. If she did not, she would not believe in anything else she said either. This kind of testing out may be more apparent with social work than other similar professions because social work tasks are, as we have seen, at the crossroads of service provision and interpersonal treatment. Knowledge conveyed by a psychologist or a doctor, for example, may be more easily accepted because it is represented as treatment expertise, whereas social workers claim to help clients adjust to the 'normal' world, where what is considered 'normal' might be contested and alternative views might be regarded as an equally valid knowledge. Clients might also question knowledge validity in political ways, as well as in interpersonal arenas. For example, the disability movement has sought to invalidate medical, dependency-creating models of disability in favour of social models.

Hierarchies of Knowledge versus Validation Processes

Processes of validation are among the social mechanisms by which existing power and authority is maintained, and change is resisted or pushed forward. If only one type of knowledge is validated or one type of validation process accepted in a particular arena, a hierarchy of knowledges arises, in which one type or source of knowledge is privileged against others. An example of this is how evidence-based practice privileges particular ways of validating knowledge for professional purposes through 'random controlled trails'. It takes for granted that knowledge is ordered in rational ways rather than in interpreted and culturally influenced ways.

Since we have noted that several knowledges originate in different arenas, attempts to create such a hierarchy subordinate some validation processes to others. However, interpersonal validation is substantially different from validation through political, academic, professional or research processes. Commitment to particular knowledges sometimes leads to rejection of alternative validation processes. Sainsbury (1987) argued, for example, in the agency-professional arena, that commitment to practices because of organizational requirements, or training inculcated early in a social worker's career, might limit acceptance of even strongly-evidenced knowledge. In the interpersonal arena, clients might reject what research says is effective because they find it uncongenial; this may make it impossible for a social worker to implement evidence-based knowledge. Therefore, evidence that is better validated according to professional or academic processes may be impossible to implement in practice if it does not fit with the social worker's capacities and skills or is unacceptable to the client.

We must therefore reject the idea that, in practice, knowledges can be formed into hierarchies by the strength of their validation. If different ways of creating knowledge have their own assets depending on the circumstances in which they contribute to action, then it is irrelevant to classify them in a hierarchy. *In practice*, such hierarchies may come up against completely different forms of validation. If a hierarchical analysis of different knowledges is not practically possible, how are we to understand the relationships between different types of knowledge?

Knowledges in Social Work

Knowledges are debated within social work. Various kinds of knowledge have been considered. Schön (1991) argues that knowing *that*, knowing something about the world, is given a higher status than knowing *how*, knowing how to act upon the world. A further example is the rural-urban context (Briskman, 1999). Most social work literature is developed and written about from an urban perspective, both in relation to social policy, problems, and how to understand and deal with them. Academics producing social work knowledge are mainly situated in urban environment. Any writing they do about rural issues will have visitors' or outsiders' perspectives. Countries, such as the USA and UK, where much professional literature is produced, are more urban, whereas countries where the international literature is used, such as Africa, Asia, Australasia or Scandinavia have strong rural communities. Urban-based knowledge may be difficult to use in rural settings. These examples suggest that in a practice activity such as social work validated knowledge will need to take account of different settings and situations. So, knowledge for practice must incorporate different sources and validations of knowledge, which, we have argued above, cannot be set in a hierarchy.

Therefore, in social work as in other professions, validation processes constantly adapt and structure different types of knowledge between different arenas. To understand how this takes place, we now explore how different types of knowledge interact. In our analysis, we use Jensen's (1993) three types of knowledge relevant for professional people: life-historical, traditional professional and scientific knowledge. These three types of knowledge are constructed in different arenas of social work discourse.

By scientific knowledge, Jensen means knowledge produced through formal research and scholarship, mainly in the professional-agency arena, rather than limiting this to evidence-based knowledge production. Life-historical knowledge is what students and social workers have acquired through life experience, deriving from political-social arenas. It is similar to Polanyi's (1983) concept of tacit knowledge. It is taken-for granted understanding about the world acquired in normal living, and not formulated in an organized way, but available to be used for practical purposes. The important difference is Jensen's emphasis on life-historical knowledge being obtained from experience relevant to professional action and understanding. Life-historical knowledge is not necessarily conceptualized and accessible for analysis and reconstruction, but becomes visible in practical situations. Jensen (1992, 1993) maintains that if life-historical knowledge is not made conscious during education, students might not be able to combine it with other knowledges. Instead of contributing to professional development, it might then unconsciously create uncertainty and aggression. When life-historical knowledge is made accessible to students during their learning process, it becomes possible to use this knowledge to go beyond the alienation that often characterizes professional relationships (Eriksen, 1990; Jensen, 1992, 1993: 7). Critical reflection may raise consciousness of how life-historical knowledge influences professional practice.

Professional knowledge is based in the traditions and experiences collected and formalized within a profession, mainly in the social worker-agency arena. It becomes accessible to others in a profession. Through considered and accountable participation over time, members of a profession create a specific culture, containing shared knowledge. An example in social work is knowledge acquired through professional supervision, where a student or inexperienced social worker gains understanding through a close, reflective relationship with a supervisor. To be professional implies, in addition to becoming familiar with such 'traditional' knowledge, taking a critical perspective so that a profession is able to renew, improve and develop itself (Jensen, 1993: 40).

Jensen proposes that scientific knowledge is a prism through which a professional might interpret, organize and consequently validate the knowledge gained through life-historical and professional knowledge and transform scientific knowledge into practice. Practice guidance does not directly arise from scientific knowledge, while professional knowledge consists of examples, including many situations where professional adjustment and discretion takes place (Jensen, 1993).

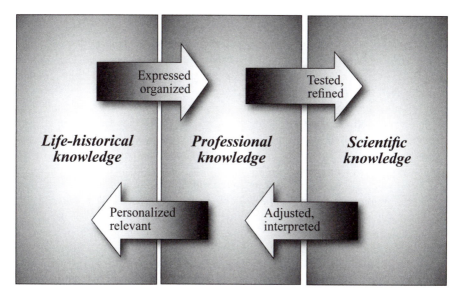

Figure 5.1   Jensen's three aspects of professional knowledge

Source: *Jensen (1993)*

Considering these three forms of knowledge together, scientific knowledge is inevitably adjusted by professional and life-historical knowledge, while professional and life-historical knowledge will be tested and amended by scientific processes. Figure 5.1 sets out a pattern in which life-historical knowledge is expressed and organized by professional experience and it, together with professional knowledge, is tested and further refined by scientific processes. Working the other way, scientific knowledge is adjusted by discretion and practical requirements arising in professional work, and personalized and made relevant to clients by being adapted through life-historical experience.

Any profession creates processes for institutionalizing different forms of practice into professional usage. For example, in social work, life-historical knowledge is mediated through professional supervision, where personal experience in relation to practice is discussed. Professional knowledge is originated through discussion and planning between colleagues and scientific knowledge is produced in processes around journals and books. These processes overlap. For example, ideas developed in supervision may be shared with the team and used more widely, and scientific knowledge may be conveyed through agency and post-qualification training, and professional journals interpreting academic dissemination.

Each of these processes is a validation process. Scientific knowledge is validated for practice by being adjusted and interpreted. Being made personally relevant allows it, and professional knowledge, to be used in working with clients. Life-historical and professional experience goes through formalizing, testing and refining processes, to become, possible, scientific knowledge.

Influences on the Validation Process

Interpretation and refinement also takes place between other arenas of social work discourse. For example, professional journals and agency manuals may not be considered as valid as academic research validated by publication in leading journals. Nevertheless, they may have direct relevance for practice. Equally, agency manuals may be valid guidance for professionally qualified social workers, even though their language and form is designed to be more relevant for other staff in social care services. Life-historical experience may help social workers to understand clients' experiences, even if they cannot be formulated in academic terms.

These processes are affected by various power relations, which arise in the social processes when knowledge is adapted and validated. Many journals publish more work from male rather than female writers, even though social work has a strong female membership. The validation processes of academic journals and books may be assumed to have universal application, but reflect the particular cultural preferences and the English language of academic globalization. In social work, for example, there has been criticism from Africa and Asia of its individualized approach and failure to recognize the social needs of countries in the South or more interdependent cultures.

A Norwegian professor describes his dilemma about where and how to publish data from a four-year joint research project between the University in Bergen, Norway and the University of Kathmandu, Nepal (Aase, 2006). Promising outcomes led him to suggest having a book published by a well-regarded European or American publisher. However, the book would become so expensive that Nepalese students and libraries could not afford it; they decided to use a publisher in Nepal. The Norwegian government's financial support system for universities partly depends on students' achievements and publications. But only what is published by internationally recognized journals and publishers is counted. Anglo-American journals and publishers dominate the approved list. The consequence of publishing the book in Nepal is that the University in Bergen will not get state support and the researcher will personally not have his research achievement acknowledged and it may contribute less to his career. To meet the requirements of his university, data would be collected in a poor country, published in a rich country and read by highly-educated wealthy audiences. Thus this academic support system reduces poor countries to raw data deliverers, and the analysis, publication and use of the material takes place in the rich parts of the world. The professor concludes that this reminds us of colonial treasure-seeking.

In these, and many other ways, the social and power context of life and practice creates variations in the validity of particular forms of knowledge. Social processes privilege certain kinds of knowledge or information. Life-historical and professional knowledge is often undervalued. In many countries, books are few and the accessible theoretical and professional literature is not contextualized because it is written for a different culture and experience. Often, as we saw in Chapter 4, postcolonialism means that this will be a Western knowledge development context drawing on data and understanding from the South.

As such contextualization takes place in local situations, traditional practice knowledge transferred via working in a professional setting and by supervision becomes important. Everywhere, knowledge transferred through books and journals is likely to lag behind professional knowledge and life-historical knowledge, which is more contextualized. Scientific knowledge is created where the resources are available for research and publication; where it is not, life-historical and professional knowledge may be the main sources of practice. Such knowledge may not be validated in scientific ways, but may be more valid because of its contextualization.

This means that scientific knowledge is mainly created in rich Western countries, in urban areas, and is achieved by white people, mostly male, in command of a world language. Within such power relations, social work is not generally a prioritized area for research. An example is the EU, which emphasizes technical, scientific and business development.

So, scientific knowledge creation in social work is biased in two ways. First, it unjustifiably claims for this type of knowledge a higher status in a hierarchy of knowledge than knowledges created through experiential, tacit, situated learning. This disempowers people from the South, rural areas, minority groups, and women. Second, in failing to incorporate knowledges from other arenas, it excludes knowledge that might be interpreted into scientific, thus losing a rich source of knowledge for practice. Our focus seeks to avoid this disempowerment by seeing validation less as a process of approval leading to a hierarchy of knowledge and more interpretation and refinement between different types of knowledge required for different arenas of discourse. This is where critical reflection, discussed in Chapter 3, may help since it also opens up possibilities for knowledge to be transferred between different arenas of social work discourse.

Empowering Knowledge Validation in Social Work

How may we develop knowledge validation in social work, so that it interprets and refines bodies of knowledge and becomes empowering rather than disempowering? The concept of 'transfer of learning' usefully characterizes validation processes as a way of transferring knowledge between arenas of discourse about social work. Macaulay (2001) suggests a number of factors that may facilitate transfer of learning. These include providing an initial context for transfer of learning by, for example, focusing on learners with explicit attention to their learning styles and providing a safe environment for learning to take place. Learners need to see and understand the connections between the original learning and the new situation. So learners need to have structured, organized and practical experience of the old learning in the new situation and to reflect critically on the transfer experience; see Chapter 3. Thus, validation through learning transfer needs to be effectively situated within the social and political context of the stakeholders, and draw explicit links between different forms of knowledge, anchoring and integrating them in well-understood social practices. These social processes include local community expectations dealing with the life-historical knowledge, agency practices dealing with professional knowledge and academic validation dealing with scientific knowledge.

Education and training, management and supervision, teamwork and collaboration, and interpersonal work with clients all enable interactions between different knowledges to be cemented. Each of these implies different priorities. Thus, the researcher aims to influence the educator and the practitioner, the educator aims to improve the learner's professional competence, the manager is concerned with the quality of the social worker's practice and the practitioner is concerned with users' progress. However, within these priorities, the overall purpose is transferring knowledge through learning, benefiting a service that helps clients. The client's benefit is not only achieved interpersonally with them, but also by change in their social environment, within the agency's service, within the range of services provided in society and by general social changes that alter the historical context in which the work is carried out. While working with clients, it is hard to keep all these possible developments in view. Focusing on differing priorities does not exclude the client's direct benefit, but interprets it in the different contexts. Transfer of learning through knowledge validation in different contexts ensures that varieties of knowledge affect each other within the overall context of service to clients.

Social work validation processes include different but overlapping stakeholders; see Chapter 8. The overlap between stakeholders permits knowledge to be transferred, so that, for example, a social worker transmits the knowledge originated in the agency-professional arena to clients, while an educator transmits knowledge originated in the professional arena to social workers. All stakeholders become mutually important in developing valid knowledge for social workers. In multiprofessional settings, often the modern context for social work practice, learning transfer may also need to be undertaken across professional boundaries, involving a wider group of stakeholders.

An example of how arenas may overlap each other has arisen in Norway when multi-systemic therapy (MST) was introduced in work with young offenders. Debate about adequate treatment of delinquency had led to a growing market for private institutions. In the late 1990s, the Ministry of Social Affairs after some inquiry decided to recommend MST as an approach. The childcare unit in some counties carried out a pilot project. MST is now offered all over the country. MST was developed at the University of Carolina. It is an evidence-based treatment, integrating different methods of working into a holistic approach. The purpose is to strengthen parental functioning, and treatment takes place primarily in the family home. The parents are considered equal partners, and have the main responsibility for goal setting and implementation. The therapists, mainly social workers or psychologists, work in teams. In addition to seminars, the teams had weekly supervision from MST therapists in the USA. The University of Oslo, Department of Psychology held the professional responsibility (Ogden, 1998). Social work programmes have not been considered competent to teach MST, since one has to be a trained therapist to do that.

Situated learning is a concept created by Lave (1991) who observed learning through apprenticeship in an African setting. It is a participative learning model where teaching takes place in real life surroundings outside the classroom, making visible a range of perspectives that influence practice, including the cultural, economic and political context. The advantages of such an approach are that 'distinctions between learning and doing, between social identity and knowledge, between education and occupation, between form and content' (Lave, 1991, 1997: 43), are broken down. Fieldwork teaching in social work education uses an apprenticeship model, which is meant to promote situated learning and where critical reflection can be a means. It is an example of learning transfer for life-historical knowledge. Situated learning is equally relevant in professional and scientific knowledge. Scientific knowledge is revalidated for use in professional settings by being resituated through agency guidance, professional education and team discussion and professional knowledge is resituated, but less commonly, for use in scientific knowledge by being accumulated, aggregated and tested in an organized way.

Conclusion

In this Chapter, we have examined ideas about knowledge validation in social work, emphasizing validation as a social process of approval incorporating power relationships rather than as an end-state producing a hierarchy of knowledge. Social work is constructed in different social arenas. We have suggested that each arena will have different validation processes, which, in turn, validate different knowledges. Validating social work knowledge, therefore, involves processes of refinement and interpretation of knowledges between the arenas. This transfers learning between the different arenas, different knowledges being resituated to be relevant to each arena. This occurs within an overall context in which knowledge in social work must permit both action within practice and the formation of structures of the social work profession. Using ideas about learning transfer, we have proposed a process of validation that focuses on situated learning, which incorporates a focus on application in real-life situations at different levels.

Why is this important? We want to emphasize three crucial issues.

- Debates about social work knowledge have often focused on validity as part of an attempt to create a hierarchy of knowledge, as in evidence-based practice. We have argued that this imposes existing power relations of different countries, social statuses and gender relations on the use of knowledge.
- It is more empowering in an international setting to focus on validation as a social process resituating different kinds of knowledge as relevant to different arenas within social work discourse. This hears different voices in different arenas.
- Knowledge may be made practically useful in different arenas through learning transfer and this avoids incorporating globalized power relations that privilege dominant cultures through using scientific communication processes.

Chapter 6

Social Work's Identity in Postmodern Agencies and Universities

Introduction

While doing a joint project with a university, a non-governmental organization and a municipal social administration bureau in China, Gurid and a colleague were invited to attend a women's conference. At the conference, several women from another European country presented papers on comparative studies of the female workforce in Europe. Gurid and her colleague enthusiastically told the conference about their project to develop an educational programme in community nursing and social work. The target group was women in their forties who had been laid off when China converted from a planned economy to a market system. These women had been victims of the earlier 'cultural revolution', when schools and universities were closed, and thus lacked education. China has a policy of limiting families to one child and there is increased geographical mobility, so many families are no longer able to look after their elders and there is an increasing demand for care for older people. In the midst of the introduction, one of the European participants interrupted: 'Are you academics?'

Some time later, Gurid attended a party in a European city with a colleague from another country. There were no other social workers and the colleague introduced them both as academics. Gurid was surprised, as she would usually introduce herself as a social work educator.

These two incidents might illustrate something about social work's identity and highlight the demand for critical reflection on it. Should we not be regarded as academics when doing community development and not empirical research? A protest against how academic work is privileged over societal engagement was clearly expressed in an initiative taken at the IASSW conference in Santiago in 2006. A network was created to support practitioners and educators in engaging as political social work activists and demanding that it should count alongside research in university staff appraisal. Social work is practical and, without action, there would be no social work profession. Social workers have influence on decisions about their professional identity. We should not accept some stakeholders deciding that research should have higher status than practical work. The examples seem to show that '... the written word tends to be more highly valued than the activity it describes ...' (Hunt, 1995) and that this affects the regard in which social work is held.

In the year 2000, the United Nations (UN) adopted a resolution on social and economic development of the poorest people in the world. Eight goals are listed aiming to alleviate poverty by 2015; one is to promote equality and strengthen the position of women. Educated women have usually fewer children and when self-supported it has extended effect on other family members. The resolution lists education as a means to this end. International Save the Children in 2006 started a five-year education campaign for children in countries at war or in conflict to break the circle of war and poverty (Redd Barna, 2006). Education is a priority for children in refugee camps. Internationally renowned pioneers in social work like Jane Addams, Alice Salomon, Sybil Francis and Sattareh Farman Farmaian were all engaged in promoting women's rights. Social work practitioners and educators should be proud of taking part in organizing education for women and children around the world.

Perhaps Gurid's colleague introduced them as academics because social work has low status or she did not want to get into defending social work against a popular negative opinion of it. Social work practitioners and educators need to fight against a feeling of inferiority that has invaded social work. Because social work agencies and academic departments have merged with other organizations with a wider focus, social work activity has become less visible in services as well as in education. Social work is perhaps overlooked in the public arena. For example, after devastation caused by a tsunami in the Indian Ocean in 2004, social workers took part in disaster work alongside other professions, but they were hardly mentioned in media reports when their skill and focus is a valuable asset (Askeland, 2007).

In Chapter 2, theories of globalization and postmodernism were described that seek to explain social changes around the world. In this chapter we explore how globalization, postmodernism and postcolonialism have made social work and its context more complex, uncertain and ambiguous. These processes change and challenge the identity of local and international social work practice and education.

Identity, Context and International Social Work

Identity through International Statements

Social work's identity is created in a historical, political and economic context. This means it responds to what is happening in the society in which it is performed. If social work's identity is socially constructed, this implies that we may reconstruct it. Debate continues about what social work is, what social workers do and what constitutes social work education. In an effort to create a common platform and identity, IFSW and IASSW have adopted Ethics in Social Work: Statements of Principles; a Definition of Social Work; and Global Standards for Social Work Education and Training. To call something 'global' implies its validity wherever in the world social work takes place. Global validity is based on universalism. We saw in Chapter 5 that postcolonial hegemony may derive from assumptions of universal validity. The standards for education and training are called global, while the statements on ethics and definition are not. The Global Standards for Social Work Education and Training have been criticized for embracing a Western ideology (Yip, 2004). We suggest it is too prescriptive and detailed to permit the kind of cultural flexibility proposed in this book.

Modernist thinking led social workers working internationally to formulate ethical guidelines, drawing on principles of social work built on some of Biestek's ideas (1961). These were debated until, in 2004, the General Assemblies of IASSW and

IFSW adopted 'Ethics in Social Work: Statement of Principles' for their members. From being normative and prescriptive codes of ethics, based on Western ideology, postmodern thinking has changed the approach to offer principles. Each regional or national association is encouraged to contextualize them.

Debate also continues over whether the current definition may be regarded as internationally valid. The present definition will again be debated in the two associations from 2008 onwards. According to Healy (2001) it has not changed much since the definition formulated by the first International Conference in Social Work in 1928. This may seem astonishing, as the participants in this conference were all Europeans and North Americans, while since then, social work has been established around the world within different cultures and political systems. If social work is socially constructed and contextual, this either tells us that the definition is still heavily influenced by Western thought or that what is considered social work is stable and universal.

Payne (2006) reviewed definitions of social work from Richmond's definition of social diagnosis in 1917 onward. Except for a Japanese one from 1961, these are all Western definitions. This analysis shows how the definitions have changed over time. It has not occurred deliberately, but in accordance with political and ideological trends of the time. Payne argues that social work is a three-way discourse, containing the three elements therapeutic, social order and transformational approaches. Although these three elements interact, he finds that over the years they have influenced social work definitions to various degrees. We argue, following this analysis, that there are divergent influences on social work's identity. The complexity and fragmentation caused by globalization and postmodernism make it hard to formulate what social work is (Kunneman, 2005). Postmodernism promotes indigenization and contextualization, contrary to postcolonialism, which promotes universalism and thus endorses conformity with Western assumptions. For example, social work in Africa deals with mass poverty, HIV/AIDS, lack of socio-economic infrastructure, conflicts, political insecurity, lack of human rights and social justice. Social work practice might therefore be different from that in the West (Osei-Hwedie et al., 2006: 69). It emphasizes community-based approaches, which must be distinguished from community organization and development. It implies that poverty, HIV, teenage pregnancy, youth employment, school drop out are all community issues that have to be understood contextually and be solved as such (Ibid.: 574).

Critique of the definition has evolved around the focus of most Western social workers to adapt people to society rather than promote change. Structural change and political activism, which people need more than individual empowerment, are not specifically identified in the definition. It contains nothing about how social workers intervene. Historically to varying extents, Christianity; philanthropy; feminism and socialism (Lorenz, 1994) influenced European social work. However, the definition fails to acknowledge assumptions such as a common language, history, religion, educational and legal systems, press or media, which contribute to a shared culture (Webb, 2003: 93).

Africa, Asia and the Middle East have fundamentally unlike cultures from the Western countries. Yip (2004) maintains that the Definition of Social Work and the Global Standard of Social Work Education and Training assume that there are universal components in social work and social work education. If diversity is acknowledged at all, it is based on how cultural, ethnic and gender differences are experienced in Western countries. Differences in how concepts such as human rights, oppression, equality, social change and empowerment may be defined, interpreted and applied are ignored. Yip uses Asia as an example of how traditional cultures are influenced by Confucianism, Buddhism, Hinduism and Islam. All these traditional Asian cultures emphasize collectivity rather than individuality, responsibility rather than individual rights, social norms and order rather than equality, family stability and security rather than social change. From this, harmony follows rather than conflict. How can a social work definition that starts with promoting change, guide local social workers? Western cultures split mind, body, spirit and the environment, a different approach from cultures with a holistic view. Many African, Asian and other indigenous cultures in Western societies, consider mind and body, and people and nature, a unity. They would view the Definition's distinction between people and their environments with puzzlement. A consequence might be that Asian social work practice and education needs to be designed differently from Western social work. If Western social workers were to learn from other colleagues, the mobility of clients and social workers caused by globalization and the uncertainty, ambiguities and complexity of postmodernism might lead them to perform social work according to Asian models. The social work definition and ethics are based on human rights, equal rights, freedom of speech and democracy, derived from Western values. Today the role of human rights in Islam is also discussed among Muslims (Gule, 2006). Some would incorporate human rights into Islam, seeing them as part of Sharia, the Islamic law system, while others find them irrelevant. Gule argues that human rights are not highly esteemed in Islamic societies where politics and conservative religion are strongly intertwined.

Social work was launched in African, Asian and Caribbean countries as a colonial activity, founded on Eurocentric and American social work models. This has contributed to a failure in developing a local identity (Maxwell et al., 2003; Osei-Hwedie et al., 2006; Muleya, 2006). Western knowledge, skills and values have not always been found useful in the local African context (Osei-Hwedie et al., 2006, Hutton and Mwansa, 1996) since for example, issues social workers are faced with have to be dealt with in a community context rather than on an individual basis. The result is that social work has become alienating to people and the local social workers. American and British models have been borrowed in countries like Armenia, Japan (Healy, 2001), Poland (Szmagalski, 2004), Taiwan (Harris and Chou, 2001) and in Western countries like Finland (Satka, 1995) and Norway. American literature has traditionally influenced British social work (Harris and Chou, 2001). Norwegian social work is closely connected with the implementation of the welfare state, and practitioners who are trained in Anglo-American treatment models have found it hard to identify their work as 'real' social work.

Comparing Social Work Around the World

What comes under the umbrella of social work varies from country to country. Healy (2001), leaning on Hokenstad et al. (1992), compares social work in Denmark, Jamaica, Mauritius, Armenia, Argentina and Japan. Both similarities and differences in conceptualization, organization and practice exist in these six dissimilar countries:

- Social work roles and contexts in which social work takes place vary widely. Government policy on welfare, complementary professions and the structure of social institutions affects how social work is defined. An example of contextual influence is Jamaica, where migration has been extensive due to economic stagnation, under-investment and unemployment. Children have been left behind (Williams, 2007), and many social workers are employed by NGOs, focusing particularly on children. In Japan, social workers perform residential care work, which would be para-professional work in the many Western countries, and complementary professions as police officers and juvenile inspectors take on child protection in Zambia.
- While social workers share a commitment to social change and an optimistic belief in people's ability to change, it is difficult to operationalize (Reid and Edwards, 2006). The opportunity to pursue it depends on organizational and political contexts. An example is Argentina's repressive government where social workers have been unable to follow their ideologically radical commitment due to a repressive government (Healy, 2001).
- Social workers work with poor people everywhere; however poverty might vary. They are also concerned with child and family issues, cultural diversity and conflict and social exclusion. As the scope and seriousness varies, so do the approaches.
- Social workers share values concerning people's dignity and worth, are against discrimination and for equal treatment. Social workers support participation and self-determination. However, there might be differences in practice between individually or collectively oriented societies.

Healy concludes that although the social work literature used around the world incorporates human behaviour and social environment, social services policies and programmes and social research, the philosophical and ideological theories underpinning it vary (Healy, 2001: 02). To conclude there is no common global theoretical base for social work; see also Chapter 5.

Status

Social work's status varies from country to country and from field to field. This also influences social workers' identities. In the US, social work has a higher status than in most European countries. Among the reasons for this might be the following:

- In the USA, social work has been established as an academic discipline, carrying out independent research, long before it got a foothold in many European universities, where often social work education was first offered at a lower level than in the US, in separate schools, thereafter in regional colleges. However, academization is now taking place (Labonté-Roset, 2004; Lorenz, 2005a; Kyvik, 2006). Because of this slow process, in Europe leading professors and researchers in social work have until recently often been sociologists and psychologists rather than social workers. This also has influenced the content and status of social work.

- More North American social workers do therapy than is commonly the case elsewhere. According to a NASW membership survey in 2000 (cited in Reid and Edwards, 2006), 39% of the social workers worked in mental health, and only 11% with adult services, aging, addiction and international services. Therapeutic social work has higher status then welfare work with poor people. People using psychotherapy are often middle class people. In addition, the higher status of other team members like physiatrists and psychologists might colour social workers' status. Much social work literature is based on therapeutic approaches. This may contribute to social workers in welfare work not considering themselves doing 'real' social work.
- Gender plays a decisive role in determining social work's status. Compared with the number of social workers, males are overrepresented in research, in publishing and leading positions. In many Western countries, social work practitioners are female, contributing to its low status and pay. When social workers work with low status people, this also influences their status. To belong to a low status profession influences the image social workers might have of themselves and their clients.

The lack of clear distinctions between social work and other professions and disciplines contributes to the unclarity of social work's identity. Probation officers in Scotland and the Nordic countries are social workers, while in England they have a separate education programme. Youth work, considered social work in many European countries and the USA, is a separate profession in the UK, with its own training and professional body. Likewise, welfare workers are not members of the Australian Association of Social Workers even though many work in childcare and social service agencies. Their education is similar to but shorter than social work education. Welfare workers are a new occupational group in Norway, established to fit social services merged in 2006 with social security and employment agencies. The joint union for social workers, child protection workers and social educators have accepted them as members.

Social work and social pedagogy on the European continent have been brought nearer to each other, and currently many educational institutions award a joint degree. Historically social work training in these countries was based on social sciences, took place in separate schools, and prepared students for public welfare services with poor relief, social movements and voluntary work. Social pedagogy was taught at universities, based on educational theories. Its aim was to teach children and youth outside the school system to cope with life, and by means of therapy establish harmonious relations between individuals and society (Frisenhahn and Kantowicz, (2005). Pedagogy has a different connotation in the UK, having been a technical word for teaching skills. However, in recent years, European social pedagogy has been explored as a way of reforming childcare practice (Boddy et al., 2006).

Social Work in a Political Context

Social work both depends on the political context in which it is carried out, and is used in many countries to support government policy. Whether it supports the government policy or works against it, the political context will influence social work's identity. Social work's legitimacy in many Western countries derives from links to the welfare state (Harris, 2003). The building of the welfare states particularly in the 1960s, and '70s laid the ground for the development of social work as a profession in the Nordic countries as well as in Australia and New Zealand. To fill new job roles with competent people, new schools of social work were established (Askeland and Danbolt, 2005). Through the welfare regime, social work becomes applied social policy, and social workers are stakeholders both in defining social problems and through their activities legitimize how to handle them. Therefore, social workers carry out social, political and individualistic approaches in social work as well as create them.

Former communist regimes, like China, Eastern European countries and Ethiopia among many had well-established social work before communist governments took over in the 1940s. Over the 30–40 years of the communist period, longer in Russia, different social work was regarded as unnecessary, with social problems being dealt with through work units, or through comprehensive state provision in, for example, childcare and housing. Different Eastern European countries developed varying policies and practices and the position of social work changed over time with some countries reintroducing some aspects of social work. After the fall of the communist governments, social work has been rebuilt, although again with varying aims and policies, and social work education has been rapidly re-established (Ramon and Pathak, 1997).

Some former communist states in central Europe, are making a transition by adopting a Western-style civil society. Poland, where social work education which started in 1925 and was reintroduced after 1990 is an example. It is particularly seen as a tool for implementing the renewed social welfare system (Szmagalski, 2004). The Social Welfare Act 1990 prescribes the professional activity as assisting individuals and families as well as creating conditions for their adjustment to the society. Szmagalski discusses dilemmas for social workers as social work and social welfare values, as for example self-dependence and empowerment for individuals and communities, do not correspond with values of an authoritarian Polish society. Less well-educated people confuse material equality with egalitarianism, and many people see social welfare as a state obligation alongside the government obligation to secure people jobs.

By being available to and associated with the welfare state, social work contributes to maintaining social order. In this role, it has been accused of being used as a means to silence suppressed groups. It does this by mediating through individualistic work the tension between the citizen and the state (Dominelli, 1996; Harris, 2003; Lorenz, 2005). Yu (2006) describes how an individualist perspective permeated the Philippine social work during American colonial rule. For social workers to propose structural explanations to social problems might have invoked penalties. During Marcos's rule, social work flourished and by not criticizing the dictatorship, rather supporting it through the professional journal, social workers legitimized it. However, there were exceptions: some social workers promoted their views by working for NGOs, a few joined the revolutionary movements, and educators and students took part in protest actions and advocacy for the victims of the political system. This was not without threat to own safety (Yu, 2006a). Further, Yu (2006) points out that to this end,

Filipino social workers have not criticized changes to the social services during the 1990s, the decline in government spending and quality and the ideology behind it. Social work practitioners and educators have been slow in criticizing the effect of globalization on social work (Dominelli, 2004).

Social work professionals, both responding to criticism of their social order role and also as part of their commitment to social justice, have criticized established systems that disempower people. Therefore, many countries have seen a trend for social work to become less attractive to governments. Positions that earlier were mainly for social workers are open to other professions that are less politically oriented, and new professions, like welfare and care workers, have been established.

Organizational Changes

Economic changes of globalization and market orientation have made it difficult to maintain the funding and socially liberal approach of welfare regimes in many countries. The strong development of social work in the twentieth century has been linked to the emergence of the welfare states. The profession has continued to grow in spite of retrenchment in the welfare state. Neo-liberal political regimes, however, claimed a need for greater competitiveness in globalized economies (Harris, 2003).

New Public Management

NPM was first introduced in OECD countries in the late 1980s (Cheung, 2002). Although the impression in the West is that it has had a great impact, according to Pollitt (2002) it has only been practised in public services in the UK, USA, Australasia, partly in the Nordic countries and Holland. However, Harris (2007) refers to several other sources who suggest a wider extensiveness through international economic organizations. From an Asian perspective, according to Cheung (2002), NPM is a managerial solution to political problems. These writers see NPM, which originates in the USA and UK, as a fruit of the neo-liberal system under Reagan and Thatcher and continued by Clinton and Blair as the Third Way. The American historical background is a political system valuing a large voluntary and a small public sector, little state intervention and individualism and self-reliance. The assumption behind it is that the best management existed in business and private concerns and should be transferred to public sector. Thus, the society in which NPM was developed had a different ideology and political organization than many countries in which it has been introduced where the social sector was primarily public.

Global trends such as this ignore local contexts, while at the same time influencing them. Where public services hardly exist, NPM should perhaps have little impact. Its availability as an idea gives it an impact in the South. It is part of the history and assumption behind treating agencies and universities as private companies where clients and students become consumers. Calling the trend consumerism disguises its political context. It is closely linked to private well-being based on individual purchasing power, replacing systems built on solidarity (Stjernø, 2005). The idea of consumerism is to listen to and adjust to people's needs. However, the result may be that purchasers' voices are heard, while clients become commodities.

NPM implies a change from political and professional leadership to management. Professional discretion becomes subordinated to economic and managerial decision (Newman, 2002). This weakens trust in professions, and deprofessionalization takes place, which is also a way of saving money. The system creates tensions between business-oriented managements and professional and academic staffs. Such tensions concern the priority given to:

- control, flexibility and devolution;
- social, political and economic agendas;
- the interests of various stakeholders like government, citizens, client, communities (Newman, 2002) and educators and students.

Market mechanisms are pursued, including competition, contracting, privatization and merger into bigger units. Performance-related systems are used for recruiting and payment. Accountability and strict control of financial resources, personnel and results are practised. Simplified rating of outcomes is a common phenomenon. If an agency or university fails to meet the performance criteria, they might be publicly compared and criticized and their reputation damaged (Barnes, 2007).

It has been difficult to assess the achievements of NPM, mainly because of scarce data, according to Pollitt (2002). Successes have been measured in purely financial terms, such as time and money. More qualitative indicators are lacking (Carter, 2000). Although there has been downsizing and staff reduction, it may be due to privatization or increased expenses relocated to other sectors; for example, cutbacks in preventive childcare might result in higher youth crime. Whether NPM is considered a success depends on who is asked. Senior managers are more satisfied than lower level employees (Pollitt, 2002), according to a study, this is also the case for social work in the UK (Dominelli, 2004).

Changes to Social Work Practice and Education

Changes due to NPM have appeared in both social services and social work education. Re-organizations often occur as a response to the complexities and ambiguities due to globalization and postmodernism. NPM is a rational system, and when it fails to manage unpredictable postmodern processes and successes do not appear, it calls for re-organizations. Often this fragments social service systems, by re-organizing to achieve integration with larger and politically more important services. The aim is to increase quality and efficiency and reduce costs; such aims might in themselves be contradictory. 'More-for-less' is expected (Harris, 2007: 3), even in situation with '*increased need* and *diminished resources*' (Barnes, 2007: 57). Cree and Davis's (2007) study suggests that frequent re-organizations create stress and uncertainty, imply new structures, new learning and adjustments, which cause inefficiency and are costly. It demands flexibility in social workers. A growing trend in the USA, called employment-at-will, is contracts where the employees accept being laid off at any time without reason (Pine and Healy, 2007). Malcolm once worked in an area where, to save money, large numbers of social workers in a major agency were allowed to retire early at short notice. Their cases were left unsupervized, professionally a clearly inappropriate decision, taken to achieve a financial target. Unpredictable working conditions like this may disrupt relationships between clients and social workers, and inhibit the growth of responsive professional practice. It may undermine work commitment and loyalty.

In a globalized postmodern era, both social work and its education are made insecure by the influence of political and organizational changes. In many Western countries, social work has become less visible when merged into bigger units, often dominated by health organizations. An example from Norway is the merging in 2006 of the governmental-financed and rule-based social security and employment services with the municipally financed and discretion-based social services into the New Employment and Welfare Services (NAV). Social workers had a strong role in the latter, not in the two former services. In the UK, government-inspired childcare trusts formed under the Children Act 2004 aim to coordinate child and family social work with education, but similarly create much larger organizations in which social work is submerged. While better, more integrated and accessible services for the public is the overall goal, the underlying political purpose is to provide for more clients with a reduced number of employees. A bureaucratic model seems to solve the problems of what is defined as lack of efficiency, whereas the postmodern analysis argues that the problems are of growing complexity and ambiguity. It remains to be seen how rule-based or discretion-based services will influence each other in Norway or education-focus and child and family focus services benefit from the change in the UK. It is important to examine which stakeholders gain from new structures.

A parallel is taking place in higher education, where social work often disappears into bigger units (Reid and Edwards, 2006), such as social or health sciences. The structure of the educational institutions might have a decisive influence on whether social work education focuses primarily on social sciences, social policy, law or political philosophy, rather than learning materials relevant to practice in another way like ethics, communication, relationship-building, co-ordination and collaboration. If social work merges with nursing, healthcare might be emphasized, and in teacher training, social work might lean towards education. Few social work professors have leading positions in universities (Lyons, 1999). Likewise, other professions achieve leading roles in the social services rather than social workers. Thus, social work looses authority and the opportunity for independent development, even though, as with agencies, such mergers may improve the cross-fertilization of ideas between professions and shared training may improve collaboration in professional practice.

Although the threatened death of welfare states in the West has not occurred, many countries have experienced cutbacks in social services and fundamental changes to social work. Contracting, competition and privatization are increasing, which converts social services into a quasi-market in which services are treated as commodities, rather than as responsive professional interactions. Social work and service provision shifts more to the private or third sectors, which have been politicized with a quasi-market being a tool for NPM, disguising the aim of saving public money. Packages of services are offered, rather than a holistic professional service. With care management, the social worker's task is to organize and arrange for contact between clients and service suppliers. The ideal is that the 'service users' should have better choice and more flexibility to meet their needs. An effect is that the public services may disclaim responsibility, while claiming partnership and shared commitment with users.

We argue that social work and education will never pay off economically. They are an 'investment' in social cohesion; people can never be 'profitable'. There should always be a difference between private and business sector and the welfare sector. While the aim in the former is a surplus for investment, the purpose of the latter is to invest in a country's human capital. Different success criteria are needed.

The parallel in education to service packages is modularization. Students become customers who buy courses, and educators sell their products for the highest possible price. This influences the educators' identity and role. Universities do not receive state support according to how many students they admit but for how many they 'produce'. The quality of the programme does not necessarily equate what 'sells'. What is popular fluctuates, so that small but high-quality courses might close down, and expertise built up over time might quickly disappear. The output that decides the financial outcome for educational institutions acting like businesses might be spending resources on public relations in competition for students, rather than spending on good quality experiences for students. Finances and prestige for universities are also influenced by the amount of research funding received, publications in internationally highly esteemed publications and international involvement. These are measured in accountability systems such as the UK research assessment exercise and ratings of courses and universities in newspapers. Thus, academization, which is necessary to consolidate social work as a discipline, goes hand in hand with the NPM requirements.

Project organization is another way of adjusting practice to NPM requirements. It is also a teaching method, similar to problem or inquiry based learning models. Using such approaches, students then learn to handle issues in ways directly applicable in the field. Projects in both practice and education are goal- and outcome-oriented. The problems are limited; so are time, resources and people. This is claimed to be effective in teaching practical skills in ways that are relevant to the work situation that students will experience, in the same way that projects in practice focus attention, work and resources. However, in education, it also means that students do not learn how practice might be better without resource constraints. Organizing work as projects also implies acceptance of insecure employment and services and less commitment from employers. Thus, the project model does not necessary meet long-term challenges, as for example in development aid, described in Chapter 8. It is a way of making a situation manageable in a complicated world, which fits well with the NPM ideas.

With the privatization and market orientation in the Western society, a business terminology has influenced social work's ideology and practice (Harris, 2003) as well as education. Social work and university leaders have become managers. Social workers have seemingly accepted without much opposition, to become entrepreneurs. As providers of care packages, they sell their products to customers or as purchasers estimate the cost-benefit. The language and concepts used influence the social workers' identity. If we believe that people create themselves and the world around them in interaction and through language, as the social constructionists claim, we have to use the power of language to recreate social work practice according to the values underpinning the definition of social work.

When complexity increases due to diversity, the NPM response is standardization as a tool to minimize flexibility and direct contact (Harris, 2007). Technological development has accelerated this possibility. However, efficiency through standardization should never be a criterion for assessing work in human relationships. Success in social work often depends on establishing rapport and support over time. This is a time-consuming process. Likewise, as we argue in Chapter 9, social work students need face-to-face training to become qualified for this kind of work.

NPM requires efficiency, and people may be related to as rational beings forgetting about a holistic approach, which include emotions and body. Relationship-based social work, which combines an individual and structural understanding of social problems, distress and dysfunction has lost influence compared to procedural and legalistic responses to issues presented by clients (Ruch, 2005). When situations become complex, ambiguous and uncertain as in a globalized postmodern world, risk assessment and evidence-based practice are required. However, this could be contradictory. Risk assessment might end up as bureaucratic time-consuming procedures and delay an immediate, flexible and updated response. Evidence-based practice may call for a modernist data collection inappropriate to inform action in a postmodern era.

New patterns of accountability require frequent and time-consuming reporting, which may compete with direct work with clients or facilitating students. Successes may be converted into facts like numbers of consultations, referrals and meetings in case management teams. For example, the annual report on English social care services reports on the number of assessments carried out by care managers, but not on the care that results. Increased numbers may be regarded as efficiency while in fact it disguises sacrifices of time-consuming counselling and treatment, or cross-cultural contacts.

Lorenz claims that social workers not only face changes in the social policy regime, but also a 're-ordering of social relationships and attempt to model them in neo-liberal ideas', meaning here 'less state, more market, more individual responsibility' (Lorenz, 2005a: 93). He suggests that social workers possibly unthinkingly avoid taking a political standpoint concerning the changes and challenges in government welfare agencies. Instead, they then either withdraw to privatization and therapy or accept NPM service delivery without opposition. He emphasizes that neither of these two solutions responds to the 'social' in public social work. Reflection is often proposed as a way of improving practice, but the critical reflection reviewed in Chapter 3 goes further than this, to address the political context. Brookfield (1995: 8) claims that a reflection becomes critical when it meets two distinct purposes, which may be used in social work:

- to understand how power is exercised in the processes on which we reflect
- to question assumptions and practices that go against clients' best longterm interests, but that seem to make social workers' daily lives and practice easier.

Therefore there is good reason to reflect critically on the professional practice of adjusting to or escaping from the changes NPM requires. If social workers continue to respond as Lorenz claims, then social work has stagnated and is not fulfilling its definition.

Postmodernism and NPM

Postmodernism is a Western phenomenon with a variety of interpretations informed by core assumptions (Meinert et al., 2000); see Chapter 2. Among these are: individual freedom, autonomy, choice, the right to personal expression, acceptance of diversity, and a right to self-fulfilment, to individual wellbeing and leisure time activities. These values only have relevance in affluent societies (Gross, 2006). Nevertheless, they fit well with the ideology underlying NPM, which highlights self-reliance, responsibility, self-help and participation. Postmodernism claims that there are no reliable truths or reality, knowledge is relative and has to be deconstructed, by incorporating into our understanding of social phenomena who created it and in what circumstances. Thus, for social workers, clients, educators and students, uncertainties, ambiguities and risks characterize postmodern life.

Postmodern social work is similarly characterized by alternative practice models from which to choose, based on a variety of theories. In a constantly altering world where changes and experimentation have a value in themselves, many social workers find that what they learned as students, others might consider professionally or politically outdated.

Postmodernism claims that every culture has value. It challenges ethnocentrism where we judge others' opinions and actions from our own framework. Social workers must balance accepting everything as valid on its own premises and cultural relativism. To avoid ethnocentrism by knowing and acknowledging others' cultural values is not the same as accepting everything as equally valid. This accords with social work values, which demand acceptance and understanding, and which provides for clear standpoints on issues. Postmodernism does not contradict this, since it posits awareness of the alternatives.

Social Work under Postmodernism and Globalization

Values Conflicts

Postmodern and NPM values have displaced solidarity, the original base of many welfare systems (Stjernø, 2005). These values have permeated society, including social workers' and clients' identities in the West. However, social workers deal with people who have not adjusted or are unable to meet the requirements. Short-term social work models are used in NPM agencies that might empower people individually, but fail to question structural and political issues.

While social workers and many clients in the West have imbibed postmodern values, in poor countries and communities and among poor people in rich countries, survival values persist. According to Gross (2006), such societies esteem traditional family ties, authority and absolute moral standards, show less tolerance to others, report low well-being and poor health and are materialistically oriented. Gross's commentary from American society has a parallel in Szmagalski's (2004) Polish analysis.

Globalization has widened the gap between rich and poor people and rich and poor countries; see Chapter 2. Reduced public services and benefits make some people dependent on temporary solutions such as soup kitchens in big cities in rich countries. Referring people to such provision defeats social work's long-term aims and values. Social workers work with people temporarily or permanently without the resources to be self-supporting or to have free choice in their lives, because their social and political environment obstructs economic, social and psychological independence. Some may need time for trial and failure, personal attention and support or care, rather than the quick fixes of NPM care systems. Defending needs for time and emotional space to help them commits resources in solidarity, securing more long-term equal outcomes (Hagen and Lødemel, 2005).

NPM values, on the other hand, revitalize the outdated philosophy of helping only 'the deserving poor', excluding from social care people stigmatized by thoughtless prejudice. Demands for financial and organizational efficiency reduce time for long-term relationships, discretion, flexibility and empowerment. Such practice cannot be prescribed by administrative systems, but builds up over time. Social workers are bound to be split between the fundamental knowledge, skills and values of their practice and the focus on market efficiency (Cree and Davis, 2007).

Another example, workfare, in which claimants work in exchange for social security allowances, applies all the pressure of change to individuals. It often aims simply to reduce welfare costs rather than help in more structural ways the people affected when globalization has caused changes in employment markets. Because it is 'an offer you can't refuse' (Lødemel and Trickey, 2001), the lack of choice for and engagement of people affected by such changes in employment make social work involvement contrary to social work values. Consequently, social work may be criticized both for failing in accountability to market imperatives and at the same time also for failing to use discretion, flexibility and professional judgement. An impossible conflict is presented as social work's failure, when it is a failure in management of globalized market pressures.

Social Workers' Mobility

Globalization makes social workers mobile as well as clients. Clients move primarily from South to North and from South to South, while social workers move from North to North and from South to North. The main exceptions are INGO employees, whose work and aims are managed from outside the culture and policies of the country they work in. In UK, employers are actively recruiting overseas social workers to fill vacancies. In 2004, there were 2,534 overseas social workers in the UK, more than ten times more than in 1991 (Firth, 2007). Most foreign social workers work in childcare, where there are most vacancies and the job is stressful. They have to learn quickly about the culture and proper use of language, social policy and law in the context in which they operate, before being able to assess the situation appropriately (Firth, 2007). Some Americans are overwhelmed by the lack of professional status, low pay and huge workload compared with social work in the USA (Batty, 2002).

What Now? Empowering Social Work to Empower

Welfare states developed in part to make up for the drawbacks of capitalism and markets. The welfare state was a modernist creation, relying on a belief that future development would solve social problems. Postmodernist analysis implies less optimistic and ambitious objectives. We have argued that organizational changes such as NPM lead social work to contribute to inequalities, oppression and discrimination and the failings of manageralism. How, instead, might social work combat and compensate for the drawbacks of globalization? First, we argue that social work must be political in its practice. Then, we will highlight ways in which social work, its management and its education might implement its values and renew its practice to achieve empowerment. Working in an empowering way needs to maintain a balance between stability to achieve security for clients, practitioners, educators and students and the flexibility to be open to diversity and change. The main elements of the practice we propose are:

- pursuing openness and flexibility;
- participation to create partnership in practice, education and management;
- incorporating awareness and integration of community perspectives in practice;
- a focus on culture, religion and spirituality as a potential strength rather than an obstacle to practice.

The concept of empowerment has permeated social work (Braye and Preston-Shoot, 1995; Lee, 2001) but lacks a clear definition (Fisher, 2005; Sewpaul and Hølscher, 2004; Askheim 2003). Implying a redistribution of power from powerful institutions, social groups and individuals, it aims for less powerful people to feel emancipated, self-confident and self-effective, that is, able to achieve control over their own lives.

Fisher claims that knowledge is empowering when it is produced in a non-oppressive way and used to reduce social inequalities. To utilize their knowledge and understanding in performing social work, therefore, practitioners and students cannot work in oppressive environments. They need to be empowered in their exchanges with managers and educators to stand up for themselves and influence their own working conditions. Without this, inequalities and oppression affecting clients is likely to limit their capacity and destroy their commitment to being open, advocating, negotiating, or promoting social justice. Non-empowered social workers are unable to support clients in their empowering processes and, furthermore, may become scared of assertive clients. Pursuing empowerment in social work will lead to more powerful clients, and this affects how practitioners, managers and educators can do their work. Thus, empowerment has not only individual consequences. It also has consequences for practice and services. This is because structural implications for the organizations and the social structures they are part of follow from the empowered capacity of clients. It is therefore political.

Social Work as Political Work

The public perception of social work in Western societies is that of individual and family-oriented activity (Payne, 2006). Social work is expected to serve government interests, and in globalizing welfare regimes to implement policies favouring the status quo of oppressive and unjust societies, contrary to social work values. However, postmodernist analysis makes it clear that value neutrality is a modernist assumption that never exists. All actions are political, even those that favour the status quo because they all emerge from particular views and analyses of the world.

There has been an ideological change underneath the organization of social work. For example, in the nineteen seventies growing juvenile delinquency in the UK was seen to arise because of poor parenting and met with prevention and united family services, while in the nineties the approach is more punishment (Morgan and Payne, 2002; Parton, 2006). This is clearly a political issue where the social work profession should not hold back from using their competence to passing on what they know and see as the effect.

An individual perspective on social work makes social workers lone workers. Social workers see themselves as change agents both on an individual as well as on a societal level (Healy, 2001). The definition also states this as a characteristic of social work. However, individual changes might cause societal changes, which are political changes. It might require collective contribution, strong local and international professional associations and affiliation with like-minded to withstand resistance and under some political systems even threats to own security.

The international definition states that human rights and social justice are fundamental to social work. Action on this demands awareness of and critical reflection on power relations in both practice and education, in relations between individuals and groups and among groups in society and in cross-border relations; see Chapter 3. Social workers as a professional group in globalized relations between countries also need to consider how to relate to regimes that violate human rights. Examples are: many aspects of political rights in China and the way the USA has imprisoned people claimed to be terrorists at the Guantanamo base in Cuba. Decisions may be difficult: should social workers from other countries assist the Chinese government in developing social work in China, as social work might make a contribution to improving social conditions? Alternatively, should they avoid becoming involved in Chinese affairs, so that a boycott raises awareness? However, to have a useful effect, professional bodies need to be enjoined to draw attention to the actions of individuals. In their own countries, social workers might be unaware of human rights violations, because social workers may also have values that unthinkingly accept their own cultural hegemony. Well-thought-out action, however, can raise awareness and have useful effects. The heads of schools of social work in Australia, for example, were one of the many groups outraged at the Australian Government's policy of mandatory detention of asylum seekers. The heads subsequently convened a national people's inquiry into immigration detention, holding public hearings throughout Australia (ACSSW, 2006). Based on professional commitment, this was clearly a stance that social work is political.

Being involved in such activity might be seen as irrelevant to the direct work of social workers. We suggest that social workers might focus particularly on issues where their practice or services may be involved, or on the effects on social groups that social workers serve, hence the importance of the Australian example focusing on asylum seekers. Many social groups served by social workers are affected by various social injustices and human rights abuses. It is valuable to be able to point to these issues in a clear way, and to press professional bodies to remain alert to such issues as a way of supporting the daily work of social workers helping clients affected by injustice and oppression.

Therefore, seeing practice in a political context may permit local action, or work in alliance on a wider scale, even in the international arena. In western countries, such activities can lead to difficulties in employment or treatment of social workers. It therefore requires careful planning and thoughtful engagement with these issues, using collective mechanisms such as professional bodies or membership of campaigning groups. Social work in a political context therefore may involve:

- careful consideration of their individual position;
- awareness of and action on issues that raise human rights issues;
- joint work through professional bodies;
- alliances with other organizations.

Social workers raising issues in an authoritarian regime may be exposed to considerable danger, even though raising them may be even more urgent than in a Western country. Social workers in the West need to support the appropriateness of interventions in political contexts as legitimate professional actions.

Empowering Practice

In postmodern practice, social workers do not have expert roles derived from universal knowledge, for three reasons:

- Empowerment means renouncing knowing what is best for clients.
- Population mobility brings together diverse cultures, languages and ethnicities.
- Postmodern practice needs to respond to participants' multiple realities.

Therefore, social workers must claim expertise in redefining the issues that clients and communities face and develop knowledge about how to transform the situations in which clients and communities find themselves. They also need to find new approaches when previous work qualifications are no longer relevant after changes in society and employment brought about by globalization. (Karvinen et al., 1999; Gould and Baldwin, 2004).

Openness means not only willingness to listen to people non-judgementally as social work's values require, but also to be intrigued, curious and willing to learn as part of enabling people to empower themselves. Social workers, therefore, need to be open to the validity of several knowledges; see Chapter 5. These might be different political perceptions about the value of social work from service commissioners, from clients, carers, neighbours and other social workers about the world that they inhabit. It may be particularly challenging to identify and respond to experiences, knowledge and potential solutions from marginalized groups, which might be unfamiliar or exotic to the social worker. Openness is also seeing lifelong learning as a lifestyle and attitude for personal and professional development and growth and not as an extra burden forced upon by NPM.

Participation and partnership with clients and colleagues follow from this (Braye and Preston-Shoot, 1995; Taylor, et al., 2006; Pine and Healy, 2007; Seden and Ross, 2007; Warren, 2007). Participation has been rendered harmless through adoption by NPM values; in an NPM organization, it may mean consultation, or providing information. Slettebø and Seim (2007) suggest the concept should be reserved for active involvement and influence through all stages from deciding whether there is a problem and its nature, selecting means of intervention to whether to terminating the contact. Seden and Ross (2007) take this further to make user participation include taking active part in the management of service delivery, however, admitting that this is very complex with philosophical, ethical and practical implications.

A precondition of user participation and partnership is equal information and access to knowledge. This requires social workers to be up-to-date, trained, willing to share information, and the skills to communicate it, even where it is contrary to their own opinion. The challenge of communicating in relevant language and through relevant means is also crucial. It demands reflexivity to position oneself in the client's situation as a subject, influenced by the client as well as seeking to influence the client and others; see Chapter 3.

A study of participation in child protection showed that children, young people (Seim, 2007) and parents (Slettebø, 2007) lacked information to enable them to participate in decisions, particularly where they belonged to minority ethnic groups and where compulsory powers were used. While participation implies redistributing power, protecting children and others from risk does not mean giving up the use of powers to remove children from abusing parents or others from risk. Social work offered through public services will have duties to act on behalf of the public to protect people at risk of causing injury to themselves or others. As citizens, parents subject to childcare interventions agreed that it is a social responsibility to protect children's interests (Slettebø, 2007). Cree and Davis (2007) also found in their study that clients might see that there are occasions when hospitalization against their will to protect them is necessary. Using compulsory powers, however, does not mean removing all participation in decision-making from the client. There are usually many aspects of their care where they may continue to have a choice. Empowerment is both a necessity for and an outcome of participation.

Social workers need flexibilities in:

- *mind*, to find ways of identifying and responding to people's needs even where these do not fit within the assumptions of NPM agencies;
- *time*, to be prepared to manage the time available to build relationships and to enable clients to think through and present their problems;
- *work-life balance*, to protect their own lives outside the agency's office hours, while maintaining openness to clients' needs, which may be more easily achieved using new technology;

- *place*, so that practitioners can gain a picture of the full circumstances of clients' lives, including their home and living environments and by means of new technology bring the office to the clients.

Contextual social work implies understanding how ranges of factors, such as housing, health and lifestyle, environment and poverty, have emerged from the social issues that affect clients. Social workers in the West might helpfully relearn community-based strategies from Africa, building networks and alliances (Gilchrist, 2004). The challenge of giving up the safety of the agency is also an opportunity to understand people and their surroundings from their different perspective on more equal terms.

Social workers might see culture, meaning tradition, art and religion, as a means to effective communication and intervention, rather than an obstacle because of difference. Resilience focuses on the potential for reconstructing the meaning of life by fostering positive emotions, affirming coping strength and flexibility (Chan et al., 2006; Monroe and Oliviere, 2008). This implies working not only with descriptions of experiences given by clients, but sharing a variety of cultural experiences with clients to gain direct understanding of their world. Løfsnæs (2006) describes a project for women in Afghanistan using art, story telling and traditional celebrations to build the capacity to overcome and survive traumas, threats, adversity and start anew. It is important to recognize how culture and traditions can be an important part of people's lives and affect how they see the world (Graham, 2002). Yip (2004) describes as an example how it enabled the first generation Chinese migrants to Australia to cope better with their life circumstances when the cultural preference for integrated norms and values was acknowledged by the social workers, for example seeking harmony instead of conflict to obtain individual rights.

Conflicts between cultures are not only cross-national phenomena. Within every country, there are contrasts between majority and minority cultures, between male and female cultures, and elderly and young people's cultures. A middle-aged social worker may be alienated from children's and young people's cultures. Using culture as a resource in social work means not only acknowledging difference and tradition, but also being open to new and unknown ideas. It is also important not to reject the fashionable as a fad; this plays into pressures of globalization to see the need to renew 'lifestyle' regularly; see Chapter 2. Particularly for different generations, lifestyle differences may represent genuine difference in ethnic or social self-expression. So, whatever an adult may feel about the music or constant mobile telephone use of young people, these represent an important aspect of their values; see Chapter 7.

Social work was a product of modernist secular movements towards rationalism (Payne, 2005a) Spirituality and religion were therefore often excluded from social work and its literature. Postmodernism practice needs to incorporate spirituality within a holistic approach to clients' lives. Studies in the USA and UK (Furman et al., 2004) as well as in Norway (Zahl and Furman, 2005) show that many social workers see religion and spirituality as fundamental in people's lives but are uncertain about how to approach it in practice. Social work has historically focused on religion's contribution to creating social problems, by oppressing people or causing conflicts. However, religions also have potential to mobilize and empower both individuals and communities (Healy, 2005). Through globalization's increasing impact on people's mobility, social workers in many countries are faced with a new variety of religious and spiritual beliefs and practices. Social workers might be confronted, even provoked, in their own outlook on life.

One of the crucial elements of NPM is its emphasis on accountability, but this is focused on accountability through financial and management requirements to the organization. For social workers, this replaces accountability for meeting clients' needs with that of meeting organizational objectives defined politically or managerially. While NPM organizations view changes positively, this is about adjustment to the financial and managerial requirements of globalization, rather than the inequalities derived from its impact on people. For social workers, this means that NPM agencies focus on listening to and changing to meet the needs of stakeholders that finance, commission and purchase goods and services rather than people who use them.

Empowering Organization

The agency context in which social work is provided influences how social work is organized, what services are offered, what approaches are chosen and social workers' identities. NPM requires change-oriented organizations to adjust to the market and people's demands. This will influence the social work. To be efficient it is not enough to be change-oriented. An organization needs committed and loyal staff that feels secure in their own workplace. Then there is a fine balance between stability and flexibility. Thus, in social work agencies, the need for participation and participative leadership and management, is a parallel to the clients' needs for this in social work. Only empowered employees can pursue client empowerment. Thus, if the goal is participation, meaning active involvement and influence, and empowerment implies power and control over our own lives, the management of social work agencies has to model this, as social workers have to model it in their practice with clients. As for clients, it is a prerequisite that social workers are well-informed, which again contributes to a feeling of security.

Pine and Healy (2007) emphasize transformative leadership and participation as a model that fits social work. It has four characteristics (Bass, 1985; 1990):

- Leaders have charisma in the ability to create a vision for the organization, becoming a strong model for others, enjoying their respect and trust.
- Leaders inspire and convey high expectations alongside motivation to commit themselves to teamwork.
- Leaders stimulate employees intellectually and encourage them to question assumptions, using creativity and innovation.
- Leaders see everybody as individuals, give personal attention and support, and create a thriving work environment, where everybody grow and develop.

The transformative leadership model parallels feminist leadership styles where both process and outcomes are important and collaboration, sharing power and joint decision-making are crucial elements (Healy et al., 1995).

A management representing these four characteristics is important in social work organization to keep up a commitment and steer a steady course under constant changes due to globalization and postmodernism; see Chapter 7 on chaos piloting. An organization with this kind of management gives social workers an opportunity to keep hold of what is fundamental in social work according to the definition and ethical principles, and to be able to balance stability and flexibility.

Empowering Education

Social work education has to incorporate understanding of how globalization and postmodernist changes in the society affect social workers and their clients. Rapid technological developments offer new opportunities for quick access to new material and for alternative ways of teaching and learning. In education as in social work, educational institutions and teachers balance such change against the need for stability and certainty to deliver quality and equitable education (Punie and Cabrera, 2006: 9).

In the same way that social work practice is more sensitive to the impact of cultural and linguistic hegemony, social work education needs to incorporate cultural issues into learning. According to an English study, social work practitioners were not aware that their culture influenced their practice (Muleya, 2006). It is not enough to learn about different cultures, like a cultural tourist; see Chapter 8. Challenging and reflecting critically upon students' culture and how it effects relationships with others and may be used to oppress others in education is an important basis for future practice. Membership of a particular cultural group, possibly a majority culture, means that social workers might make clients feel marginalized or excluded, without constant critical analysis of their practice. The flow of information and input about different cultures that globalization may expose students to might falsely convince social workers, students and educators that in postmodernity they know about a wide range of cultures. Nevertheless, they may fail to empower clients to pursue their own cultural directions.

NPM management approaches and the political context of practice mean that identifying the impacts of policy on practice helps students and practitioners to analyse these and other developing ideologies underpinning the context of social work practice. Critical reflection is needed to understand ways in which they may conflict with the definition of social work and its ethical principles. This enables social workers and students to understand and influence working conditions to promote empowering practice, organization and education. They need to understand the balance between professional and political work, distinguish between politics and policy and how to combine it and when and how to get involved. We have argued that such ideological influences equally affect social work education. Therefore, educators need to challenge themselves and students to see their own education's political context, and strengthen their ability to use it in their studies and future work for the benefit of clients. The basis for empowerment and participation has to be laid during their studies. This challenges educators and affects how they teach and model appropriate critical reflection.

Social workers, as part of a practice profession in postmodernity, need to learn to meet, empower and build relationships with individuals in different situations and social positions. If relationship-building is lost because of a focus on procedural accountability to organizations, then something vital is lost in the profession (Ruch, 2005; Cree and Davis, 2007). Therefore, education has to prepare social workers to practice effectively within the limitations of a procedural organization. Since, as we have suggested, similar social processes are required in practice, organization and education, educators may usefully model parallels in work with clients and colleagues in agencies in demonstrating relationship-building in their work with students (Askeland, 1994).

A specific competence in social work is to have an overview of the network of organizations involved in work with a client and the client's own social network and community. Alongside this, social workers have the capacity, using cooperative and collaborative skills, to link areas in which other professions take the lead. Professional self-confidence will be an effect of empowerment, but students also need to learn to know their professional boundaries in order to achieve these overview and linking roles. Social work education might usefully highlight and develop these skills, emphasizing their importance to the overall social work role, and thus contributing to greater awareness among social workers and other professions.

Conclusion

In previous chapters, we identified globalization and the way it is managed internationally as creating inequality, social injustice and individual difficulties. We argued in this Chapter that it also forms the agency and university context of social work, and therefore is in tension with the identity of social work practice. This is because practice is drawn from a professional identity based on values committed to responding to the needs of clients within their social context. A particular area of tension is the way management in transnational organizations developed in response to the needs of globalized economic development. This has had an impact on welfare agencies through a collection of managerialist approaches characterized as new public management. These give priority to accountability through financial mechanisms and management structures to responding to politically- and economically-defined objectives, rather than developing professional discretion and responsibility for meeting needs identified by clients. Postmodernism argues that a wide range of structures and policies are available, and might be used to respond to a variety of social and cultural needs and wishes. Limiting practice to what is defined through NPM accountability structures fails to open up the possibilities offered by our complex societies. Neither does it enable social workers to extend their practice towards the boundaries of the definition and ethical standards established internationally through the professional bodies. These increasingly offer the opportunity to respond to local contexts within social work's wider general approach.

Therefore, in the latter part of this chapter, we have argued for practice that responds to the opportunities of postmodernity and reacts against the organizational limitations of globalized managerialism. Social work always responds to and interacts with its political context, so its practice must incorporate analysis of the impact of social factors on clients' lives and the organizations within which social work is practised and learned. Empowering practice, agencies and education seeks to balance certainty and security against change and development. It pursues openness and flexibility in participative partnerships that incorporate an awareness of the needs of individuals, families and communities in cultivating their culture, religion and spirituality.

In the next chapter, we extend this analysis of the organizational context of social work practice and education by considering the impact of the experience of postmodernism on practitioners, students and educators.

Chapter 7

Piloting through the Challenges of Globalization

Postmodern Social Workers, Students and Educators

Postmodern people may be seen as updated nomads. Like traditional nomads, postmodern societies require people to be flexible and mobile, making what they can of their environment, and to settle temporarily rather than permanently. Postmodern nomads need to relate to complex social situations in constant flux and to contradictory knowledge which is provisional rather than certain, unstructured rather than organized, and oriented towards the future, rather than backward-looking. Practitioners, students and educators face the struggle to relate to a lot of information and various and sometimes contradictory knowledge. Agencies as sites for social work practice face us with this challenge. So do higher education institutions together with agencies as sites for learning and teaching social work. Postmodern people are all affected by commodification and consumerism, but not everyone has equal opportunities to make free choices (Edwards, 1996).

Atherton and Bolland (2002) among others claim that focusing on postmodernism will have negative consequences for social work because of its relativism and that the benefits of doing so are illusory. However, we argue that some aspects of postmodernism can be used in developing thinking about social work practice and education. The postmodernist analysis permits an examination of how strengths in different generations and in different cultural groups may vary and how growth in possibly opposite directions may be facilitated and incorporated into one society.

All countries are affected by the social changes of globalization, but richer countries in the West may be more affected by technological change than poorer countries, where people cannot afford the same amount of technology. Sometimes, though, new technologies may allow poor countries to leap one or more generations of development. For example, in poor rural countries in Africa, mobile phone networks can be developed where it would be too expensive to build links with wires. People can club together to buy used handsets, and maintain communication among families split up by migration or the need to work away from home. A newspaper article indicates some of the possibilities that affect the lives even of rural peoples:

> One pilot program allows about 100 farmers in South Africa's northeast to learn the prevailing prices for produce in major markets, crucial information in negotiations with middlemen. Health-care workers in the rural southeast summon ambulances to distant clinics via cell [mobile] phone. One woman living on the Congo River, unable even to write her last name, tells customers to call her cellphone if they want to buy the fresh fish

she sells. 'She doesn't have electricity, she can't put the fish in the freezer', said Mr. Nkuli of Vodacom. 'So she keeps them in the river, tethered live on a string, until a call comes in. Then she retrieves them and readies them for sale' (LaFrantiere, 2005: 1).

Piloting through Chaos: The Challenges of Globalization

Our model pursuing practice in this context is the idea of the chaos pilot. A three-year Nordic study programme for creative project leaders, called 'chaos pilots', has taken this seriously (Institute for Social Inventions, 2003). Chaos education aims for students to learn how to cope in different contexts, cultures, traditions, and organizations, under different historical, economical, political and social conditions. They must deal with their own values, attitudes and skills. The programme argues that students should be in command of academic competence, social competence, competence to act and solve problems in reality, and competence in achieving change and flexibility. During the first year, students study in a Nordic country, originally Århus Denmark, (UddannelsesGuiden, 2006), with the second in San Francisco, and the third in Beijing, enabling them to get to grips over a significant period with a range of cultural contexts, rather than a brief exchange. A lengthy involvement in alternative cultures might be more appropriate than a brief exchange for preparation for social work. Now the programme has expanded to other parts of the world as well. This alternative leadership education teach how to 'navigate in unknown terrain', and to think in new terms, be creative, visionary and agile at high tempo. Part of it is trial and effort. In a continually-changing world, it is important to be observant and able to combine intuition and knowledge (MRB Bedriftsutvikling, 2001). We argue that having been through an educational programme like this would help students to find more creative and better solutions in partnership with clients. This is because they will have learned how to respond with agility to different contexts, cultures, traditions, and organizations, under different historical, economical, political and social conditions.

The immediate environment in which we work seems constantly in flux. Government and management constantly reorganize, people's lives are stressed and difficult. It seems chaotic. Chaos theory is not sufficient for understanding chaotic behaviour in complex social systems (Halmi, 2003). However, understanding the trends and consistencies within chaos allows, in scientific theory, ways of responding to it. We seek to focus on social changes that are damaging to our clients, to our practice and to our education. They are damaging because they strengthen, rather than overcome, inequality and oppression. Resolving problems by a simple intervention is impossible. Ideas such as an agreement with clients for a limited period of task-centred practice, or by negotiating a response from another agency do not deal adequately with the complexity of the social factors that create clients' difficulties. Simply lecturing to provide information and studying to identify evidence does not help us to apply the oversimplifications we have been given in social work education. We have to teach and learn in ways that help us deal with complexity and flexibility. Focusing on just one priority is impossible in the complex of difficulties that families and communities face, and yet pressures of finance and management seem to make dealing with complexity difficult.

Piloting through chaos involves accepting a general background of constant change, seeking to ride the currents of change, responding where the winds blow, swerving round dangerous areas, but maintaining progress towards our objectives. Chaos piloting requires:

- Identifying general long-term objectives for our work, to guide movements as we shift in response to change. These objectives will reflect our fundamental values. In particular, 'zooming up' and 'zooming down' will be required (Algie, 1975). That is, people have sometimes to look at broad social issues and conflicts and sometimes at the minutiae of their effects on people's lives.
- Identifying values to guide us as we work alongside clients in the complexity of their lives and our own lives and alongside trends that may push us off course. In this book, we have focused on the useful values of contextualization, criticality and flexibility particularly in cultural and linguistic translation. Trends towards inequalities, cultural hegemony, and managerialist responses to economic pressures are all potentially disruptive to social work, and need to be understood and challenged as they arise.
- Identifying and using skills to understand and respond to change in ways that help us to understand and exploit underlying flexibilities in our societies. We must not accept practice that is determined by globalization, but instead look for alternative modes of understanding and working with people.

Therefore, in this Chapter, we examine how to pilot through a globalized postmodern world. A tension exists between the openness of postmodern thinking and the way globalization requires practice to be determined by modernist, universal, evidence-based knowledge and understanding. To talk about people as postmodern implies that their experience of life now would have been different a generation ago, at least in economically developed countries. Also it implies that now there is greater openness, while then their world would have been more determined. These comments are phrased as comparatives – 'greater' 'more' – to indicate that this is not an absolute change, but a trend in which some modes of thinking and working would continue in a deterministic way, while openness and flexibility would have been available previously.

While postmodernism is not, therefore, a complete break from other modes of thinking and working (Dobson and Haaland, 2000), a comparison of Swedish and American young people suggests that each generation creates itself as different from previous generations in its historical context (Glans, 2003). The generation of the 1960s and '70s in much of Europe saw itself as liberated from the stress of the economic depression of the 1930s and the grey uniformity of the war years through the development of post-war welfare states. Some of the generation of the 1990s saw their parental generation as undisciplined visionaries who failed to achieve economic security. The generation of socialists who achieved independence from colonial powers in Africa in the 1960s saw themselves as different from their parental generation some of whom accepted the advantages of colonialism. Therefore, the millennial generation, that is, the one coming to adulthood in the early twenty-first century, differs from previous generations because of its particular political and social experiences. If there have been changes, they have consequences for people in social work and its education today. Our aim here is to identify some characteristics of postmodern social workers, students and educators and discuss some consequences for the training that prepares present students for future social work.

Social workers, students and educators experience globalization and postmodernism every day as part of their work, because these social trends affect every part of society. We saw in Chapter 6 the effects of globalization in three trends within social work:

- The commodification of welfare provision, with welfare services and education becoming like goods and services in the commercial market, for example as packages of care, rather than as therapeutic services. This arises because of the power of transnational corporations in the economy to influence ways of thinking about activities within welfare and to invade the management of service provision that was previously largely within the public sector.
- The priority given to market mechanisms and economic development over social development to respond to poverty, social exclusion and inequality.
- The emphases that managerialism and new public management (NPM) give to the way services and education are provided.

These factors derive not from within social work or welfare, but from wider economic, political and cultural changes. We have suggested in previous chapters that globalization presents social work with important challenges because these factors conflict with the flexibility and openness required of social work to respond to the inequalities of welfare systems. Globalization creates or emphasizes inequalities, and so adversely affects the economically and politically excluded social groups that social work mainly deals with. In a sense, we can say that the modernism of economic globalization and its political and cultural aspects has invaded a profession that valued flexibility and openness, and that postmodernism seeks to open up renewed possibilities of openness.

Postmodern Practice

We argue that postmodernism creates flexibilities within globalizing societies that gives social work the political and social space to respond to the challenge of globalization. In Chapters 3–6, we picked up the major features of postmodernism in Chapter 1 and discussed various ways in which social work may respond to the challenges of globalization by using the flexibilities of postmodern thinking. For example:

- Avoiding meta-narratives means that social work rejects universalizing explanations of the social factors that it deals with. Instead, critical reflection allows a range of factors to be brought to bear, see Chapter 3. The International Definition of Social Work discussed in Chapter 6 shows how both social and psychological knowledge and both social justice and human rights explanations and values must be integrated within social work. We cannot use just one or the other of each of these two alternatives.

- Accepting instability and complexity in social relationships; and avoiding oversimplification. Social workers deal with correcting inequalities and injustices that arise in societies, through empowerment and anti-discriminatory practice. In Chapter 4 we argued that incorporation of different cultures is not a simple process.
- Focusing on language, signs and symbols as important carriers of the meanings of social phenomena are important aspects of responding to inequalities through cultural translation and through transfer between different forms of knowledge; see Chapters 4 and 5 respectively.
- Understanding the world through different forms of knowledge and through contextualizing understanding so that it is relevant to particular social and cultural groups; these have been issues in all our discussion so far.
- Detailed examination or deconstruction of behaviour and uses of language, signs and symbols in our social environment is important for understanding social and power relations through critical reflection, cultural translation and transfer of knowledge.

In this Chapter, we bring together these postmodern responses to the challenge of globalization, by showing how by being a postmodern social worker, student or educator, we can use the flexibilities in our situation to respond to the social complexities created by globalization.

To understand this, Brenda, an African woman aged 47, illustrates some of the complexities that arise as a result of migration in a globalized world. She had just separated from her West Indian husband when she came into contact with a disabilities social worker, an education social worker and eventually care managers for her mother and daughter. The family owed rent, from the time of the marriage break-up, so she was also in contact with a housing welfare worker. She had two children aged 14 and 12 years at school, one son aged 16 years just seeking work, and one daughter with learning disabilities, aged 21 years living in special housing. Housing welfare workers and carers from a specialist learning disabilities agency supported her. Nearby, her elderly mother lived alone, who had just been diagnosed with Alzheimer's disease. Brenda provided a great deal of support for her, and assumed she would be doing more for her in the future. While the expectation that she would provide help is typical of many cultures in Britain, it was given added force by the fact that in her African culture, care for family members was part of the important interdependence among family members. Her mother was a recent migrant and had no other relatives in the UK.

Brenda was diagnosed with multiple sclerosis, which progressed fairly rapidly. Soon her son, who had been attending further education college with a view to training as a chef, had to give up his course and prospects of a job for the time being to care for her. Her social worker from the social services disabilities team initially assumed that her older daughter and mother could help her, until she realized that the learning disabilities and Alzheimer's would preclude this. The frail elderly team social worker became involved with seeking a care arrangement for Brenda's mother. Not wanting to worry the daughter with learning disabilities, her carers had decided not to tell her of her mother's diagnosis or prognosis, which was poor, so she did not understand her mother's sudden deterioration. The education welfare service became involved when the 14 year old began staying off school to be with her mother. The estranged husband reported to a child protection agency that the mother was no longer able to care for the children, and announced that he would like to resume the care of the younger children and take them to the USA, where he had family. They did not want to leave their mother or the country. Soon, the son was providing physical care for Brenda. This was considered unhelpful to his sexual, social and personal development, although he was happy to do it, again pursuing the interdependent culture of the family. Brenda hoped that her sister could come to support her, but the house was too small to accommodate her, and she could not get a visa to come to the country to care for Brenda.

The complexity of this situation is by no means exceptional in social work caseloads. Care agencies in the UK generally do not call on social workers unless this level of complexity arises. In addition to raising the impact of globalization leading to migration and families spread across the world, there are multiple problems and agencies involved. Although there are healthcare and housing implications, many of the issues are psychological and concerned with social arrangements and relationships within a private arena, the classic arena of social work action. During the 1970s, reorganization in the UK social services tried to provide one door for multiple problems of this kind, and many countries in Europe including Norway developed similar coordinated agencies, with a focus on social issues and responses. However, it was always optimistic to believe that one worker, one group of workers or one focus could achieve results with this degree of complexity, which arises from the complexity and fragmentation of modern lives and societies. Instead of relying on social workers and groups of social workers for collaboration, although this is still required, coordination between agencies and policies is also necessary. Furthermore it is unrealistic to expect wholly consistent policies, responding with unity to rapid and often disputed and debated social change.

For Brenda's family, each social worker will need to create varying alliances among them and between them and family members to achieve:

- A clear long-term objective for their joint work: a stable and supportive family during the present situation that can develop resilience among the younger people who will take the current experience forward to strengthen them to deal with difficulties in later life.
- Clear short-term objectives for each individual family member, which contribute to or at least do not impede the long-term objectives.
- Strengthen values, increasing the capacity to care for each other among all members of the family, and contribute to its resilience, even those with disabilities.
- Developing the skill of linking the different specialist knowledges of the social workers, for example in disability, Alzheimer's, in marriage problems and in learning disabilities. Also, their capacity to confront difficulties in relationships between family members and to respond to the emotional and practical consequences of the changes affecting the family will be important.

Increasing complexity is also a consequence of social change arising from globalization in the South as well as in the West. Clashes of culture, groups of the population being left behind, migration to the cities away from rural areas, rapid industrialization, changes in working practices and work roles, all these and many more lead to complex social issues for societies to deal with. However, resources to deal with the social consequences of change are more limited in poor economies than in Western economies. However, all societies face a 'care deficit' (Hochschild, 1995). Nowhere in the world, and at no time in history has a society had the capacity to deal with all the social and human issues that its people faced. We argue that the chaos piloting approach will help to focus on both the psychological and social, zooming up and down between them, and on the inequalities and cultural conflicts that globalization produces.

Postmodern Student

Postmodernism affects students and educators because it refers to changes in how knowledge is generated and understood in societies. Local cultural and social understanding is transformed by the impact of the increasing new communications technologies discussed in Chapter 9. These bring people into close contact with other cultures.

To connect with postmodern students, changes and adjustments are required compared with previous generations, but for education to be effective as a preparation for social work, some postmodern trends need to be challenged. We need to think about how educators from a different generation may meet postmodern students' needs with respect and curiosity. We seek to identify how social work education must change to take advantage of, but also to challenge, present trends.

As updated nomads, postmodern students are flexible and mobile, making what they can of their environment. They settle down only temporarily. They are used to relating to a lot of information and various and sometimes contradictory knowledge. They are competent in using a range of technological tools to manage the uncertainty and complex world around them.

The conditions for being a postmodern student may not be found everywhere in the world, only in some countries. To become a postmodern student requires

- financial, material and technological resources such as technical equipment for communication and travelling;
- electricity, mobile phone and Internet coverage;
- libraries and access for individuals to affordable professional literature (books, CD-roms, videos and the Internet) in a comprehensible language.

We saw in Chapter 6 that issues about identity are crucial in understanding how postmodernism is expressed. This is also true for student experiences. Identity in postmodern societies does not imply being rooted in a specific role or profession, such as social work (Castells, 1997), but it cannot be rooted in insecurity either. Giddens (1991) claims that in a postmodern era people's constant seeking identity is a restless hunting for a narcissistic 'who am I' rather than a commitment. According to Giddens, a narcissist is unable to distinguish clearly between the self and the environment. The compression of space and time contributes to loss of grounding and changes in personal identity (Edwards, 1996). Continuous seeking for identity in this way might make students rootless, in the West, where such personal identities are important. However, in some societies, seeking to maintain social identities with family or community will be more important than establishing an individual professional identity as a student or as a member of a profession; see Chapter 6.

In postmodern societies, people have diverse, multiple sources of identity: what they consume, whom they communicate with, where they get information, what they experience through travel, what this symbolizes to them and the culture of their generation. People are what they know or can find out; this is what gives them personal or professional power. If postmodern students create in this way an individual, personalized identity rather than relying on a professional identity, they may not gain a common identity through their professional studies, and the focus of the education has to be more on the students' own production of knowledge (Kvalbein, 1998; see also Chapter 5).

Rapid change makes knowledge like consumer goods, easily bought on the Internet and thrown away when it is no longer of any use. After all, it can be found again, if required. Students' individualized identities may also be thrown away, displaced by new knowledge. The importance of life experience may be rejected in favour of evidence drawn from academic studies that may not connect with the student. Feminist writers, such as Gilligan, (1993), for example, have argued that structured, logical moral reasoning aiming towards an ethics of justice may not be relevant to women whose experience leads them to an 'ethics of care'. This respects connections and relationships as equally important aspects of life alongside fairness.

Postmodern Educators

Postmodernism may or may not lead to generational difference between students and educators. Educators may also be flexible, open, fragmented, globalized, market-oriented travellers and technology freaks. Academics like the freedom of responsibility for a few modules rather than a whole programme, like to test out new technology, to be artistic performers. They may also compete in the higher education market and become academic tourists. The ageing of populations in many Western countries means that many present social work educators have a background different from that of postmodern students (Glans, 2003). Their theoretical background was originally positivist, education being aimed at making people increasingly expert in their field. However, their role has become more fragmented and complex, with many competing aims and demands. Professional and academic literature has exploded in volume making them more specialized. Varied pedagogical approaches add to the demands. To relate to students as consumers requires new pedagogical competence to meet managerial and commercial aims (Solstad, 1997). There may be demands to earn research grants. A higher proportion of staff may be part-time or short-term. In these ways, higher education is changing educators' ways of working.

Postmodernism has changed higher education. Modularization of courses, globalization of contacts and communications, increased use of information and communication technology, mass universities increasing the range of courses have all raised issues for debate. Students are active consumers in the global market society, and higher education costs add to their financial burdens. Continuing professional education and mid-life career changes to professions such as social work also implies increasing family and financial responsibilities. Eritsland (2001) suggests that the only thing the next generation is certain about is that their adult lives will be very different from those of their parents. Present-day students cannot assume continuity of experience throughout their lives. The likelihood of constant change cannot be avoided. There will be changes both in the student's experience and in social work for which students are being prepared to work.

Because education has become a market product, it is expected to produce events and happenings as if it were entertainment. Radio, television, mobile phones and the Internet all treat sensitive material with elements of entertainment, and this is also expected of educators. Edutainment does not promote reflection and contemplation. It may be useful for learning facts and functional behaviour, but it is questionable whether it will be useful from a critical learning perspective (Bang, 1997) and it may not provide sufficient contextual information of evidence for theorizing or for action (Eraut, 1994: 69) and for skill training (Dreyfus, 2001). Students may not engage with complex and difficult material or allocate time to develop skills and practice techniques. Learning may be provocative and challenging; it may provoke feelings and adverse reactions; it is more than entertainment (Moxnes, 1992).

Social work and education are parts of a consumer market system influenced by business approaches and ethics (Harris, 2003). Agencies compete, so postmodern students need to learn how to participate in that competition. However, in education for social work, we retain an identity for social work that focuses on service and welfare. Students compete in a market for expertise for example, social workers might compete for jobs with people in cognate areas of expertise such as counsellors, psychologists, or nurses, while agencies compete in a market for roles, tasks and ultimately clients, since unless they can demonstrate a role with a client or problem group, in a market system, they will not survive.

Political attitudes are ambivalent there is to the social services. On one hand, between a wish to provide a welfare system oriented to people's needs and welfare. On the other, there is a movement towards providing social care through markets. In the globalized, consumerized market, constant renegotiation of the relationship between the market and the state goes on, incorporating not-for-profit agencies. Social workers will be involved in a mutating system in which they will have to understand and renew their position. Education for social work needs to prepare for work within commercial, volunteer and corporate state welfare systems negotiating with people with varying motives and assumptions for offering services.

Postmodern Social Work Education

If social work is a profession it has to be linked to the university (Reid and Edwards, 2006). Pressure for academization rather than professionalization in social work derives from higher education markets. Newspapers across the world, for example

Times Higher Education Supplements and Shanghai Jiaotong, publish league tables comparing universities around the world. On the former list, the University of Oslo (UiO) fell from number 101 in 2004 to number 177 in 2006, while at the latter list it rouse from number 69 in 2005 to 68 in 2006. According to the university president (Ellingsrud, 2006) this does not mean a quality deterioration. It must be seen in relation to the criteria, which change from year to year. For example, the Times Higher Education Supplement's rating list in 2006 included the number of article citations written in several Asian languages. Consequently, this moved some of the Asian universities forward on the list, while others, like the UiO, fell down. Numbers of citations is a commonly used criterion. However, it is not objective, since it varies from discipline to discipline, and depends on whether a university's researchers primarily publish in English or another world language or in local languages, which also depends on the discipline. Ellingsrud also claims that the rating in itself is self-reinforcing as 50% of what counts is the university's reputation without any further explanation.

The academization taking place in European social work education may be good for the status of the profession. However, will it be better or worse for clients? How does the deacademization that occurs in the UK, with political impetus to emphasize practice against theory, influence social work's identity? What is the policy behind establishing new social professions? Does it serve people's interests because society has become more complicated or is it an effort to minimize the influence of a profession that does not always adhere to structural and political changes?

Contrary to trends in the UK, in most European countries, social work education is moving from professional training towards academization (Labonte-Roset, 2004; Lorenz, 2005a). In Finland, except for one Swedish speaking school of social work, social work education has for decades been a six-year-long programme within the social policy faculties, and until fairly recently the social work staff has had to fight for their right to teach social work theory and skills.

Social work education developed to train people to fit into modernist organizations; this conflicts with the postmodern life experience of students. Managerialism actively contradicts current social trends towards openness and flexibility that postmodern students have come to expect. People in social work education need to develop an awareness and analysis of how they can educate students to handle it constructively. For example, assessment of detailed competences as part of social work education permits a more explicit and defensible statement of practice assessment, but makes it more difficult to see students' attainments as part of their holistic development as practitioners.

Social work education in Europe varies from lower level occupational training in technical colleges or separate schools to post graduate university degrees (Hamburger and Wøbcke, 2005). The length varies from one to five years. The American educational model of bachelor, master and doctoral are gaining ground particularly in countries where social work is a fairly new or renewed profession or in Europe through the Bologna process (Ashford, 2004).

Because of these trends towards or away from the academization of training, it is important to ask how educators meet the postmodern student. Are they traditional students or postmodern students with no clear boundaries between education, training, work, consumerism, entertainment and leisure (Edwards, 1996)?

Special Needs of Postmodern Social Work Education

Three aspects may be highlighted:

- *Emergence* – postmodern education is a shared process of creating knowledge and identity.
- *Professional identity* – students need to gain mastery of complexities in holistic practice to overcome insecurity generated by postmodern trends.
- *Transfer* – constant social change means that students need to gain skills in transfer of knowledge and values.

Social work education should value building students' knowledge and skills so that, as they practice, they will be able to gain mastery of an area of study and practice. Because postmodern knowledge is created, constructed between students and educators working together, postmodern education extends beyond a banking model in which teachers provide knowledge. This is because it is about the joint creation of identity: the educator must be visible and engaged as a person, as much as the student. Both are influenced by their life-historical knowledge; see Chapter 5. Neither teaches the other about different worlds, they create the world together in their work together. They jointly create personal and professional identities. Through doing this, the parallel process of identity-creation with clients within social work is jointly modelled (Askeland, 1994; Askeland, 2003; Askeland, 2003a). Such an educational process is a more dialogic form of education, than education where one person teaches the other by modelling expertise.

Postmodern students are well-prepared to gain access to information resources about their area of work as information is increasingly accessible. Having a lot of information is not all that is needed to gain mastery of practice; this requires knowledge to be used well. Students will throughout their careers need the capacity to reflect critically on their practice, to integrate into a coherent system of thought and practice and to apply knowledge skilfully in the context of a professional value system. Pearson (1998) shows American social work faculty are pulled between two different learning styles and value bases, mastering and mentoring learning approaches. This tension has also entered European social work education alongside academization.

As information resources have grown, acquiring and assimilating information has begun to compete for time with the processes of reflection and integration. Students must be educated to make judgements about the validity of the source and to understand the values and cultural assumptions that inform those judgements.

All education has to build on students' strengths. Education for mastery must confront and challenge students' experiences with mature and complex understandings of social work. It must lead students to appreciate and enjoy the process of in-depth study. To become holistic practitioners implies the need to seek understanding of connections and coherence. Therefore, challenging present skills is crucial to building on strengths to achieve in-depth mastery. Educators have to model engagement, to stimulate in students a curiosity for alternative conceptions and understandings, and appreciate how ability to practice emerges from this process. Creating understanding rather than teaching knowledge requires more responsible and closer educational relationships than edutainment. Creators cannot walk in and out of a creative process, but like the sculptor they can return to it at different times over a period from many different directions. In this way, the education process practises and models user participation and empowerment. A learning community is where interdependent and interdisciplinary learning and involvement are encouraged (Tinto, 1997).

Individual, Collective and Professional Identity

Identity is eroded by globalization, postmodernism and postcolonialism; see Chapters 2 and 6. The unclear identity of the profession and social workers' uncertainty about their identity mutually reinforce each other, affecting social work practice. Social work's identity is influenced by the social workers' personal and professional identities. People create their identity through interaction with others in a social process (Payne, 2006). Whom we identify with, meaning being the same as, and whom we are different from therefore becomes important. From a postmodern perspective, individuals do not have a core identity. On the contrary, postmodernism sees identity as fragmented and in a process of constant development in frequently changing contexts. People may choose among various personal and professional identities. This may cause uncertainty for some while it gives others opportunities to create consciously a coherent identity. This is true for clients, practitioners, students and educators.

In a process of mutual influence, clients become co-creators of social work's identity (Payne, 2005). In Western cultures, identity is related to the individual; while in other cultures, like the Asian cultures, collectivism has priority over individualism. In cultures influenced by Confucianism, Taoism, Buddhism, Hinduism and Islam there is not a sharp distinction between the self or an individual identity and others (Yip, 2004: 604-5). In the Philippines, the self does not even have a separate identity, but shared identity with others of the inner self. The African *ubuntu*, means humanness, that people are people through other people. This would influence the social workers' and clients' identities as well as the understanding and solutions. If not, social work would become alienated from both the social workers and the people it is to serve.

Working as described above also helps students understand the process of continuous identity creation as they become professionals. Clients may no longer accept the authority of the 'social worker' so they must define themselves to their clients, to their employers and to society in a way that is authentic. This has consequences for the professional identity for students. Postmodern ideas produce a politics of the self. 'The postmodern conception of community is ... based on difference in the sense that the self is perceived through the recognition of otherness and is therefore incomplete in itself.' (Delanty, 2001: 140). The postmodern student cannot identify their 'self'; they can only see their self by seeing that they are different from others. To maintain their self, they must always search for and maintain their differences from others. Yet to join a profession and implement knowledge, they must integrate their self-identity with that of social work.

Capacities such as the ability to change students' social environment and circle of acquaintances (Bauman, 2000; Meland, 2001) will influence students' identity creation. Chaos pilots need similar capacities. Their postmodern life experience provides opportunities to develop and hone such skills, but it also has to be nourished during professional studies to create mastery of complexity.

Social Change – Knowledge Transfer

One of the characteristics of postmodern societies is constant change. Critical reflections and reflective learning is an educational approach that fits postmodernism (see Chapter 3; Taylor, 1996). Postmodern students, according to Fook (2002: 44-145), must learn the 'skill of transferability' and 'cultural competence' so that they are able to 'read' 'the cultural climate of contexts' and have the skill to get involved in and appreciate the cultural climate of the contexts in which they operate. Opportunities are available in every classroom, but this requires educators to bring them out as part of their work, as Mumm and Kersting (1997) propose in discussing teaching critical thinking. For example, if experience of ethnic difference is not available in a student group, educators might raise ideas about cultural transfer between different age generations, or people with rural and urban backgrounds.

Re-establishing and Renewing Social Work Education

Postmodern trends pose to social work education two important practical issues: incorporating students' skills with newly available information and communication technology, and responding to students' needs for identity within a constantly changing environment.

Communication

Three characteristics of present-day communication compared with the past may be identified. First, mobile phones are in the public arena. Second, the mobile phone is personal, and the threshold for contacting others at any time has decreased. People's accessibility has increased as mobile phone calls have gained priority over other activities. To reach young people as clients and students we have to learn from them about how to communicate efficiently by symbols and icons. Postmodern students are accustomed to expressing themselves in writing, sending text messages, photographs, emails and participating in chat rooms. Such communication may be impulsive, but implies thinking and sorting out ideas, presenting them attractively and engaging in debate. In postmodern education we have to take advantage of the confidence students gain in writing in this way. These forms of writing may stimulate reflection just as effectively as face-to-face debate.

While postmodern students may be individualistic, they also develop group thinking and team spirit by turning to friends and media for information and advice rather than the adult world (Glans, 2003). Their loyalty to their peers and to their reference group emphasizes the importance of using various group approaches in social work education.

American tests of comprehension of material show that students who study with the aim of teaching others, get a better result (Bargh and Schul, 1980; Annis, 1983). As postmodern students use various communication media, the opportunity for teaching others interpersonally are legion. Helping other students learn should be encouraged, and parallels to working with social work clients might be made. Study materials and guides might promote student experience of educating others as a means of interacting with the material they study. Through this, they might also learn that to relate to other people's experiences, may be a rich source for creating new knowledge.

Flexible Uncertainty

Social work education must learn how to bring out more clearly the skills and understanding required to develop flexibility and transferability. Social workers, students and educators, like chaos pilots, need to handle situations from a range of cultural perspectives and within a range of contexts. Western social workers might benefit from learning more about how others who cannot rely on a well-funded welfare regime, as with some African and Asian countries, are able to make the most of the available resources. American social workers might experience the gains, strains and challenges of welfare state environments for practice. To transfer competence from these different situations, critical reflection on the experiences is necessary, and a structure of learning that permits effective international experience; see Chapter 8.

Social workers thus become process pilots able to negotiate uncertainty and development through reflection and action, by transferring understanding from one situation to another. The content of knowledge becomes something that is adapted for transfer, rather than established and taught. The educator's role is to manage knowledge transfer so that knowledge remains true to the research and scholarship that developed it. The student's role is to learn process piloting, using the framework of knowledge and understanding to the point where they can join professional colleagues in piloting through the uncertainties of a rapidly changing world. Educators have to master uncertainty in their organization. Managerialist processes such as global standards inhibit the flexibility that permits mastering uncertainty and educators need to balance flexibility objectives against that. Since postmodern education involves preparation for piloting through uncertainty, constant updating is required. Postmodern educators are not experts in the content of knowledge, but need to model the capacity to transform experience from one situation to another. They model how to source and treat information, how to research, develop, integrate, and incorporate knowledge into understanding for practice. For knowledge and understanding to be useful, it must then be reconstructed as the framework from which current learning emerges through transfer processes into action (Kolb, 1984).

Postmodern?

Social workers, educators and students are piloting through uncertainty. Practitioners are experiencing a changing welfare system apparently chaotic because of its complexity and the complexity of the lives that clients experience. Therefore as students they need to learn ways of piloting through these complexities. Educators are experiencing change through knowledge transfer from their starting point, students from theirs. Creating a joint process of education that integrates with practice is like beginning to fly in formation. Students can identify their own positions with reference to the journeys of their educators.

Since social workers, educators and students are piloting from different starting points, they are, in the postmodern way, alike in the manner they do things but what emerges will always produce individual differences. Postmodern students are something they and their educators are unable at present to define.

Who thought of postmodernism? – the present academic generation (Callinicos, 1989). Who experiences chaos? – the present managers and educators. Once secure, the older generation now see the world as less secure. They see societies and students as postmodern because the current practice and student experience create insecurity for managers and educators. The postmodern idea is that people cannot impose ideas on others; they have to transfer knowledge so that it emerges into identities relevant for themselves. Managers and educators are telling practitioners and students that they are postmodern; perhaps they will find out that they are not. The next two chapters examine ways of dealing with postmodern experiences in cross-national contacts and in the use of technology that show in a more detailed and specific way how we can handle the issues we face in postmodern globalizing societies.

Chapter 8

Exchanges and Cross-national Activities: Broadening the Mind

Introduction

'Travel broadens the mind', goes the English saying. More cross-national activities such as study visits, international placements or cross-national research have been taking place during the past decades. This expansion has occurred on the assumption that such activities do broaden the mind, and that this is valuable for social work, its organization, management, practice, education or theory, skill and knowledge development. As we saw in Chapter 1, cross-national activities in their professions are one way in which people experience globalization. This chapter looks at some conditions for cross-national activities as a way of understanding the impact of globalization on social work practice and education.

Arntzen's (1998) Swedish study found that participants in development aid projects abroad felt that their home agencies did not value and make use of their international experiences. A literature study of international students' impact on domestic students and host institutions shows that although international students expected and wanted greater contact with domestic students, interaction was limited (Ward, 2001). Social work students in field placements in an exchange programme funded by European Union (EU) and the Canadian government had similar experiences; this project also involved practitioners and academics (Dominelli and Bernard, 2003). Ward suggests that the benefits for host educational institutions are often rhetorical rather than real and influence neither content, nor teaching methods. She argues that to promote intercultural interactions, situations must be structured. Dominelli and Bernard found that the home educational institutions did not recognize the knowledge, values and skills the students acquired in their placement. Nevertheless, the students claimed to have grown personally and professionally, by learning to think differently about themselves and their own culture. Dominelli and Bernard concluded that among issues that need particular attention in international exchanges are: agreed procedures, collaboration on a mutually beneficial basis, engaging the whole team of practitioners, academics, students and administrators and structures for the collaboration.

In a study Shardlow and Cooper (2000) found 76 publications in English about comparative social work in Europe published between 1980 and 2000. Of these, Shardlow and Walliss (2003) drew out 14 qualitative and quantitative empirical studies and found that the majority was about social welfare providers. Most of the researchers had a reflexive attitude towards their research methods. However, only 'around a quarter of the studies demonstrated even the smallest awareness or sensitivity towards cross-cultural issues' (p. 935). English authors predominated, and over half of the studies did not have a native author from the country in focus. This issue was rarely discussed in the studies. Postmodernists would question outsiders' interpretations of material from another culture.

Such studies suggest that social work has not developed a clear-sighted assessment of the value of cross-national activities. We argue that success in cross-national activities requires a good understanding of the structure, organization, purposes and participants as an appropriate basis for this work. This chapter aims to create a model where these needs are meet.

Cross-national activities, as we refer to them in this chapter, are part of international social work. As we saw in Chapter 1, there are a range of views about what international social work is. Educational institutions undertake or promote much of this activity, as part of teaching, learning and research. Therefore, we focus here on policies and structures in social work education. However increasing numbers of service users and practitioners move between countries to live and work. As a consequence, more services are being set up to meet welfare needs that arise from migration, asylum seeking, movements of refugees and social problems of families who have members in different countries, with different legal and cultural expectations. Therefore, increasing cross-national activity in education has an impact on practice because it adds to the proportion of people working in social work with international experiences and contributes to their understanding.

Some Experiences

Considering the outcomes of cross-national activity we must decide what aims and achievements we most value. Clear evidence about the effects of cross-national activities and their consequences is rarely available, so we often fail to assess rigorously the gains against the resources, in money, time and competence. Frequently, getting involved in cross-national work is a matter of personal preference or accident.

We start to explore some of these matters by using our experiences to raise some of the issues we intend to address.

Experience 1: Participants

Gurid co-headed a project with Chinese and Norwegian partners in developing an educational programme in China including social work and nursing. Chinese partners were invited to visit Norway. The Norwegian partners suggested a visit by the staff that was going to run and teach on the programme. However, the Chinese partners indicated that senior staff in the university and senior officials representing the agencies involved in the project would need to come on the first visit.

Exploring this difference, it seems that the Norwegian participants gave priority to fulfilling the educational objectives of the project, where senior administrative and political representatives could make less of a contribution. Norwegian participants wondered if the Chinese preference came from a cultural assumption that prestigious projects were enhanced by participation of senior people, and had a cultural preference themselves for including lower-status staff to benefit the experience and learning of those who were going to be directly involved in the education. Chinese participants focused on the need to ensure careful nurturing and recognition of organizational and political support for the programme, which Norwegian participants took for granted as the project had already been contracted. On further consideration, they could understand this way of thinking. We argue that the difference was initially seen as a cultural phenomenon rather than a more reasoned disagreement about strategy. This leads us to focus, below, on the importance of the difference between stakeholders, like the teaching staff, who are participating in a project and ringmasters, such as senior Chinese officials, who provide resources that may condition the success or failure of the activity.

Experience 2: Objectives

Two senior academics from different countries planned a joint research project and applied through Malcolm to various funders for grants to pursue it. This was unsuccessful, so they organized the first phase of the project on a cheaper basis, funding it from available resources. The project took a long time to complete and was not as comprehensive as they had hoped. Some publications emerged but these were delayed and did not contribute to the research assessment exercise, an important external assessment of the work of Malcolm's department.

This experience illustrates how a project might achieve some of its objectives, which may not be enough for all the participants. We emphasize later, in our analysis of the roles of stakeholders and ringmasters, that conflicting and uncertain objectives are sometimes incorporated into cross-national activities to their detriment. These academics compromised their original aims, so limiting their achievements. However, we might argue that Malcolm's requirements for achievement were unrealistic in the first place. Full grant aids, and publications to a timescale when something is not fully funded, were perhaps unrealistic.

Experience 3: Planning and Organization

In an African country, Gurid's teaching session was set for 10.00 am. Hearing about possible hold-ups, she asked an African colleague, who then informed her that the start would be delayed until midday, to enable people from the field to arrive. It had not occurred to him to tell her in advance. Some students appeared on time, but uncomplainingly went off to other activities, and came back to check from time to time. At 5.00 pm the practitioners arrived and the session eventually went ahead.

Gurid and Malcolm attended a conference in southern Europe where start times were delayed throughout and arrangements constantly changed. Northern European attenders complained about inefficiency, while the organizers said that, as visitors, the northerners should adjust to the modes of organization in the host country.

At the time, we interpreted these differences in approach as both cultural, and in the African example, also as reflecting poor transport infrastructure. We saw the difference as about efficiency and inconvenience and a different view of planning and organization from expectations in our home countries. However, all the activities actually occurred. With hindsight, we acknowledge that Western and Northern European countries often have to overcome infrastructure difficulties as well. Our initial response was to make a value judgement that these differences reflect cultural difference. However, our Western/Northern assumption that advanced planning is more effective than flexible accommodation to events was not borne out by the outcomes, which were successful.

Cross-national Work: Experiences of Difference

Our position, deriving from such experiences, is to be cautious about how we interpret apparent differences in cross-national work, and yet exploring difference is at the heart of it. Perhaps the fact that we set off to find difference causes us to find it where it does not exist. Visitors to the South assuming that these countries may have poor infrastructure or exaggerated deference to senior officials may need to question their assumptions about their own countries. Visitors to the North may need to question their assumption that resources will be more easily available in Western countries. Greater demands for planning and control of resources may reduce flexibility, rather than increase the availability of resources.

However, many people assume that the main purpose of cross-national activities is to experience and understand difference, which would be useful in a globalized postmodern era. The 'broadening the mind' purpose assumes that we will gain intellectually and practically by experiencing social work in different countries. The argument seems to be:

- Social work, social services and social policy within any one country are fairly homogeneous.
- Ideas and ways of working are directly transferable between countries.
- Experiencing different practices will illuminate understanding of our own practices.
- Therefore, cross-national work enables alternative practices to have an impact.

All of these points reveal modernist and universalizing assumptions that may not be true. We should therefore be cautious in assuming that all cross-national work is worthwhile. At least, it will need careful planning to make the experience more effective in its impact on our work.

Merely experiencing difference may not be enough to achieve learning that goes as far as valid knowledge for practice, which we discuss in Chapter 5. What is required is to develop ways of learning from difference, to which we have a critically reflective approach, as we elaborate on in Chapter 3. For effective learning to take place and for it to be used, three issues might be considered, covering the structure, content and process of learning.

- Structuring cross-national experiences by focusing on objectives, participants and organization.
- Identifying and building on difference to strengthen knowledge, skills and attitudes.

- Identifying and developing learning techniques that can make use of international experiences of difference.

Here, we will particularly concentrate on the structure. To develop ways of learning from cross-national work requires an understanding of the opportunities it offers, and we look at this in the next section.

Participants in and Types of Cross-national Work

Cross-national work in social work education, research and practice may involve a variety of participants and activities. In order to structure the activities so that they contribute to the participants' objectives more effectively, we must understand this variety of involvements.

We can distinguish different participants and different types of work. Figure 8.1 identifies six different groups that might participate in cross-national work. All these groups might potentially take part in activities shown in the box on the right. Particular groups may be more likely to take part in the activities in the smaller

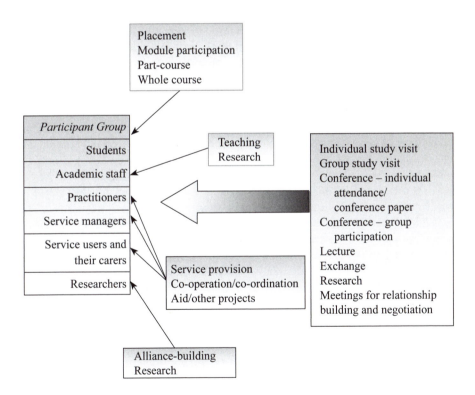

Figure 8.1   Participants in and types of cross-national work

Source: Askeland and Payne, 2001

boxes, the particular connections being shown by the smaller arrows. Although these likely connections are displayed, they are not exclusive. For example, academics and students may provide some elements of services when undertaking cross-national work, and practitioners and managers may well undertake research or teaching. Also, cross-national work might involve only one or several of these activities.

Academic and student activities are an important aspect of cross-national activity. Exchange or one-way educational visits and participation in courses or placements abroad and the staff activity which surrounds this has been an important aspect of the development of international social work. Many educational institutions, particularly in the North, support student exchanges.

There are more exchanges in education than in social work practice. Nevertheless, they do exist even if there is not a lot published about them. The American National Association of Social Work (NASW) has its Eileen Kelly exchange program for social workers. CIP (2007) has for 50 years run its exchange programme for social workers. Originating in the USA, it has spread throughout the world. Some exchanges in practice combine solidarity and mutual professional development. For example, the branches of the three northern counties of The Norwegian Union of Social Workers and Social Educators have an exchange programme to assist Russian colleagues to build their professional union combined with mutual exchanges for professional development. Another county branch has had long-term cooperation with Palestinian social workers in Bethlehem to strengthen their union, support them financially to become members of IFSW, as well as exchanges for mutual professional development and support a child culture centre (Ingdal and Kamal, 2005). A third county branch has supported financially locally organized social work with children with learning disabilities in Tanzania as well as an organization where women sell their own products.

Related to exchange programmes, particularly in academia, has been a tide of cross-national research, mainly done by academics and more often focusing on welfare than on social work (e.g. Palier, 1995; Lødemel and Trickey, 2001). However, while this has led to better understanding and exploration of social service systems, it is less clear that it has led to similar development in social work practice, which is still largely bounded by national legal, policy and administrative systems.

Another distinction is between different kinds of countries: whether the countries are fairly similar or different in locality, character or development. Countries in the same region, for example Europe or Latin America, would be closer together culturally than countries in different regions and continents. The more different the countries are the greater are the demands for reflection about the structure of the cross-national work if it is to secure a satisfactory outcome. In a cooperation project to develop contextual social work in Ghana, also mentioned in Chapter 3, between a 'Queen Mother', who is the biological mother or close relative and adviser to the chief, and local social workers, the 'Queen Mother' suggested that instead of going to Western countries, social workers should make exchanges with other West African countries. Then they could learn about social work from an African point of view, which could make their work easier (Kretzer, 2005).

Cross-national work raises ethical and policy issues, which need to be taken into account. Scholarships in Africa, for example, are fewer than in the North (Oduaran,

2006). Where exchanges are between North and South, Northern participants may take up a higher proportion of resources in the South. On the other hand, the partner in the North may contribute more financially. The participants in the South may experience the relationship as exploitative or may experience being dominated or patronized in a financially unbalanced relationship. How each looks upon the connection will also depend on whether the aim is a one-way or mutual benefit.

The Construction of Cross-national Work

The particular model of cross-national activity established by participants creates constraints and requirements that construct the form of cross-national work that they undertake. In this section, we explore factors that construct arrangements for cross-national work.

To do cross-national work implies certain social constructions. It implies the existence of social, and probably organizational, structures in each nation involved. The emphasis on 'national' implies assumptions that national differences in these structures have an impact on social work and its organizational and policy context. Such assumptions embody or imply social understandings of the nature of social work, the identity of the nations and of what it means to act cross-nationally. Supra-national social and organizational structures may exist, such as the European Union, the Fulbright Awards or the international social workers' (IFSW) and social work schools' (IASSW) associations. These represent a further range of social understandings. Finally, the different kinds of cross-national work are again understood differently in the various countries and supra-nationally. For example, a project perceived by Western participants to assist the development of social work in an Eastern European country may be seen as patronizing imposition of a Western model by Eastern European participants. The different social understandings may have implications for the cross-national activities and how they are carried out. What happens in cross-national activities will have dissimilar implications for the social and organizational constructions and for social understandings about social work.

We have organized this analysis of cross-national work by first looking at participants, whom we describe as 'stakeholders', that is, we are concerned with groups, individuals and organizations who have or need some involvement in the process of cross-national work. Second, we explore different purposes for taking a stake in cross-national activities.

Stakeholders in Cross-national Work

We propose that there is a continuum of interaction between individuals and their participation in cross-national work and the institutions from which the individuals' participation springs.

Cross-national work in the social work field involves a variety of people, who may be considered stakeholders. In Table 8.1, we divide stakeholders into four categories and give examples of individuals and organizations that fall into each category. First, we make a distinction between organizations and individuals and, second, between

Table 8.1 Stakeholders in cross-national work: Education and developmental aid and relief work

Examples of :	Ringmasters		Stakeholders	
	Education	Developmental aid and relief	Education	Developmental aid and relief
Organizations	Employer organization EU University Research funder	UN organizations National political org. and governmental ministries International and national humanitarian and religious organizations	Professional organization Service user organization Social agency University department/school Research funder	UN organizations e.g. UNICEF, humanitarian organizations e.g. Save the Children, political organizations e.g. ILO, religious organizations e.g. Caritas, professional associations e.g. IFSW, grassroots' organization e.g. Attac, interest groups e.g. Disability Alliance
Individuals	Manager Political leader	Manager Political leaders Board members and directors of national international humanitarian and religious organizations	Academic Researcher Professional practitioner Service user Student	International social workers, Representatives for different professions in various organizations and institutions, members of interest groups and grassroots movements

Source: Askeland & Payne (2001), Askeland & Døhlie (2006).

two types of stakeholder, described as 'stakeholders' and 'ringmasters'. Ringmasters 'hold the ring', that is they define the context, in which the other stakeholders operate, but the ringmaster's stake is in the context rather than in the cross-national activity itself.

We have divided the columns of stakeholders and ringmasters into education and development aid relief work to exemplify who might be involved in two different kinds of cross-national exchange work.

Organizations and Individuals as Stakeholders

This section examines relationships between organizations and individuals involved in cross-national work. Organizations contain individuals whose stakes may be different and perhaps at odds. Both organizations and individuals may be stakeholders and ringmasters. Individuals may pursue cross-national work alone or as part of an organization's programme.

Different ends of the cross-national arrangement might perceive it differently. To give a commonplace example, Malcolm was appointed to a regular visiting role by a foreign university as part of their institutional international programme. However, the home institution regarded the arrangement as personal, since it was not part of their international programmes. At the time, he was visiting several other institutions as part of a series of staff and student exchanges, where there were written agreement between the partner institutions, which seemed to perceive the programme in the same way. However, more complexities emerge if the situation is examined closely. For example, one of the partner institutions has similar links through agreements with three institutions in the academic's country, but the academic's institution has only this one link. Therefore, the 'stake' in the link is likely to be different. Also, in the same network, with some links only staff is exchanged, whereas with others, students also exchange. In other links, institutions participate in conferences but not in the exchange. The extent and nature of the stakes therefore vary at each end.

Institutions' and constituent individuals' cross-national work may be closely or quite distantly linked. Moreover, the link may be single-ended or double-ended and the strength of the stake in the link may also vary at each end. There will always be a personal aspect to the strength of the stake, as cross-national activity demands investment from the individual and often their family whether or not the organization is involved.

There might be ringmasters only at one end. Organizations are neither equal in material and personal resources, nor in power, status or the strength of their interests. A ringmaster might impose an activity on another, and in particular might exert power or status to impose activity on subordinates or client organizations. There might be ringmasters from different areas at different ends. In student field placements, one ringmaster will be an academic and one from the social agency. Finally, the nature of the link, for example the activities undertaken or the personnel involved, may vary.

Stakeholders and Ringmasters

In the previous section, we saw that individuals and organizations involved in cross-national work may have a variety of relationships with a range of factors affecting how their relationship develops. Table 8.1 also distinguishes between two types of stakeholder relationship that individuals and organizations may have with each other. Ringmasters have an important impact on how individual and organizational relationships develop, since the ringmaster sets and controls the context in which relationships develop. A ringmaster may be an individual, such as the manager of a person involved in cross-national activity. Alternatively, ringmasters are often organizations that provide funding or systems for relationships.

Even if there are ringmasters in both countries, their power may vary. Ringmasters in the North or with good resources will have more power to influence and decide, than ringmasters in the South or where they have limited financial resources. Relevant resources may not only be financial. For example, an organization whose government strongly supports an initiative will have more influence than one whose policy is less concerned with international exchange.

The ringmaster's objectives may differ from those of the stakeholder. For example, EU authorities finance activities primarily to increase cross-national understanding and promote greater unity and understanding among populations in different parts of the EU. An academic might accept the finance in order to pursue a research interest, with the aim in the longer term of enhancing the academic career. A student might accept the finance to gain an interesting experience, which might enhance a later career, or help provide a comparative element in academic assignments. The EU is probably uninterested in the development of social work at all, since the subsidiarity principle that the lowest possible tier of government should bear responsibility for policy and actions excludes social work from much of its role, which is focused on the economy. The academic or student may be largely uninterested in the future solidarity of the EU. Nevertheless, the EU context affects the nature of the social work cross-national activity.

Individual ringmasters and their support may also be relevant to the nature and success of particular programmes, as in the Chinese example, outlined above. A particular manager or politician may give priority to a cross-national approach to their objectives. However, a characteristic of ringmasters is that their contextual role influences how cross-national work affects the construction of social work, but they do not necessarily have a concern for the nature and practice of social work within either a national context or internationally. An agency training officer, for instance, refused to offer fieldwork practice placements to a university, complaining that this university gives priority to international work for their academics in pursuit of international standing and research opportunities. This was irrelevant to what the training officer conceptualized as the main concerns for social work education. Here, ringmasters setting priorities for universities focus on matters that appear of low concern to an agency, whose priorities are set by different ringmasters. Yet both are ringmasters with influence on the context of the university, since it requires both international links and fieldwork practice placements. These conflicts impinge directly on people trying to build relationships, but are rarely dealt with by exploring how priorities might be aligned. For example, agencies might come to accept the long-term advantages to the profession of wider international understanding, while universities might balance their international and local priorities better.

Again we propose that there is a continuum of consistency between the interests and stakes held by ringmasters and stakeholders. Their aims and activities may be more or less consistent with each other, and the aims and activities of individuals and organizations will also interact with more or less consistency. This is true at each end of the cross-national relationship, so that the interaction of ringmasters and stakeholders may be extremely complex, and require careful analysis and clarification. In our experience, people involved in cross-national activities are often unclear about such issues, and therefore are not able to be proactive in reducing tensions and difficulties.

Objectives in Cross-national Work: The Five 'i's

Clearly, stakeholders might have varying interests in pursuing cross-national work either at all or in particular activities. Also, as we noted in the introduction, resources are required to play a part in cross-national activity. These might include finance for research grants, for travelling, including exchange programmes, for lecturing or for conferences, for administrative links to meet practice and clients needs and for aid and relief work. However, we should not limit the consideration of resources to financial or organizational aspects. Personal interest, motivation, available time and commitment may be important resources both within organizations and for individuals, and are always factors in how cross-national work is pursued. Stated objectives may be belied by complexes of additional, covert or understood objectives. By examining some examples of activities, we have constructed a model of objectives that we call 'the five i's', set out in Table 8.2.

The 'five 'i's' model suggests several progressions from the earlier to the later objectives:

- *In time* – Generally, later objectives require greater periods of time for achieving them successfully.
- *In commitment* – Generally, later objectives require greater personal and organizational commitment of both stakeholders and ringmasters and greater commitment of resources.
- *In mutuality* – Generally, later objectives require more mutual commitment of the participants; earlier objectives may be pursued more individualistically. Moreover, the earlier objectives are more capable of being imposed on recipients of visits or of services, while later objectives require a greater degree of mutual consent
- *In complexity* – Generally, later objectives are more complex in the demands that they make on the participants and on the organization of the cross-national activity.
- *In equality* – Generally, the later objectives require greater equality of power between the parties.

Table 8.2   The 5 'i's: Objectives in cross-national work

Objective	Definition	Examples	Typical participants
Interest	Providing a well-rounded understanding – cross-national work as hobby or human and professional development	Study visits; exchanges; visits to agencies; student or staff placements; conferences	Students; people's early participation
Information	Gaining information that may be used to pursue our own objectives – cross-national work as a support to our own work	Study visits; exchanges; visits to agencies; student or staff placements; conferences	Researchers, managers, academics, students, service users
Instruction	Providing information that helps the other – cross-national work as education or development of the other	Teaching; aid work; practice relationships	Students, social workers, aid workers, long-term academics
Interaction	Providing an opportunity for human relationships – cross-national work as personal, intellectual or social development	Exchanges; joint work; joint research, development or teaching	Long-term academic, research, training or research, practice partnerships
Integration	Achieving joint development, research or education enabling progress for both or all parties	Jointly developed and funded practice, research, learning partnerships	Long-term academic, research, training or research, practice partnerships

An international exchange programme for students might be time limited, stimulate low commitment and mutuality, be simple and lack equality. Accordingly, its objectives might only progress as far as interest and information.

To give an example of a more complex situation, Malcolm became a visiting lecturer with a university in a foreign country. An instruction objective was satisfactory to them, but his home institution hoped for the development of wider links, including research. Because the visiting lecturer programme did not offer these opportunities, his home university, his ringmasters, began to resist the arrangement, and pushed him towards an agreement with another university that offered broader objectives. Here, there was a conflict between objectives of the stakeholders and ringmasters. The ringmaster on one side and the stakeholders on both sides are satisfied with the objective of instruction while the ringmaster on the other side would like to see interaction and integration as an objective and accomplishment.

The example suggests, first, that if cross-national work is to be sustained, it will generally need to progress towards more complex, mutually satisfying links of longer duration. Cross-national work that does not progress in this way is more likely to be lost over time. For example, both Gurid and Malcolm have experienced exchange projects in which some participants from both countries were consistent over several years, while others were only involved on particular occasions or for a shorter time. Because occasional or new participants wanted to renegotiate objectives each time and had to be briefed and re-engaged whenever they appeared, the longer-term participants became frustrated by the time taken from pursuing agreed objectives in these repetitive interactions. In such situations, consistent participants may withdraw because they feel they are not making progress, or occasional participants may feel excluded by the 'permanent' group. Where fleeting participation is inherent in a programme, whether staff or students, to be replaced by different participants next year, organizational structures will have to be well-established in order to maintain commitment to the long-term objectives.

Second, objectives may not be achieved. Cross-national activity may set out to be, say, integrative but only interest or information may be achieved. For example, one of Malcolm's links involved contributions to developing social science programmes with an institution in the South (instruction objectives), with the secondary aim of building research relationships. However, these did not develop, and the institution providing the aid felt that in some ways they had given up teaching resources for the benefit of the partner institution, without receiving the research and integration benefits they desired. The gap between aims and achievements, while commonplace in development activities, may be another important factor for long-term maintenance of cross-national work. We saw this in the unfunded research example outlined above as experience 2. It may be particularly important for the ringmasters whose interests may not lie directly in the development of social work. Ringmasters may seek objectives broader than the interests of the actors in cross-national work or may even be in conflict with those interests. Therefore, they may be particularly liable to disillusionment as a result of failure to achieve objectives, even though stakeholders might be satisfied with their benefit.

Third, long-term objectives, such as better relations between countries or the development of professional understanding through comparative work, may clash with short-term objectives, such as raising the specific skills of social work students on practice placements. A balance between the long- and short-term may need to be specifically negotiated, or at least understood by the participants.

Social exchange theory (Loxley, 1997) would suggest that cooperative relationships work best where there is reciprocation that is acceptable to all parties in meeting their objectives. Reciprocation may not develop because of differences in power, resources, culture and language. There may be different timescales for reciprocation. For example, ringmasters with higher-level objectives, such as EU funders of research collaborations, may be willing to wait longer to achieve their outcomes than dissatisfied participants in a student exchange. However, where complex arrangements between numbers of parties exist, differing levels of acceptance of objectives and achievements may be hidden from many participants. They might carry on in links for some time before becoming aware that their interests are not being met.

Five 'i's in Developmental Aid and Relief Work

Developmental aid and relief work are kinds of exchange work in which social workers are often engaged. Our 'five 'i's model has been developed further by Askeland and Døhlie (2006) in Table 8.3 to show progress towards sustainability. It gives an example of who needs to be involved to obtain objectives in different stages.

Four African social work master students had all worked for international NGOs. Gurid challenged them about what an international social worker should know when coming to their country, and they shared their experiences from being involved in projects. Firstly, although a baseline is demanded for assessing the needs and plan a project, no resources are available for research. Secondly, the period between the design of the project and the available grant might take several years. The situation may then have changed, but the original plan has to be followed and relevant adjustments are usually not accepted. Thirdly, short-term projects may make local communities more dependent than empowered and do not promote sustainability. Fourthly, projects are often initiated to meet transitional problems like drought and hunger, and not aimed at sustainability by alleviating chronic problems like, drought, poverty and HIV/AIDS.

What is exemplified here is a lack of reciprocation between the local and international ringmasters and stakeholders, and the power to make decisions is unequally distributed. The objectives clash as the international organizations do not commit themselves to go any further than instruction, while the local ringmasters and stakeholders want sustainability.

Different Time Systems

In our 'five 'i's' model, time is one of the criteria for fulfilment of the objective. As an example of the complexity we would like to draw attention to how differently time can be perceived and how it effects how people and situations are treated. It may cause clashes and misunderstandings in exchanges as well as in practice when social workers, clients, students and educators belong to different time systems. To function effectively in another culture it is just as necessary to learn the time language as the spoken language (Hall, 1989: 3).

Table 8.3   The 5 'i's: Progression in developmental aid and relief work

Objective	Definition	Examples	Typical participants
Interest	Contact and exploring mutual interests	Assess needs and possible partnerships	Policy makers and non-committed performers
Information	Purposeful information collection to explore tentative relations for cooperation	Discussing tentative contract, including target groups, work forms, financing	Policy makers, leaders, consultants, researchers, performers
Instruction	Premises set by donors	Organizing and implementing ventures by donors	Implementing institutions, organizations and people
Interaction	Premises set in mutuality between receivers and donors	Organizing and implementing ventures jointly by receivers and donors	Implementing institutions, organizations and people
Integration	Premises set by the receivers for sustainable development	Organizing and implementing ventures with local anchoring and responsibility	Implementing institutions, organizations and people

Source: Askeland and Døhlie, 2006.

Time reveals how people experience the world. It is a core system of cultural, social and personal life. Some run their life by light and season. The pace might be set by nature, weather or infrastructure. The clock, in addition to other technical development and equipment such as electric light, created a whole new way of organizing people's lives. Western people go by the clock, and externalize and treat time as a continuum, from past, present to future. Thus, people manage, control, spend, save, waste and run out of time. That is why people can be late or early, feel the 'time squeeze' and have 'quality time'. Western people go by urban time, which is an external time and might not be synchronized with the biological internal clock, which explains jet lag. Westerners are uncomfortable with silences and seem to think that because nothing overt is happening, nothing is going on (Hall, 1989).

In new public management (NPM), that we discuss in Chapter 6, time is used to measure competence, effort and achievement. In some countries in the South, the

Table 8.4   Different time systems

Polychronic time	Monochronic time
Involvement in many people and issues at the same time	Follow a schedule
Appointments not taken seriously, commitments are: 'see you before an hour'. 'see you after two days'	Appointments on time
People seen or cases are handled in no recognized order	People line up and are dealt with accordingly
Many things/many relationships going on at the same time (business and private)	One thing at the time Distinction between work and private life
Context and relationships, involvement with/engagement in people are core Important to have the right contacts Take their clients with them to their new jobs	Context-free, rule-oriented, not influenced by personal relations, strict division between work and private life
Management exercise strict control over the individual employees and their time Hierarchical, centralized	Decentralized, responsible for their own activity
People-oriented	Task, schedule and procedure oriented

Source: Hall, 1989.

bureaucracies are influenced by former colonial countries' systems, while the people the social workers are dealing with go by their own cultural time. This has its parallel to when refugees' and immigrants' relation to time clashes with that of the Western social workers.

Once teaching in Ethiopia, Gurid presented the schedule to the students when they asked whether it was set up by Ethiopian or Western time. Gurid became confused until the students explained that the Ethiopian clock is divided into twelve hours, not twenty-four, and it is 01.00 Ethiopian time when it is 05.00 Western time. Each month has 30 days and a year has 360 days.

Hall, an anthropologist (1989, see also Mattock, 2003) has compared French with German people and matched them with North-Europeans and Arabs and Turks. On this background he has developed a model that he calls polychronic and monochronic time. The former implies relating to one thing, while the latter to many things at the same time. Both have strengths and weaknesses, but are difficult to combine as the two systems are logically and empirically quite distinct. These are not strict categories, but tendencies that can be recognized in various cultures and organizational systems and may influence the outcome of the exchanges.

Conclusion

In this analysis of the construction of cross-national work, we have argued that a variety of stakeholders exists in complex relationships in cross-national activities. To some extent, these are consciously constructed. However, the different roles of ringmasters and stakeholders, and the range of potential objectives that we have identified suggest the possibility of hidden, uncertain partially understood stakeholders and objectives. The complex factors involved may lead to the interests of some participants and the pressure of some objectives being in conflict with and imposed upon others. Understanding and analysis of potential or actual conflicts may help us to plan or to deal with obstructions and opportunities in the structure of relationships that develops. We suggest that clear understanding of objectives, their distinction from achievements and whether they are single- or double-ended and short- or long-term is essential in negotiating and clarifying cross-national activities.

To use cross-national work to develop social work practice and thinking, 'broadening the mind' through travel is not enough. Maintaining and developing activities through progression to more complex and mutual objectives is likely to be required to strengthen innovations sufficiently for them to take hold and affect practice and education more widely in a new setting. In addition to focus on the structure, we also have to pay more attention to the content and the process of learning from the experiences, which has not been the focus of this chapter.

We have argued that 'travel broadens the mind' cannot be a complete justification for cross-national work. If globalization leads to increasing cross-national activity, resources may be wasted and postcolonialism may occur unless we jointly clarify our aims and what arrangements will best facilitate them. We suggested that more careful understanding and analysis of cross-national activity would help us to achieve more valid outcomes, without imposing one participant's priorities upon others.

Our first main point argued that much cross-national work focuses on exploring difference. However, we have argued for caution in analysing difference as coming from cultural or national differences. Critical reflection on sameness and difference may be required. Second, we proposed that the construction of cross-national work has important consequences for the outcomes of activities. Analysis of potential stakeholders, ringmasters and objectives suggests that conflicting factors and power relations may render cross-national activity uncertain, ineffective and postcolonial. Eventually, this must have consequences for the continuing support of cross-national work by stakeholders involved. Therefore, sustainable cross-national work will generally need to progress towards more long-term, complex and mutually satisfying links.

We believe that lack of clarity means that values and objectives of some participants, such as we have discussed here, are imposed on others. This is just as important for practice agencies, international aid organizations as for educational institutions with student and staff exchanges and research. As we have seen in previous chapters, it is easy for Western universities and agencies with their priorities, and assumptions to dominate. Better resources, a more established profession, more systematic government, better infrastructure all seem overpowering in any cross-national relationship.

The best way of dealing with this is to progress to more mutual, equal and committed objectives in cross-national work, building on initial phases where objectives are more single-ended and short-term. For cross-national work to survive in an appropriately ethical form, we need to bear in mind long-term mutual aims rather than short-term exploitative objectives. To do this, we need to reflect critically on our cross-national work and set aims pursuing equality in understanding and mutual benefit rather than simply exchange of information, instruction, data collection for research and offering short-term assistance on own premises.

Chapter 9

Technology-based Social Work Education and Practice

Introduction

'Nearly everything a social worker does face-to-face could be done online', McCarty and Clancy (2002: 153) claim. Although technology has changed the society and invaded social work practice as well as education, we would question this statement, particularly in an international arena. According to Maidment (2005), cultural implications of online teaching and learning in education generally has only received limited attention, and it has not been an issue in social work education. This Chapter starts from considering social work education, but also includes consideration of online social work.

Thinking about technology and how we use it is important to understanding the impact of globalization, postcolonialism and postmodernism in social work practice and education because technology is an important driver of the current round of globalization. Through computer, television and mobile (cell) telephone technology, international communication has become quicker and widely available. This form of communication increases the globalizing effect of rapid travel, which promotes quicker, cheaper and more extensive movements around the globe; see Chapter 8 on increasing cross-national activities.

As this technology develops, it becomes more flexible, allows more interaction and will become more appropriate for interpersonal practices such as social work and its education. An important issue to address is how increasing use of information communication technology (ICT) discriminates between rich and poor countries, rich and poor people and rich and poor social agencies and educational institutions. Generally, the poorer, the less accessible technological resources will be. The quality, flexibility and usability of the technology available is poorer, and poorer countries or local areas are less likely to have the infrastructure to provide good technology, so fewer benefits are gained from technological advance.

ICT can also be used for social control. In the workplace, it can be used to monitor clients, social workers, educators and students. The possibilities are legion; registering and checking information, how people spend time, where and how they are using the Internet and who they are communicating with. Some monitoring is for security reasons, but mainly it is for management.

Technological development leads to increases in surveillance in society as a whole. This may be seen both as beneficial, to protect people against crime and terror, but also as a threat to people's privacy. Child pornography is a serious abuse requiring child protection action. Prosecutions for downloading child pornography from the Internet have relied on the electronic records of Internet service providers. Extensive closed circuit television (CCTV) surveillance of public areas means that people's behaviour can be supervised. While these developments are matters of wide social change and controversy, which are beyond the scope of this chapter, they are of concern to social work. CCTV surveillance may benefit poor people, the users of social work services and social workers, because they improve public safety in poor, high-risk areas. However, it also mean that their privacy is more compromised than richer people, who have private cars, live in less observed areas and do not move around in highly-supervised locations.

Another example is the way that some countries, for example, China, control public access to the Internet, in cooperation with big companies like Google, to avoid people using information contrary to the interests of the ruling party. In emergencies, it has also been possible to prevent access to mobile phone networks to avoid communicating between protesters. This happened in Ethiopia in the summer of 2005 during student riots against how the government interpreted the result of the parliamentary election. At the time of the bombings in London in July 2005, priority was given to emergency services in using mobile phones. Others could not use their phones for private communication. While this might be seen as a social benefit, these examples illustrate the capacity of the authorities to manage technologies in ways that support their objectives and limit social freedoms.

The Internet may play an important role in spreading information about social injustice and political situations that otherwise would not become known to the world. Support can be organized in worldwide activist or interest groups. For example, Roxana Setayesh, an Iranian poet, was in 2007 using a weblog http://www.ipetitions. com/petition/CEDAW/signatures-16.html to collect signatures to influence a change of laws so that women should be treated equal to men in Iran.

There is, of course, always a danger that such opportunities could be abused. 'The flexibility of the new electronic media is being exploited skilfully by many groups that can rally support or protest quickly and across country boundaries to become powerful political groupings' (Lorenz, 2005: 6).

What this Chapter is About

In this chapter we make three main points about how consequences of globalization that promote technological development might promote postcolonialism and counteract local contextual social work education and practice. First, in a commercialized education environment, a large audience is needed to gain the economic advantages of distance education technologies and practice programmes. This means that distance education often has to be offered internationally, competing for the best students (Punie and Cabrera, 2006). Second, the majority, so far, are national developments of distance education in social work and social work practice, which are on a small scale, and which therefore meet the particular needs of the local context of practice. Third, however, since the commercialization of education and practice leads to attempts to achieve a more global reach, in the future, achievements in social work distance education and practice may be pressed to develop internationally, putting at risk their success in meeting local and national cultural and professional needs.

In Chapters 4, 5 and 8 we address the risk that in the future increasing globalization of social work education and practice might impose a Western linguistic and cultural hegemony on other countries. In this chapter we argue both that this risk exists for all technologies in itself, and also that using the Internet to distribute distance social work learning and practice exacerbates the problems. Moreover, we argue that while the problems are raised by the way in which distance learning technologies affect the learning process for both students and clients, these factors are likely to affect the particular content that is typical of social work. Therefore, it is important for social work education and practice to consider strategies to respond to the issues raised.

As distance education in social work is more widely dispersed than computer-based programmes in social work practice, in this chapter we focus primarily on distance education. However, many of the issues we raise are also relevant for practice.

Distance Education Technologies

Distance education, where students and their teachers are separated in space and time, is a well-established concept. Learning materials are provided by an education organization, which offers students support-services via individual or group-communication by using various technical media. Use of distance education has been promoted within social work for more than twenty years. For example, a comprehensive study of the possibilities was produced by the British social work education council in 1985 (Osborne, 1985). Since then, new modes of flexible distance learning have developed through several stages that are increasingly technology-based and automated. This development will also influence the distance education in social work, and we seek to examine the consequences of this expansion.

Distance learning technologies offer an important contribution to social work education (Siegel et al, 1998). In some countries and where audiences for education are widely dispersed, for example by geography, such technologies may offer the only opportunity for higher education, in social work as in other subjects. Programs have been positively evaluated by students of social work courses (Ligon, et al, 1999; Petracchi, 2000) and studies that have compared student outcomes from similar traditional and technology-supported distance learning courses have revealed no differences (McFall and Freddolino, 2000; Petracchi and Patchner, 2001; Dalton, 2001; Kleinpeter and Potts, 2003; Faux and Black-Hughes, 2000).

As far as we are aware of nothing has been published about cross-national distance education in social work. We would claim that social work has special characteristics requiring linguistic and cultural diversity, and particular forms of skill development that are not provided for adequately in distance learning technologies. Care is therefore required in implementing distance learning in social work education and also in social work practice, particularly if it is intended for an international audience (Maidment, 2005).

The first point about these developments is that the focus on developing technology overlooks potential inequalities created by its use. Technological development has dominated distance education during the 1990s, because creating new technologies for delivery and support was the main focus of activity. New technology seems to promote equality. This is because it may reach some groups of students who might otherwise never have access to education, due to full-time or part-time jobs, family responsibilities, disability and immobility for various reasons or who cannot afford to move to a university town or foreign country. The problem is that for this to work, the infrastructure needs to be accessible, for example for students to be able to afford and operate the necessary electronic equipment, and know the language of the education course. Language can be a powerful means of oppression and ICT may reinforce this as English is by far the dominant Internet language; see Chapter 4. Jackson's (2003) analysis of the weaknesses of distance learning technology for Western post-experience students, alongside many strengths, included:

- lack of access to the technology and equipment needed
- the presumption of technical knowledge
- 'techno fear'
- impersonal communication
- disempowerment through dependence on technology
- lack of commitment by students to using the technology.

For many students in the North these weaknesses are almost overcome, since increasingly they are familiar with using advanced technology from an early age. However, such weaknesses may create or increase a knowledge gap between rich and poor people and North and South. Selectivity in favour of the use of technologies by already rich people and countries is likely to be the outcome, rather than greater equality.

The second point is that the use of technology is constantly changing because new forms of technology will strengthen the commercial imperatives towards automation, which in turn may increasingly disadvantage poor people and countries in the South. Distance education has now reached its so-called fourth generation. Taylor (2001), a major figure in distance learning development, claims that the technology to achieve the fifth generation is imminent. The distance education generations have to be distinguished from the technological generations used in electronic colleges (Rekkedal and Møystad, 2002). The generations imply different models of distance education:

1. A *correspondence* model based on print. This has a long history in distance education.
2. A *multimedia* model, based on print, audio- and videotapes, interactive video and computer-based learning (disk and tape). An example is the well-established UK Open University courses.
3. A *tele-learning* model with opportunities for synchronous communication such as audio, tele- and video-conferencing, TV/radio broadcasting combined with teleconferencing and audiographic conferencing. These enhance contact with the producers of the original material from remote locations.
4. A *flexible learning* model, based on interactive multimedia online, Internet-based access to the worldwide web and computer-mediated synchronous and

asynchronous communication. This makes use of knowledge resources on the world-wide web and allows interaction with teachers from remote locations, as well as through intranets within universities.

5. An *intelligent flexible learning* model, based on automated cross-media courseware production from a single document, automated pedagogical response and advice systems and automated business systems (Taylor, 2001). This means that when a student uses a learning tool on the Internet, help and support will be generated automatically from the learning package. Consequently, costs will not increase when the number of students increases or the amount of help they need increases.

Taylor's (2001) crucial point about the fifth generation is that the economic gains are guaranteed by automated responses as part of the learning package; this has not been possible in previous generations. Technical development and equipment has made global expansion of distance education possible economically. The fifth generation strengthens the commercial argument still further. Thus, economic and commercial pressures for moving towards greater automation would become more powerful than with previous generations of distance learning development. We would suggest that the fourth generation, called flexible learning, is the model that will suit distance social work education best, and this applies similarly to social work practice.

Debate on Distance Education as an Entrepreneurial Market

The concern is not solely one of technologies, because technology-based distance education seeks to disseminate knowledge through a market, due to globalization, see Chapter 2. We suggested in Chapter 5 that acceptance both of universal knowledge, skills and values and also universal teaching and learning methodologies is a prerequisite for a global market in education and for distance education as part of it. Knowledge, sold through distance learning programmes, contributes to creating a knowledge market, which reproduces the economic market. Relationships between powerful countries and cultures in the North and less powerfull countries and cultures in the South create postcolonial relationships.

Education, including a growing market for foreign students and distance education, has become one of the biggest economy sectors of Western countries (Ljoså, 2001). In Australia, education is the third largest service export and the eighth largest export overall. Computer-based learning is considered a growing market and of great interest for professional investment (Ibin.). Distance education has become big business, where corporate money is involved, and the actors, including the universities, have become technological, industrial, rather than local and interpersonal concerns. To achieve economies of scale, distance education increasingly standardizes study materials, so that the student cohort grows larger and extends worldwide.

Distance education has come to be seen as a market (Lea and Nicoll, 2002), requiring an entrepreneurial approach to 'sell' acknowledged expertise, since forces leading towards automation are economically and not pedagogically founded. For example, Kreuger and Stretch (2000: 458) suggest that social work is currently often seen as a passive recipient of advances in technology, and changes in social work are determined by the technology, rather than application of technology being directed by the needs of social work and its education.

The market also presses education towards the industrialization of production processes for learning materials. The more the automation the larger are the student groups that can be served. Distance education holds out the promise of being cheaper than traditional education because production processes can be industrialized, even McDonaldized (Ritzer, 2000), for a wider market. If education is no longer seen as an interpersonal, interactive process as it is in the flexible model that we think social work education should hold on to, it may be divided into easily reproduced modules, to be delivered in separate packages. Such modules are the hamburgers of distance education. When education becomes an industry, universities are more like industrial production lines, courses are produced in standard forms and students become commodities competed for internationally.

A comparative study of 130 institutions in 26 countries worldwide offering web-based education showed that none of them made any substantial profit from student fees (Paulsen, 2000). Converting traditional to distance education is not a simple and cheap process, neither in general, nor in social work. ICT does not in itself make education more efficient, it requires changes and new pedagogical approaches (Lea and Nicoll, 2002). The development and renewal of programmes is an expensive, never-ending process. Small fields, such as social work education, and practice as well (Weiner and Petrella, 2007), are unlikely to attract the finance for developing and maintaining courses. Instead, standardized materials and learning processes are more likely to be used; by for example, using standard social science modules rather than creating modules directly relevant to social work practice. Cost pressures may also prevent the development of new teaching approaches taking advantage of technical possibilities and adapt them to needs of social work education.

Such developments deny the crucial importance of human interaction between a teacher and a learner in general but particularly in social work education. In subjects like social work, where students are learning interpersonal skills, substantial aspects of any course will require human judgement and interpersonal learning. Effective technology-based flexible learning resources may only offer the chance of enhancing expensive human resources, rather than substituting for them, reducing financial arguments and institutional support for it.

So, in addition to the costs of maintaining learning materials, the cost of the student support systems in distance education, increases with the number of students (Rekkedal, 2001). This will also be the case for social work practice programmes as more direct social worker involvement develops.

Technology developments in social work education are currently about facilitating admission for students without access to campus studies, or about strengthening courses in university or continuing education settings by increasing resources of information or staffing or making their use more flexible. However, as globalizing economic and market pressures on universities grow, social work education might be pushed in the direction of hamburger social work modules, made available for commercial reasons to a wider and potentially global constituency. An example of this process beginning is Kleinpeter and Oliver's (2003) argument that distance education in social work will help to achieve 'university goals'.

Almost all ICT programmes are commercial and expensive products; it is easy to be left behind. Globalization has increased the use of English. Often it is used as if it is neutral to the cultural context (Mayor and Swann, 2002). An overview of accessible 'net-learning programmes' in 1998 showed that they were almost without exception in English, were based on a very traditional understanding of teaching and learning and were static (Alexandersen, 2001). This implies an inflexible organization of and positivist approach to learning where next to nothing could be changed to take account of local conditions and culture. Technically based distance education programmes can only be made in such a commercial environment where promoters have the power to command resources. This primarily means in Western countries, and consequently they promote Western cultures, even though programmes are claimed to have universal relevance, and to be based on universal knowledge. What is considered relevant is so only from a Western perspective.

As education on the Internet is a growing market, there are many options to choose from and there are many poor quality or inappropriate courses. It is difficult to select a good quality programme (Ljoså, 2001), or to get advice on what would be best or be able to assess a program without paying. Once connected, Internet access is almost free. However, access to learning material such as journal articles has to be paid for and therefore excludes people who cannot afford payment. The price might thus be a decisive quality factor (Punie and Cabrera, 2006), which might mean that poorer students, as well as poorer clients served by social workers from poorer agencies, from poorer countries, will get lower quality. This means that access by poorer countries and minorities to the potential of distance education is disadvantaged (Rafferty et al., 2005). Elite universities, whose graduates might have the best access to future power, seek to charge premium prices (Ludvigsen and Lundby, 2002), which might exclude able students who cannot afford the fees and work in favour of rich people or those supported by employers. In summary, the globalized commercial market and industrialization of distance education treats students as a commodity (Lea and Nicoll, 2002), and raises many technical, practical, legal and ethical issues (Quinney, 2005; Weiner and Petrella, 2007).

Likewise, rich people might seek online treatment and social work programs from well-reputable institutions that poorer people cannot afford. Education and counselling should both promote emancipation and empowerment. With unequal opportunities it might instead contribute to exclusion and postcolonial oppression.

Communication as Crucial to Social Work Education

The market arguments for distance learning have implications particularly for the face-to-face element that is crucial to the success of distance education (Keegan, 1996), and especially social work education, which can never be totally technologically based. It will always have to be supplemented with flexible learning in which people interact with each other in person and face-to-face and within their social contexts (Huntington and Sudbery, 2005, Madoc-Jones and Parrot, 2005).

Non-verbal communication is perhaps the best example of why this is so necessary, and why social work education cannot be fully delivered through distance learning. In particular, it shows how cultural variation requires culturally appropriate education materials. Various parts of the body are used as channels for conveying a message in non-verbal communication. Non-verbal languages and channels have various meanings and significances in different cultures. Nuances are impossible to communicate in a written or graphical communication. Therefore, technological transmission will always be inadequate, and the more advanced equipment, the more expensive and therefore also exclusive. Pearson (1991) demonstrates in a study of groupwork in Hong Kong that Western people tend to feel uneasy about silence, and there is a tendency to fill the pauses quickly with talking. Since modesty and humility are very important for the Chinese, it is considered rude to be the first speaker. In Western culture, on the contrary, to talk first is a way of showing self-confidence, a highly valued virtue in these societies. Wong's (2004) study of Chinese learners in a social policy course using elements of a 'virtual classroom' emphasizes the cultural importance of teacher interaction to combat passivity in Chinese students' learning. Because dealing with silence and similar issues are important aspects of social work training in any culture, training for social workers operating in Western societies has to be different from those operating in some eastern cultures.

The issue for globalized distance education, therefore, is not only that ICT cannot convey many nuances, but also that different cultural requirements need to be addressed. If distance education or computer-based social work practice fails to address such differences, it is being culture-blind. In the same way that being 'colour-blind' to differences in skin-colour is regarded as racist, being culture-blind is also racist. In discussing Western or Eastern cultures, we disguise variations within these cultures. The more similar they seem to be or the more different from our own cultures, the more difficult it is to distinguish the nuances that might have great impact on our teaching and learning and social work practice. In Chapter 3 we therefore emphasize how important it is to be reflexive, which implies to position and reflect critically on ourselves as both subjects and objects in the situation.

Both social work and learning make use of spoken language. In distance education, communication mostly depends on written words and graphics, which are often metaphorical. The very process of writing or creating graphical images produces a different experience from an oral communication, even within a single culture. Huntington and Sudbery (2005) draw attention to the inherent tensions in using virtual classroom teaching across national boundaries with students from various language groups. Furthermore they emphasize the importance of having local bilingual tutors. However, using a distance education or social work practice programme from abroad also requires a tutor or social worker who could serve as a cultural translator; see Chapter 4. To perform an adequate job necessitates acquaintance with both the local and the foreign cultures.

Distance Education in Social Work

Technology-based distance education has an increasing impact on social work education as well as in lifelong learning. In addition to several comprehensive distance education courses in social work (for example Siebert and Spaulding-Givens, 2006), many educational institutions offer specific courses like for example:

- research statistics courses (Bolen, 2006);
- interactive video disks for interviewing (Reinoehl and Shapiro, 1986);
- multimedia training in child protection work (Satterwhite and Schoech, 1995);
- direct practice (Coe and Elliott, 1999);
- critical thinking skills (Huff, 2000);
- critical reflection (Oterholm, 2005);
- inquiry-based learning (Cooner, 2005);
- supervision (Bourn, 2000);
- field placement (McFall and Freddolino, 2000; Bourn and Bootle, 2005; Roberts-DeGennaro et al., 2005; Wolfson et al., 2005; Quinney, 2005).

These examples and the surveys and evaluative studies already cited indicate strong interest. Discussions of potential and future prospects in social work education hold out optimism about the possibilities (Hollister and Mehotra, 1999; Schoech and Helton, 2002; Cooner, 2004; Weiner and Petrella, 2007).

Consequently, the technical requirements of ICT are crucial issues for all education and particularly for social work. Feminist 'polyvocalist' perspectives propose that ICT restricts the representation of female and minority voices (Kreuger and Stretch, 2000), an area to be particularly aware of since the majority of social work students and educators, clients and social workers in many countries are women. Although some uses of technology offer opportunities for empowering involvement and appear to engage men and women equally (Gasker and Cascio, 2001), 'technology is not gender neutral' (Rafferty et al., 2005: 03). Thus women might become disadvantaged in using ICT (Huntington and Sudbery, 2005; Roberts-DeGennaro et al., 2005). Machines and computer programs are racist; they operate as though white, Western behaviour and priorities are standard; they conceal diversity; they often assume male priorities (Lund, 2000). The jargon is American English. The organization of the screen, from left to right and top to bottom, is Western. Clip art collections contain mainly American and occasionally European images, with the occasional token black person. Machines and computer programs are also market oriented. The programs are designed for business purposes and have to be adapted for educational and practice use. The design of programs such as word processors and spreadsheets focus on business first. Presentation programs offer business-focused templates and 'wizards'.

However, teaching methodology and social work methods and ethics are important to securing progress (Weiner and Petrella, 2007), instead of merely focusing on the technological limitations and possibilities. How we teach using technologies may counteract many of the technical problems or exacerbate them. There is a difference between learning as a quantitative and qualitative change (Rekkedal, 2001). The first occurs through information collection, while the latter by integrating the knowledge and values. This shows that *information* and communication technology (ICT) should not deceive us into believing that everything it offers is a *learning* technology. As published examples demonstrate (Stocks and Freddolino, 1998, 2000; Harrington, 1999; Wong and Law, 1999; Faux and Black-Hughes, 2000; Petracchi and Patchner, 2001; Roberts-DeGennaro, 2002), the use of technologies focuses on the relatively 'hard' knowledge of social policy and research methods, which can also be applied to teaching other professional groups. However, as commercial and globalizing pressure continue, these uses of technology-based distance learning that research shows are valued may be pushed beyond the capability of the technology into aspects of social work education and practice that involve effective communication and cultural responses.

Learning is an individual as well as a social process. Clearly, individual learning processes may be supported by information collection available through Internet. To increase their flexibility students may use audio and video, podcast and mobile phones to download material for later use. The social learning process may be stimulated through all the opportunities that the technology offers. Students may:

- be involved in chat groups and forums;
- create networks, where they can exchange information or work on joint assignments synchronously or asynchronously;
- use weblogs to inform or test their own opinions;
- organize video-conferences;
- get in touch for exchanging news 24 hours a day by Short Message Service (SMS), Multimedia Message Service (MMS), via mobile phones and Wikipedia for open software.

Some authors would claim that students learn best in interactions with others (see for example Rafferty et al. 2005). The opportunities for social processes of learning to take place and be used to its full extent, however, have to be structured, and much more so than on-campus learning (Nickelsen, 2002; Siebert and Spaulding-Givens, 2006). There need to be arrangements for specific feedback, for Internet forums and timetabled opportunities to communicate with course tutors. Finally, since learning is a social process, the courses needs to be created so that the students can become co-producers of their own learning material (Punie and Cabrera, 2006), be able to critically reflect on what is presented and contextualize the material to transform it to their own reality. This is a particular requirement for programs that are aimed at an international audience.

The quality of the teachers' work is, however, essential for all learning, including that via the Internet (Rekkedal, 2001). In a student evaluation, Rekkedal found that communication with teachers was more important to students than peer relations. However, most of the time in distance education, students have no opportunity to communicate directly with teachers. While traditional teaching may allow for clarifying, filling in, elaborating and changing opinions, teaching on Internet demands that teachers are able to express themselves precisely and consistently, and students are able to gain from the teaching what is intended. Alternative interpretations are not allowed for, only the sequence of learning anticipated by the teacher, so that students' unclear or creative ideas cannot be tested out with the teacher. Interpersonal dialogues between students and teachers in conventional education may help to confirm students' understanding of the material in relation to their own context. While this may be achieved with distance learning technologies, they need to be structured to permit it; it does not happen as a by-product of work in the classroom.

In distance education adult and/or constructivist learning are widely recommended, also in social work (Cooner, 2004; Madoc-Jones and Parrot, 2005; Bourn and Bootle, 2005; Rafferty et al., 2005; Punie and Cabrera, 2006; Glen and Moule, 2006). In social work education different teaching methods are used without necessarily having specific pedagogical objectives. These include various participatory approaches as part of the process of developing relationships that facilitate learning of competences. Social work courses would have to be transformed for ICT, including some that today are taught face-to-face. However, the learning goals and outcomes should decide whether ICT can be used or not (Rafferty et al., 2005). According to Dreyfus (2001) context-free facts, rules and procedures are suitable for learning by technology-based distance education. However, he maintains that for students to incorporate fully within their repertoire professional skills and competence requires bodily involvement and the imitation of role models. Such learning has to be done in relationships to others. Bodily involvement includes motivation, courage, responsibility and risk taking, and technology does not offer a satisfying opportunity for such learning processes. Internet is in itself a low context medium, while it operates as a high context medium. It reaches out to people from very different cultures without elaborating on the context in which the material is created. It lives its own life as if the material is neutral and universal.

If the needs of social work education, rather than technology, are to direct students' learning, the technology has to be chosen accordingly, depending both on students and teachers and also on their culturally influenced learning styles. Western adult learning principles suggest that we should regard students as active and responsible for their own learning.

However, this might not be true in practice neither in all Western countries, nor in countries in the South. For example, the American philosopher Herbert Dreyfus claims that French, German, and Greek philosophy are contemplative and interpretive, while the American approach, which comes from James and Dewey, is more pragmatic. American pragmatism again is different from the European one. European philosophers, according to Dreyfus, are interested in how thinkers' texts relate to each other, while Americans are concerned about how to apply the philosophy to the real world (Duesund, 2000). While teaching in Europe, Dreyfus found that French and German students are more passive than Danish students. In France, the professors give very polished lectures, and the students learn to listen and take notes. When Dreyfus offered an opportunity to raise questions, they could not, while in Denmark students were able or willing to engage in a conversation, as they had not been lectured to all their lives (Duesund, 2000). We may also find such differences in social work education around the world and must be prepared to meet them in distance education.

Globalized educational and social work practice programmes might not be sensitive enough to the local community and the economic and political system of the home countries of the students or clients. Social work models presented in distance education programmes might be developed for Western individual approaches to social work and their focus on exposing and confronting conflicts. A cultural mismatch will arise where training for such perspectives is offered to regions where family, tribal or community approaches, indirect communication and consensus and harmony are prevailing values. Social work education via globalized distance education might therefore cause chaos and bewilderment in many countries, increasing the low status that social work already has.

To illustrate this, on an exchange visit to Tanzania Gurid asked social workers in various institutions what was the most important thing they had learned during their training. Without exception, the answer was confidentiality. This was also the response from a social worker in a social service agency. The office had one chair, which was offered to Gurid, and two desks. There were three social workers and five clients, who all took part in the same conversation. One of the main tasks was to organize a lift to the home villages for people who suffered from AIDS. How can confidentiality in the Western meaning of the concept, described to them in their English textbooks or distance learning materials as a fundamental principle in social work, be relevant and practised in such a context? Rather the whole context of the materials needs to be fashioned in a way that is relevant to the needs of local social workers.

Poverty is not the same around the world. In Africa, poverty is a mass problem; in USA the minority of people is poor. It creates different political contexts in which social workers have to operate, and which may demand different approaches depending on the nature of the welfare state regime. To create global study materials and expect them to fit these various environments is very demanding. Likewise, to learn from such complex comparisons students need to have good capacity to generalize knowledge and an effective support system.

ICT-based Social Work

In the late 1950s the first video therapy via television with implication for social work, took place (Bashshur, 1997 in McCarty and Clancy, 2003). Nevertheless, ICT is still not widely used in social work practice (Robers-DeGennaro et al., 2005). It is yet at an early stage. All the learning technologies that are mentioned above for students can also be used in social work practice. It may change social work to become more interactive with increased possibilities for user-participation.

Mental health care is still the social work treatment and consultation domain in which ICT has its broadest use (McCarty and Clancy, 2002). Of Internet health programs in the USA, mental health comprises one third (Fox et al., 2000). In mental health and family counselling a variety of technology-based programs exists (Oravec, 2000). These are also fields that globalization and a market orientation may expose to professional investment and corporate money in order to be spread for sale on an international arena. Clients as students will then be regarded as commodities, where consultations have to be paid for. However, as with distance education there might be a protection in that social work practice is a small field and thus easier to control that what is offered is ethically, professionally and culturally justifiable.

We are aware of a flowering of treatment and counselling programs on the Internet that may or may not be quality assured by professionals. Social workers will have no influence on how people use the possibilities for interaction that are available on the Internet. What we are concerned with here is therefore what social workers take part in creating or using, and particularly programs where the target group would be cross-national. Our preoccupation is what may be offered worldwide as professional support and counselling systems, pretending their basis is neutral and universal in a postmodern era of apparent flexibility, which is globally dominated by Western cultures. This may have a postcolonial effect.

We argue that social work programmes have to be contextualized just as much as the distance education programmes and are therefore likely to be unsuitable for a global market. Jackson's (2003) analysis of weaknesses of distance learning technology, discussed above, might to date be more relevant for social work clients around the world then for students. Again, the best services will only be accessible for those who can afford to pay.

Through electronic management systems, the power and control aspects of social work have increased. It is timely for social workers to react to this (Garret, 2004). An example is the controversial plan under the *Every Child Matters* programme announced by the British Government in 2003 and implemented through the Children Act 2004. An aim was to list all children with basic information in an electronic system, and it was important to improve the collection and sharing of information (Parton, 2006). Social workers, teachers and the police could insert concerns about children and their families. The idea behind this was that children already, from the age of 7–8 years, could be identified at risk of a criminal future. To simplify the cooperation, the government committed itself to remove organizational, legal, technical, professional and cultural barriers to information exchange. Garret further maintains that children from poor, socially and economically marginalized families are the most vulnerable to surveillance. This exemplifies that it is important to reflect constantly and critically upon possible use and misuse of computer-based systems to promote or support government policies that would be against social work values and violate people's human rights. Moreover, in case a system like this would be offered on a global market, it is important to know the context in which it is created. For example, the age of criminal responsibility varies; in the UK it is 10, in Norway 15.

Anonymity on the Internet is a danger and an advantage. The impersonal and distant relationships in chat programs allow for young people to experiment but may nevertheless also expose them to becoming abused. It is not uncommon to make arrangements for sale or exchange of sex on the Internet. A website (www. notforsale.no) has been constructed to meet young people on their home arena. It offers counselling and information to youngsters who sell or exchange sex, or have bad experiences with sex. Relatives may also get counselling.

Internet can be used to offer services to people that are hard to reach. People, who would never show up in person to seek help, might find it easier when they can remain anonymous, for example gamblers. For this group many online therapy and counselling programs are available (Griffiths and Cooper, 2003). The hot-telephone-lines have for years had great success in supporting people in crisis. Via chat channels they may get in touch with people with the same interests for exchange of ideas and support to a more extensive degree than what social workers or other professionals can offer. Gammon and Rosenvinge (2000) describe a Norwegian pilot project where five out of eight people with serious psychiatric diagnosis benefited from having access to Internet for a year. By using email, discussion groups and seeking information they got more socially confident, less lonely. It worked as a crisis and anxiety intervention, and also gave them the feeling of meaning something to others. This result was also confirmed by a study of online self-help groups in Slovenia (Mesec and Mesec, 2004). The chatting promoted community cohesion, helped people to get included in social life, helping others with similar problems as themselves and strengthen their self-confidence. In a study of four Norwegian mental-health-related online discussion forums of 492 respondents, a clear majority wanted professionals to take active roles in the forums (Kummervold et al., 2002). This might be a guideline also for social work practice programs.

Conclusion

Technology-based development has and will continue to change our lives. ICT-based distance social work education and practice offer many opportunities and potentialities benefiting both students and clients. However, there are issues that need to be consciously considered particularly in cross-cultural activities that may be exposed to postcolonial and globalizing forces.

Social work education has embraced the opportunities offered by distance education, particularly for better access to education. It has done so through experiment with the technologies involved, research on comparability with conventional education and through debate about the possibilities for progress. Less so has been done so far in social work practice.

Our starting point in this chapter was a concern about the impact on social work education, as well as on social work practice, of future trends in ICT. These trends derive from marketization focused on the opportunities offered by new technology for commercialization and industrialization. The particular needs of minor areas such as social work are not the driver of developments, but rather must be made to conform to dominant technologies. Technology and the market of globalized distance education are not neutral; rather they are culturally oppressive, unresponsive to minority cultural and linguistic needs. This might also be the case for social work practice programs.

We have argued that neither social work education nor practice can be wholly provided through the Internet and other technologies, but they will inevitably be affected by these trends. Moreover, as relatively small-scale areas of professional education and practice, they may not be able to finance or negotiate high-quality programs that incorporate local diversity and contextualization, in an international market. On the other hand, because social work is not a prosperous field in the global knowledge economy, it may be advantaged by having opportunities to influence how distance education or ICT-based social work programs are used, to be in control of whom it is sold to and to be able to assure a contextualization.

We argue therefore that a balance requires to be struck. Social work needs to build an awareness of trends and participate in creating distance education and professional practice programs to influence how they will affect social work. Being able to respond to dangers in developing trends, by focusing on cultural, educational and linguistic diversity is part of that awareness. Social work values promote acceptance of valid alternative views; see Chapter 5, not crushing them into standardized boxes in pursuit of a false quality.

The opposite should be the rule. Standardization should only be acceptable when the target group is small enough for authors of distance learning materials and for creators of the social work practice programs to be familiar with and able to adjust the material to the social context of the students and clients; see chapter 3 and 4. When this is not possible, students' learning process should involve local tutors for cultural translation, and for clients social workers should perform the same task. However, for this to work well, the cultural translators in turn need to be familiar with the social context of the creators of the material and program as well as the students' or clients' contexts.

We have argued that awareness of the trends is important so that the opportunities may be taken up, and we avoid the disadvantages we have discussed here. Awareness is not enough, however, and social work education and practice need to pursue a number of strategies to take advantage of the opportunities:

- *Openness to joint work* – Distance education and practice programs intended to cross national and cultural boundaries should be planned and constructed jointly respecting relevant cultures and with possibilities for co-production. Joint work needs to continue through the delivery, student involvement and assessment of the course and through user participation.
- *Anti-standardization* – Language and cultural difference should demand localization and contextualization in development, production and spread of materials and programs.
- *Reflexivity* – Programs should have openings for critical reflection on both the producer and receiver's position and context in order to actively work for less powerful cultures and experience to influence dominant cultures and knowledge.
- *Anti-discrimination* – Expertise is required not only in the social work content, but also in the ability to work together with people from another culture, to understand their experience and the importance of language in constructing personal and cultural identity and to be able to work in an equal relationship to identify and share expertise.
- *Translation resources* – Distance learning resources and practice programs need translation both in language and in their cultural implications.
- *User control* – As there are currently moves towards promoting international standards in social work education, local flexibility needs to be positively incorporated; this means more than acknowledging local differences or leaving space for them. The control of objectives, content and process needs to lie with the contexts where the course or practice program will be delivered, not with the producers.

Technologies open opportunities both for social work education and practice that we have never had before, and will continue to do so but also raise new challenges. The impact of making social work education and practice a commodity in global markets and use of ICT for inappropriate elements of social work education and practice need to be countered by action to recognize the cultural and learning needs of social work students wherever distance education is used across national and cultural boundaries. The same applies to clients when social work practice programs are offered cross-nationally.

Chapter 10

Conclusion

International Social Work

In this conclusion, we bring together our arguments. We started out to understand international social work. Does it exist and is it important? This question arises because social work is usually seen as depending on local law, culture and welfare regimes in any particular state. Yet there are structures of international cooperation and communication in social work, and the claim has been made, at least by enthusiasts, that there is an international social work. In Chapter 2, we argued that there are international movements in welfare and policy that have an impact on the local interpretation of social work, and that any local social work gains from international ideas.

However, we raised further questions concerning globalization and developments in postmodern thinking. This is because globalization seems to emphasize the importance of trends towards internationalization, of which the growing importance of international social work is a part. However, there is also a critique of globalization that suggests that it leads to the continued imposition of Western economic and political power, culture and thought on former colonial societies. Inequalities across the world and within countries and regions result from this. How should social work respond to those trends? Is it affected by them? What should its critique be? Postmodernism both analyses and criticizes these trends, because it questions the universalist assumptions of an international social work, but itself is an international trend implicated in globalizing Western culture.

In Chapters 2 and 8, particularly, we identified a number of activities that are part of international social work as it is usually conceived. Several such activities are not regarded as social work practice in many countries. Practice becomes international where people from one country, usually in the West, go to provide international aid or development work in another country, mainly in the South, or where the welfare regime is not well-developed. Another form of international practice is in activities where clients cross borders and help is needed, over adoption, with child abduction and with refugees, asylum seekers and migrants. To some degree, increases in clients crossing borders has come from the greater mobility derived from globalization, as better and cheaper transport brings different societies and cultures closer together. Social work education is also an important structure in which globalization, postmodern ideas and post-colonial influences occur.

It is not, however, the only such social structure. Welfare policy and political and social regimes govern welfare provision and therefore to a great degree social work practice. All are formed in an international policy environment, significantly affected by the economic aspect of globalization. This is why international social work should be a concern for practitioners, educators and students of social work. Globalization influences and creates the social issues we deal with, it creates the context of our practice and education through its impact on the political and cultural landscape within which we practise, educate and learn.

Globalization

What are the concerns about globalization for social work? Why are they concerns? The main answer to these questions is that globalization creates and accentuates inequality and injustice that particularly affect the populations and issues that social work deals with. These inequalities and injustices arise between countries, in particular between the West and the South, and within countries, between urban and rural areas, between richer and poorer communities and people. Since social work as a profession seeks to combat inequality and injustice, these must be its concerns. This is so internationally, in policy development and where cross-border work takes place. It is also so at the local level.

We weaved through the book a number of ideas and issues about globalization that have a particular effect on social work and welfare regimes:

- *Postcolonialism* refers to the maintenance of Western power over local cultures through cultural domination of ideas, communication media and technology.
- *Linguistic and cultural hegemony* refers to the maintenance of Western power though cultural domination that relies on control of language.
- *Transnational companies and economic structures* refer to the maintenance of Western power through exploitation by Western-dominated international organizations and companies.
- *New public management and managerialism* refers to the maintenance of the priority of economic globalization by the incorporation of market structures on welfare regimes.

Such processes damage the interests of countries in the South and people in poverty everywhere, and increase social injustice and socio-economic inequalities. They are a product of economic globalization. There is debate about whether they are a necessary evil. We have argued that social concern, in search of justice and welfare, is an essential adjunct of economic globalization. There are social movements that claim that alternative economic strategies are possible. Social development is certainly necessary to meet these social concerns. Moreover, the unbridled pursuit of market forces and their cultural and managerial adjuncts have been unnecessarily damaging to justice and welfare. Constraint on these social trends is possible, necessary, and therefore important to social work.

This is all in the field of international economic and social policy: what can the minor profession of social work with its small-scale objectives and focus on interpersonal, small group, family and community relations do? We have argued that as a policy for the development of social work we need to do the following:

- Awareness through understanding and analysis of the injustices and inequalities of globalization and the pursuit of the social work values.
- Activities to enhance understanding of the political connection between globalization and practice.
- To be prepared to question injustices in society.
- The incorporation of social development as an aspect of practice.
- The development of practice, management, knowledge, education and curriculum in ways that do not accept or potentiate the impact of globalization.
- Practice and education that reflect contextualization, flexibility and openness to alternative cultural and social needs.

These are our proposal for a policy for social work practice and education to respond to globalization and its impact on the people social work serves. Postmodernism is another social trend that contributes to the opportunities to pursue this policy in social work.

Postmodernism

Postmodernism is both part of and in tension with globalizing social processes. It is part of those processes because it expresses the broadening range of knowledge and issues, contexts and cultures that emerge from cultural globalization. It is in tension with these processes, because postmodernism denies the modernist dominance of determinist universal knowledge that economic and political globalization imposes on social work and welfare regimes and education through marketization, NPM, academization and managerialism. Therefore, postmodernism offers the potential to engage with globalization, because it is intertwined with the same social structures, while at the same time it places them in tension.

There are many strands in postmodernism, which is not a coherent concept or movement. Indeed, most strands of postmodernism would reject the possibility of coherence. Instead, postmodernism incorporates diversity, flexibility and opportunity, and this is its value for social work in responding to globalization. These characteristics are at the heart of social work's concerns about the injustices and inequalities of globalization.

Critics of postmodernism complain of its relativism and cynicism, perhaps its rejection of certainty. The delights in paradox, the focus on the symbolic, on language, on cultural signs all make it seem insubstantial. Yet social work has always been concerned with communication and language, with seeking the hidden social and cultural factors affecting our clients, on dealing with the emotional and personal within their social contexts. These aspects of postmodern ideas offer a rich creativity in helping people find alternative ways through the social and personal issues that they face.

Therefore, in using postmodern ideas we seek to make its flexibility and openness practical for social work in the face of the complex social forces of the current age. Postmodern values that are relevant to incorporation into social work practice, management and education are as follows:

- Contextualization, because postmodernism recognizes that knowledge emerges from the social and historical context in which we are operating.
- Knowledge development and management through communities of practice in which, through ideas such as critical reflection, cultural translation and knowledge validation, we develop and adapt knowledge for use in a particular context.
- Objectives that progress towards diversity, complexity, equality and mutuality in knowledge exchanges to promote sustainability for local knowledge production.

As social work practitioners, educators and learners we accept that there is evidence and knowledge to be gained from formal validation and research processes. However, we argue that this knowledge will always require contextualization in the current context, for the people here present. Knowledge processes must always have practices that progress towards greater equality, mutuality and openness. Otherwise, we contribute to globalizing inequality and injustice. It is process that progresses towards context and openness that social work must incorporate.

Social Work Processes for a Globalized Postmodern World

We argued above that social work can respond to globalization by pursing four major policies. In this section, we bring together the practice and education strategies that we have proposed in this book to achieve awareness through understanding and analysis, incorporation of social development, avoiding practice, management and education that strengthens globalization and achieving postmodern openness and flexibility in practice.

Table 10.1 summarizes the processes that we have discussed in this book. Each of these processes is discussed in relation to a particular issue, but we argue that collectively they form a social work approach to globalization. We have explored some in relation mainly to education, some in relation to policy, practice and management, but we have also tried to show how these ideas may be made relevant and mutually transferable across practice, management and education. We see these ideas as creative, positive and critical. They are part of and build on the traditions of social work. But they do so in ways that deal with the issues raised by globalization and use methods that exert the pull of postmodern social experience to do so.

Conclusion

We can aim for a social work that is concerned for international and personal equality and justice. Globalizing economic, political and cultural trends contribute to inequality and injustice. In international social work, we can aim in practice to combat the personal, social and political effects of those processes. In practice and in education, we can develop our awareness, understanding and analysis to respond to the experience of those effects in the people and communities we work with, clients and colleagues, students and educators. Knowledge, understanding and curriculum

Table 10.1   Social work processes and globalization

Chapter	Process	Outcomes
2	Critical reflection	Incorporates four critical traditions, professional development and competence, social and political contextualization
3	Cultural translation	Openness to alternative cultural and linguistic requirements, availability of knowledge to facilitate indigenization and social inclusion
4	Knowledge validation	Transfer of different knowledges through validation processes
5	Empowering social work identity	Pursues openness, flexibility, participation, partnership, community perspectives and cultural strengths to empower practice, management and education
6	Piloting through chaos	Facilitaties contextualization of understanding and competence, creating flexible and open practice
7	Progressive objectives towards equality in exchanges	Develops objectives towards increasing complexity, equality and mutuality in order to secure sustainability in international exchanges
8	Diversity in ICT use	Develops technology use to permit diversity, openness and flexibility

about ways can help us avoid being drawn into the negative effects of globalization and to stand up for what we believe in and what the aims of social work and its values require us to do. The positives of markets, managerialism, linguistic and cultural hegemony and developments in technology can seduce us into participation in the negatives. The flexibility and openness inherent in postmodern societies can offer us ways of piloting through processes that express and contribute to equality and justice.

Bibliography

Aase, T.H. (2006), 'Elfenbenstårnet bygges høyere', in Hagen, E.B. and Johansen, A. (eds) *Hva skal vi med vitenskapen?* (Oslo: Universitetsforlaget).

ACSSW (2006), *We've Boundless Plains to Share: The First Report of the People's Inquiry into Detention* (Australian Council of Heads of Schools of Social Work), <www.peoplesinquiry.org.au/PIDFirstReportNov_2006F[1].pdf>, accessed 27 January 2007.

Adams, J. (1995), *Risk* (London: Routledge).

Adepoju, A. (ed.) (1993), *The Impact of Structural Adjustment on the Population of Africa: the Implications for Education, Health and Employment* (Portsmouth, NH: Heinemann/UNFPA).

Agger, B. (1998), *Critical Social Theories. An Introduction* (Boulder: Westview Press).

Ahmad, B. (1996), *Black Perspectives in Social Work* (Birmingham: Venture).

Ahmad, W.I.U. and Atkin, K. (eds) (1996), *'Race' and Community Care* (Buckingham: Open University Press).

Aldgate, J. et al. (2007), *Enhancing Social Work Management. Theory and Best Practice from the UK and USA* (London and Philadelphia: Jessica Kingsley).

Alexander, J.C. (ed.) (1998), *Real Civil Societies: Dilemmas of Institutionalization* (London: Sage).

Alexandersen, J. (2001), 'Mellom tradisjon og nyskaping – strategier og tiltak for å øke kompetansen innen fleksibel utdanning ved Universitetet i Tromsø' in Arneberg and Skare (eds).

Alexandersen, J. et al. (2001), *Nettbasert læring i høgre utdanning* (Tromsø: SOFF-Rapport 2/2001).

Alexandersen, J. m.fl.(red) (2001), *Nettbasert læring i høgre utdanning: Noen norske erfaringer* (Tromsø: Soff rapport 1/2001).

Algie, J. (1975), *Social Values: Objectives and Action* (New York: Wiley).

Annis, L. (1983), 'The Processes and Effects of Peer Tutoring', *Human Learning* 2, 39–47.

Argyris, C. and Schön, D. (1976), *Theory in Practice: Increasing Professional Effectiveness* (San Fransisco: Jossey-Bass).

Arneberg, P. and Skare, O. (eds) (2001), *Personalutvikling i IKT-basert undervisning i høgre utdanning* (Tromsø: SOFF-Rapport 2, 27–46).

Arntzen, I. (1998), *The Internationalization of Work: Psychophysiological Predictors of Adjustment to Foreign Assignments* (Stocholm: Karolinska Institutet).

Ashford, M. (2004), *Bologna Declaration 1999,* <http://www.swap.ac.uk/quality/bologna.asp>, accessed 29 December 2006.

Ashrcoft, B. et al. (eds) (1995), *The Post-Colonial Studies Reader* (London: Routledge).

Askeland, G.A. (1994), *Studium og klientarbeid. Same arbeidsprosess?* (Oslo: Det Norske Samlaget).

Askeland, G.A. and Payne, M. (1999), 'Authors and Audiences: Towards a Sociology of Case Recording', *European Journal of Social Work* 2:1, 55–67.

Askeland, G.A. and Payne, M. (2001), 'Broadening the Mind: Cross-national Activities in Social Work', *European Journal of Social Work* 4:3, 263–274.

Askeland, G.A. (2003a), 'Reality Play – Experiential Learning in Social Work Training. A Teaching Model', *Social Work Education* 22:4, 351–363.

Askeland, G.A. (2003), 'Reality Play – Experiential Learning in Social Work Training. Evaluation of a teaching model', *Social Work Education,* 22:4, 363–375.

Askeland, G.A. and Danbolt, T.F. (2005), 'Social Work Education in Norway: Three Professions – One Job Market', in Hamburger, F. et al.

Askeland, G.A. (2006), 'Kritisk reflekterende – mer enn å reflektere og kritisere', *Nordisk sosialt arbeid* 26:2, 123–25.

Askeland, G.A. (2007), 'Globalisation and a Flood of Travellers: Flooded Travellers and Social Justice', in Dominelli, (ed.).

Askeland, G.A. and Bradley, G. (2007), 'Linking Critical Reflection and Qualitative Research on a Social Work Programme in Africa', *International Social Work* 50:5, 671–685.

Askeland, G.A. and Døhlie, E. (2006), 'Internasjonalt sosialt arbeid – når sosialarbeidaren kryssar grenser', in Døhlie and Askeland (eds).

Askheim, O.P. (2003), 'Empowerment as Guidance for Professional Social Work: An Act of Balancing on a Slack Rope', *European Journal of Social Work* 6:3, 229–240.

Atherton, C.R. and Bolland, K. A. (2002), 'Postmodernism: A Dangerous Illusion for Social Work', *International Social Work* 45:4, 421–433.

Baldock, J. et al. (eds) (2003), *Social Policy* (Oxford: Oxford University Press).

Bang, J. (1997), 'Multimedier, interaksjon og narrativitet – edutainment eller læring?' in Danielsen, O. et al.

Bargh, J. and Schul, Y. (1980), 'On the Cognitive Benefits of Teaching', *Journal of Educational Psychology*, 72:5, 1253–604.

Barnes, J. (2007), 'Improving Performance in Social Work through Positive Approaches to Managing Change', in Aldgate, et al.

Barnett, R. (1997), *Higher Education: A Critical Business* (Buckingham: Open University Press).

Baron, S. et al. (eds) (2000), *Social Capital: Critical Perspectives* (Oxford: Oxford University Press).

Bashshur, R. et al. (eds), *Telemedicine: Theory and Practice* (Springfield, IL: Charles C. Thomas).

Bashshur, R.L. (1997), 'Telemedicine and the Health Care System', in Bashshur, R. et al. (eds).

Bass, B.M. (1990), 'From Transactional to Transformational Leadership: Learning to Share the Vision', *Organizational Dynamics* 18:3, 19–31.

Bass, B.M. (1985), *Leadership and Performance Beyond Expectations* (New York: Free Press).

Batty, D. (2002), 'How the Other Half Lives', *The Guardian* August 9, <http.// society.guardian.co.uk/socialcarestaff/story/0,1141,771997,00.html>, accessed 9 August 2002.

Baudrillard, J. (1987[1993]), *Symbolic Exchange and Death* (London: Sage).

Bauman, Z. (2000), *Savnet fellesskap* (Oslo: Cappelen Akademisk Forlag).

Bauman, Z., Tester, K. (2000), *Conversations with Zygmunt Bauman* (Cambridge: Polity Press).

Beck, U. (1992), *Risk Society: Towards a New Modernity* (London: Sage).

Bgoya, W. (1999), 'Effect of Globalization in Africa and Choice of Language in Publishing', in Broch-Utne, B. and Garbo G. (eds).

Biestek (1961), *The Casework Relationship* (London: Allen & Unwin).

Boddy, J. et al. (2006), 'The Professional Care Worker: The Social Pedagogue in Northern Europe', in Boddy et al. (eds).

Boddy, J. et al. (eds) (2006), *Care Work: Present and Future* (London: Routledge).

Bolen, R.M. (2006), Utilizing Web-based Databases to Introduce Social Work Content in Research Statistics Courses', *Social Work Education* 25:1, 17–27.

Boud, D. et al. (2006), *Productive Reflection at Work* (London: Routledge).

Bourn, D. (2000), 'The Challenge of Delivering a Professionally and Academically Credited Postqualifying Social Work Management Programme in Supervision and Mentorship by Distance Learning', *Journal of Vocational Education and Training*, 52:1, 31–48.

Bourn, D. and Bootle, K. (2005), 'Evaluation of a Distance Larning, Post Graduate Advanced Award in Social Work Programmes for Child and Family Social Work Supervisors and Mentors', *Social Work Education* 24:3, 343–362.

Boyne, R. and Rattansi, A. (eds) (1990), *Postmodernism and Society* (Basingstoke: Macmillan).

Braye, S. and Preston-Shoot, M. (1995), *Empowering Practice in Social Care* (Buckingham: Open University Press).

Brechin, A. and Sidell, M. (2000), 'Ways of knowing', in Gomm, R. et al. (eds).

Briskman, L. (2003), *The Black Grapevine. Aboriginal Activism and the Stolen Generations* (Sydney: The Federation Press).

Broch-Utne, B. (2006), 'Avviklingen av norsk fagspråk', in Hagen and Johansen, (eds).

Broch-Utne, B. and G. Garbo (eds) (1999), *Globalization – on whose terms?* Report Education in Africa, 8:5, (Oslo: University of Oslo, Institute for Educational Research).

Brookfield, S.D. (1995), *Becoming a Critically Reflective Teacher* (San Franscisco: Jossey-Bass).

Brookfield, S.D. (2005), *The Power of Critical Theory for Adult Learning and Teaching* (Maidenhead: Open University Press).

Bryant, I. (ed.) (1995), *Vision, Invention, Intervention: Celebrating Adult Education: Proceedings of the 25th Annual Conference* (Southampton: University of Southampton, SCUTREA).

Burgess, H. and Taylor, I. (eds) (2005), *Effective Learning and Teaching in Social Policy and Social Work* (London: Routledge/Falmer).

Burr, V. (2003), *Social Constructionism* (London: Routledge).

Carter, J. (2000), 'New Public Management and Equal Opportunities in the NHS', *Critical Social Policy,* 20:1, 61–83.

Castells, M. (1997), *The Power of Identity* (Cambridge, MA: Blackwells).

Castles, S. and Davidson, A. (2000), *Citizenship and Migration: Globalization and the Politics of Belonging* (Basingstoke: Palgrave).

Chan, C.L.W. et al. (2006), 'Developing Resilience and Competence: An Eastern Body-Mind-Spirit Approach to Holistic Well-Being', 2006 ISPA Colloquium, Hangzhow, China, July 15-20, <http://www.ispaweb.org/Colloquia/China/Chan. pdf>, accessed 25 October 2006.

Cheung, A.B.L. (2002), 'The Politics of New Public Management: Some Experience from Reforms in East-Asia', in McLaughlin et al.

CIP (2007), *Council on International Programs USA* <http://www.cipusa.org/ conference_information.asp> accessed 30 January 2007.

Coe, J.R. and Elliott, D. (1999), 'An Evaluation of Teaching Direct Practice Courses in a Distance Education Program for Rural Settings', *Journal of Social Work Education*, 35:3, 353–66.

Cooner, T.S. (2004), 'Preparing for ICT Enhanced Practice Learning Opportunities in 2010 – A Speculative View,' *Social Work Education*, 23:6, 731–744.

Cooper, A. et al. (1995), *Positive Child Protection: a view from abroad* (Lyme Regis: Russell House).

Cox, D. and Pawar, M. (2006), *International Social Work: Issues, Strategies, and Programs* (Thousand Oaks, CA: Sage).

Craib, I. (1992), *Anthony Giddens* (London: Routledge).

Cree, V.E. and Macaulay, C. (eds) (2000), *Transfer of Learning in Professional and Vocational Education* (London: Routledge).

Cree, V.E. and Davis, A. (2007), *Social Work: Voices from the inside* (London: Routledge).

Cvetkovich, G. and Löfstedt (eds) (1999), *Social Trust and the Management of Risk* (London: Earthscan).

Dalton, B. (2001), 'Distance Education: A Multidimensional Evaluation', *Journal of Technology in Human Services* 18:3/4, 101–105.

Daly, J. et al. (eds) (1999), *Annual Review of Health Social Sciences* Vol 9, 11–20, (Bundoora: La Trobe University).

Danielsen, O. et al. (1997), *Læring og multimedier* (Ålborg: Ålborg Universitetsforlag).

Delanty, G. (2001), *Challenging Knowledge: The University in the Knowledge Society* (London: Open University Press).

Derrida, J. (1998), *On Grammatology* (Baltimore: Johns Hopkins University Press).

DH (2002), *Copying Letters to Patients: Good Practice Guidelines* <www.doh.gov. uk/patientletters/issues.htm>, accessed 12 December 2002.

Dobson, S. and Haaland, Ø. (2000), 'Postmoderne pedagogikk – et forslag', in Haaland, Ø. and Dobson, S.

Døhlie, E. and Askeland, G.A. (eds) (2006), *Internasjonalt sosialt arbeid: Innsats på andres arena* (Oslo: Universitetsforlaget).

Dominelli, L. (1996), 'Deprofessionalizing Social Work: Anti-oppressive Practice, Competencies and Postmodernism', *British Journal of Social Work*, 26:2, 153–175.

Dominelli, L. (2004), 'Practising Social Work in a Globalizing World', in Ngoh-Tiong and Rowland (eds).

Dominelli, L. (ed.) (2007), *Revitalising Communities in a Globalising World* (Aldershot: Ashgate).

Dominelli, L. and Bernard, W.T. (eds) (2003), *Broadening Horizons: International Exchanges in Social Work* (Aldershot: Ashgate).

Dreyfus, H. (2001), *On the Internet* (London: Routledge).

Duesund, L. (2000), 'Teaching and Learning: An Interview with Hubert Dreyfus', in *Kunnskap om idrett: Skriftserie fra Norges idrettshøgskole* 2:4, 3–16.

Edwards, R. (1996), 'Troubled times? Personal Identity, Distance Education and Open Learning', *Open Learning*, 11:1, 3–11.

Ellingsrud, G. (2006), 'Rangeringens svakheter', *Aftenposten, Kultur,* 25 October, 11.

Eraut, M. (1994), *Developing Professional Knowledge and Competence* (London: Routledge Falmer).

Eraut, M. (1998), *Development of Knowledge and Skills in Employment* (London: Falmer Press).

Eriksen, T.R. (1990), 'Socialisation og kvalifikation til kvindeligt omsorgsarbejde', in Jensen, K. (ed.).

Eritsland, A.G. (2001), 'Lærarutdanning i den postmoderne kulturen', *Norsk Pedagogisk Tidsskrift* 85:4, 273–286.

Etzioni, A. (1995), *The Spirit of Community: Rights, Responsibilities and the Communitarian Agenda* (London: Fontana).

Everitt, A. et al. (1992), *Applied Research for Better Practice* (Basingstoke: Macmillan).

Faux, T.L. and Black-Hughes, C. (2000), 'A Comparison of Using the Internet versus Lectures to Teach Social Work History', *Research on Social Work Practice*, 10:4, 454–466.

Firth, R. (2007), 'Learning From Overseas Social Workers' Experience in the UK', in Manthorpe, J. (ed.).

Fischer, J. (1973), 'Is Casework Effective? A Review', *Social Work* 18:1, 5–20.

Fischer, J. (1976), *The Effectiveness of Social Casework* (Springfield, IL: Charles C. Thomas).

Fischer, J. (1978), *Effective Casework Practice: An Eclectic Approach* (New York: McGraw-Hill).

Fisher, M. (2005), 'Knowledge Production for Social Welfare: Enhancing the Evidence Base', in Lang. P. (ed.).

Fisher, W. F. and Ponniah, T. (2005), *Another World is Possible: Popular Alternatives to Globalization at the World Social Forum.*(London: Zed Books).

Flanagan, J.C. (1954), 'The Critical Incident Technique', *Psychological Bulletin* 51: 4, 327–58.

Fong, R. (ed.) (2004), *Culturally Competent Practice with Immigrant and Refugee Children and Families* (New York: Guilford Press).

Fook, J. (1996), 'The Reflective Researcher: Developing a Reflective Approach to Practice', in Fook, J. (ed.).

Fook, J. (ed.) (1996), *The Reflective Researcher: Social Workers'Theories of Practice Research* (St Leonards: Allen and Unwin).

Fook, J. (1999a), 'Reflexivity as Method', in Daly, J. et al (eds).

Fook, J. (1999), 'Critical Reflectivity in Education and Practice', in Pease, B. and Fook, J. (eds).

Fook, J., Ryan, M. and Hawkins, L. (2000), *Professional Expertise. Practice, Theory and Education for Working in Uncertainty* (London: Whiting & Birch).

Fook, J. (2002), *Social Work: Critical Theory and Practice* (London: Sage).

Fook, J. and Askeland, G.A. (2006), 'The "critical" in critical reflection', in White, S.

Fook, J., White, S. and Gardner, F. (2006), 'Critical Reflection: A Review of Contemporary Literature and Understandings', in White, S., Fook, J. and Gardner, F. (eds).

Fook, J. and Askeland, G.A. (2007), 'Challenges of Critical Reflection: "Nothing Ventured, Nothing Gained"', *Social Work Education* 26:5, 520–33.

Ford, P., Johnston, B., Mitchell, R. and Myles, F. (2005), 'Practice Learning and the Development of Students as Critical Practitioners – Some Findings from Research', *Social Work Education*, 24:4, 391–407.

Fox, S. et al. (2000), *The Online Health Care Revolution: How the Web Helps Americans take Better Care of Themselves* (Washington DC: Pew Internet and America Life Project).

Freitas, M. J. et al. (2005), *Children, Young People and Families: Examining Social Work Practice in Europe* (Roma: Carocci).

Friesenhahn, G.J. and Kantowicz, E. (2005), 'Social Pedagogy: A Paradigm in European Social Work Education from German and Polish Perspectives', in Freitas et al.

Frønes, I. and Kjølsrød, L. (eds), *Det Norske Samfunn*, 5, (ed.), (Oslo: Gyldendal Akademisk).

Furman, L.D. et al. (2004), 'Religion and Spirituality in Social Work Education and Direct Practice at the Millennium: A Survey of UK Social Workers', *British Journal of Social Work* 34:6, 767–791.

Gammon, D. and Rosenvinge, J.H. (2000), 'Er Internett til hjelp for personer med alvorlige psykiske lidelser?', *Tidsskrift for Den Norske Lægeforening*, 120:16, 1890–1892.

Garret, P.M. (2004), 'The Electronic Eye: Emerging Surveillance Practices in Social Work with Children and Families', *European Journal of Social Work*, 7:1, 57–71.

Gasker, J. A. and Cascio, T. (2001), 'Empowering Women through Computer-mediated Class Participation', *Affilia*, 16:3, 295–313.

George, V.and Page, R.M. (eds) (2004), *Global Social Problems* (Cambridge: Polity).

Germain, C. (1970), 'Casework and Science: A Historical Encounter' in Roberts, R.W. and Nee, R.H. (eds).

Gibbs, L. and Gambrill, E. (2002), 'Evidence-based Practice: Counterarguments to Objections', *Research in Social Work Practice*, 12:3, 452–76.

Giddens, A. (1990), *The Consequences of Modernity* (Cambridge: Polity).

Giddens, A. (1991), *Modernity and Self-Identity: Self and Society in Late Modern Age* (Cambridge: Polity).

Gilchrist, A. (2004), *The Well-Connected Community: A Networking Approach to Community Development* (Bristol: Policy Press).

Gilligan C. (1993), *In a Different Voice: Psychological Theory and Women's Development* (Cambridge, MA: Harvard University Press).

Glans, K. (2003), 'Sweden's orderly young' *Axess* 3 http://www.axess.se/english/currentissue/swedens_orderly_young.php, accessed 5 December 2003.

Globastat (2001), <www.globastat.com/o10.htm>, accessed 4 July 2002.

Glen, S. and Moule, P. (2006), *E-learning in Nursing* (Basingstoke: Palgrave Macmillan).

Goffman, E. (1968), *The Presentation of Self in Everyday Life* (Harmondsworth: Penguin).

Gomm, R. and Davies, C. (eds) (2000), *Using Evidence in Health and Social Care* (London: Sage).

Gould, N. (2000), 'Becoming a Learning Organisation: A Social Work Example', *Social Work Education* 19:6, 586–596.

Gould, N. and Baldwin, M. (eds) (2004), *Social Work, Critical Reflection and the Learning Organisation* (Aldershot: Ashgate).

Gould, N. and Taylor, I. (1996), *Reflective Learning for Social Work* (Aldershot, Arena).

Graham, M. (2002), *Social Work and African-Centred Worldviews* (Birmingham: Venture).

Graham, M. (2004), 'Empowerment Revisited – Social Work, Resistance and Agency in Black Communities', *European Journal of Social Work,* 7:1, 43–56.

Gray, M. (2005), 'Dilemmas of International Social Work: Paradoxical Processes in Indigenisation, Universalism and Imperialism', *International Journal of Social Welfare* 14:3, 231–8.

Gray, M. and Fook, J. (2004), 'The Quest for an International Social Work', *Social Work Education* 23:5, 625–44.

Greenwood, E. (1957), 'Attributes of a Profession', *Social Work* 2:3, 45–55.

Griffiths, M. and Cooper, G. (2003),' Online Therapy: Implications for Problem Gamblers and Clinicians', *British Journal of Guidance and Counselling* 31:1,113–135.

Gross, E. (2006), 'Global Values Shift and Social Work in America: Making Positive Change', *International Social Work* 49:6, 719–730.

Gule, L. (2006), *Islam og det moderne* (Oslo: Abstrakt forlag).

Haaland, Ø. and Dobson, S. (2000), *Pedagogen, teksten og selvet – et innspill til en postmoderne pedagogikk* (Lillehammer: Høgskolen i Lillehammer, Research report no. 48).

Habermas, J. (1995), *Kommunikativt handlande. Texter om språk, rationalitet och Samhälle* (Gøteborg: Daidalos).

Hagen, E. B. and Johansen, A. (eds) (2006), *Hva skal vi med vitenskapen? 13 innlegg fra striden om tellekantene* (Oslo: Universitetsforlaget).

Hagen, K. and Lødemel, I. (2005), 'Fattigdom og sosial eksklusjon', in Frønes, I. Kjølsrød, L. (eds).

Hall, E.T. (1989), *The Dance of Life: The Other Dimension of Time* (New York: Anchor).

Hall, S. and Gieben, B. (eds) (1992), *Formations of Modernity*, (Cambridge: Polity).

Hall. S., Held, D. and McGrew, T. (eds) (1992), *Modernity and its Futures* (Cambridge: Polity).

Halmi, A. (2003), 'Chaos and Non-linear Dynamics: New Methodological Approaches in the Social Sciences and Social Work Practice', *International Social Work* 46: 1, 83–101.

Hamäläinen, J, and Vornanen, R. (1996), 'Social Work and Social Security – Theoretical and Practical Challenges in a Changing Society', in Hamäläinen, J. et al. (eds).

Hamäläinen, J. et al. (eds) (1996), *Social Work and Social Security in a Changing Society* (Augsberg: MaroVerlag).

Hamburger, F. and Sänger, A. (1991), 'Annotated list of EC Social Legislation and Policies concerning Freedom of Movement, the Social Fund and Poverty', in Hill, M. (ed.).

Hamburger, F, and Wöbcke, (2005), 'Introduction', in Hamburger et al. (eds).

Hamburger, F. et al. (2005), *Ausbildung fur Soziale Berufe in Europa*, Band 2 (Frankfurt/Main: Institut fur Sozialarbeit und Socialpaedagogik).

Hamilton, P. (1992), 'The Enlightenment and the Birth of Social Science' in Hall and Gieben (eds).

Harrington, D. (1999), 'Teaching Statistics: A Comparison of Traditional Classroom and Programmed Instruction/Distance Learning Approaches', *Journal of Social Work Education*, 35:3, 353–66.

Harris, J. and Chou, Y-C. (2001), 'Globalization or Glocalization? Community care in Taiwan and Britain', *European Journal of Social Work*, 4:2, 161–171.

Harris, J. (2003), *The Social Work Business* (London: Routledge).

Harris, J. (2007), 'Looking Backward, Looking Forward: Current Trends in Human Services Management', in Aldgate, J. et al.

Hassan, I. (1987), *The Postmodern Turn* (Columbus: Ohio State University Press).

Healy, K. (2000), *Social Work Practices: Contemporary Perspectives on Change* (London: Sage).

Healy, K. (2005), *Social Work Theories in Context: Creating Frameworks for Practice* (Basingstoke: Palgrave Macmillan).

Healy, L.M. et al. (1995), 'Women and Social Work Management', in Keys and Ginsberg (eds).

Healy, L.M. (2001), *International Social Work: Professional Action in an Interdependent World* (New York: Oxford University Press).

Hesselbein, F., Goldsmith, M., Beckhard, R. and Schudbert, R.E. (eds) (1998), *The Community of the Future* (San Francisco: Jossey-Bass).

Hill, M. (ed.) (1991), *Social Work and the European Community: The Social Policy and Practice Contexts* (London: Jessica Kingsley).

Hochschild, A. (1995), The Culture of Politics; Traditional, Postmodern, Cold-modern and Warm-modern Ideals of Care', *Social Politics* 2(3): 331–46.

Hokenstad, M.C., Khinduka, S. and Midgley, J. (eds) (1992), *Profiles in International Social Work* (Washington, DC: NASW Press).

Hollister, C.D., and Mehrotra, C.M.N. (1998), 'Utilizing and Evaluating ITV Workshops for Rural Community Leadership Training', *Journal of Technology in Human Services* 16: 2–3, 35–45.

Hopkins, D.H., Lorentzen, L.A., Mendieta, E. and Batstone, D. (eds) (2001), *Religions/Globalizations: Theories and Cases* (Durham: Duke University Press).

How, A. (2003), *Critical Theory* (Basingstoke: Palgrave).

Høyrup, S. and Elkjær, B. (2006), 'Reflection: Taking it Beyond the Individual', in Boud et al.

Huff, M.T. (2000), 'A Comparative Study of Live Instruction versus Interactive Television for Teaching MSW Students Critical Thinking Skills', *Research on Social Work Practice*, 10:4, 400–416.

Hunt, C. (1995), 'Journey through the Looking Glass: Some Reflections on Crossing the Community/Higher Education Divide', in Bryant, I. (ed.).

Hunt, C. (2006), 'Travels with a Turtle: Metaphors and the Making of a Professional Identity', *Reflective Practice* 7:3, 315–332.

Huntingdon, S.P. (1996), *The Clash of Civilizations and the Remaking of the World Order* (New York: Touchstone).

Huntington, A. and Sudbery, J. (2005), 'Virtual Classrooms: Experiences of European Collaborative Teaching and Learning', *Social Work Education*, 24:3, 363–371.

Husband C. (1996), 'Defining and Containing Diversity: Community, Ethnicity and Citizenship' in Ahmad, W.I.U. and Atkin, K. (eds).

Hutton, M. and Mwansa, L-K. J. (1996), 'Social Work Practice in Africa: Social Development in a Community Context: An Overview', in Hutton, B. and Mwansa, L-K.

Hutton, M. and Mwansa, L-K. J. (1996), *Social Work Practice in Africa* (Gabarone: University of Botswana).

IASSW (2001), About IASSW: International Definition of Social Work, <www.iassw-aiets.org/>, accessed 20 March 2006.

IASSW (2004), *Global Standards for Social Work Education and Training*, <http://www.iassw-aiets.org/>, accessed 16 January 2004.

IFSW (2000), *International Federation of Social Workers: Definition of Social Work*, <http://www.ifsw.org/Publications/4.6e.pub.html>, accessed 16 January 2006.

IFSW (2007), *Historical Matters: Individual Cases* <www.ifsw.org/en/p38000166. html>, accessed 3 January 2007.

IFSW, Human Rights Commission, <www.ifsw.org/en/p38000166.html>, accessed 15 December 2006.

Ingdal, B. and Kamal, M.A. (2005), *Evaluation Report PAL-97/032: Children's Cultural Center Bethlehem*, (Final report 1 April 2005).

Jackson, P. (2003), 'Ten Challenges for Introducing Web-supported Learning to Overseas Students in the Social Sciences', *Active Learning in Higher Education*, 4:1, 87–106.

Jarvis, P. (2006), *From Adult Education to the Learning Society: 21 years from the International Journal of Lifelong Education* (Abingdon, Oxen: Routledge).

Jenkins, K. (ed.) (1997), *The Postmodern History Reader* (London: Routledge).

Jensen, Karen (1992), *Hjemlig omsorg i offentlig regi. En studie av kunnskapsutvikling i omsorgsarbeid* (Oslo: Universitetsforlaget).

Jensen, K. (1993), 'Den framtidige profesjonsutdanningen. Perspektiver på kunnskap og læring' in Kirkvold et al., (eds).

Jokinen, I. et al. (eds) (1999), *Constructing Social Work Practices* (Aldershot: Ashgate).

Jones, H. (1990), *Social Welfare in Third World Development* (Basingstoke, Macmillan).

Jørgensen, M.W. (2002), *Refleksivitet og kritik: Socialkonstruktionistiske Subjektpositioner* (Fredriksberg: Roskilde Universitetsforlag).

Karvinen, S. et al. (1999), *Reconstructing Social Work Research* (Jyväskylä: SoPhi).

Karvinen, S. (2001), 'Socialt arbete på veg til reflexiv expertis' in Tronvoll, I.M. and Marthinsen, E. (eds).

Karvinen-Niinikoski, S. (2005), 'Research Orientation and Expertise in Social Work – Challenges for Social Work Education', *European Journal of Social Work* 8:3, 259–271.

Keegan, D. (1996), *Foundations of Distance Education*, 3rd Edition, (London: Routledge).

Kendall, K.A. (1978), *Reflections on Social Work Education 1950–1978* (New York: International Association of Schools of Social Work).

Kendall, K.A. (2000), *Social Work Education: Its Origins in Europe* (Alexandria, VA: CSWE).

Keys, P. and Ginsberg, L. (eds) (1995), *New Management in the Human Services* (Washington, DC: National Association of Social Workers Press).

Kirk, S.A. and Reid, W.J. (eds) (2002), *Science and Social Work: A Critical Appraisal* (New York: Columbia University Press).

Kirkvold, M. et al., (eds) (1993), *Klokskap og kyndighet* (Oslo: AdNotam Gyldendal).

Kleinpeter, C.B. and Oliver, J. (2003), 'Site Development in a Distance Education Program', *Journal of Technology in Human Services* 22:1, 75–86.

Kleinpeter, C.B. and Potts, M.K. (2003), 'Teaching Practice Methods using Interactive Television: a Partial Replication Study', *Journal of Technology in Human Services* 22:1, 19–27.

Kolb, D. (1984*), Experiential Learning – Experience as the Source of Learning and Development* (Englewood Heights, NJ: Prentice-Hall).

Kraidy, M.M. (2005), *Hybridity, or the Cultural Logic of Globalization* (Philadelphia: Temple University Press).

Kretzer, L. (2005), 'Queen Mothers and Social Workers: A Potential Collaboration between Traditional Authority and Social Work in Ghana', *Chieftancy*, 1, 2004, University of Calgary. <http://dspace.ucalgary.ca/handle/1880/42980>, accessed 30 May 2006.

Kreuger, L.W. and Stretch, J.J. (2000), 'What is the Role of Hypertechnology in Social Work Today?', *Social Work* 45:5, 457–462.

Kummervold P.E. et al. (2002), 'Social Support in a wired world', *Nordic Journal of Psychiatry,* 56:1, 59–65.

Kunneman, H. (2005), 'Social Work as Laboratory for Normative Professionalisation', *Social Work & Society* 3:2, 191–200 <http://www.socwork.net/Kunneman2005.pdf>, accessed 15 June 2006.

Kvalbein, I.A. (1998), 'Allmennlærerutdanning som møter "moderne" lærere og 'postmoderne' studenter. Er modernismebegreper tjenlig for bedre å forstå lærerutdanning? *Norsk pedagogisk tidskrift* 82:4–5, 252–259.

Kyvik, S. (2006), *Endringsprosesser i høyskolesektoren i Vest-Europa*, (Oslo: NIFU STEP Arbeidsnotat, 7 2006) <http://www.nifustep.no/norsk/publikasjoner/ endringsprosesser_i_høyskolesektoren_i_vest_europa>, accessed 11 December 2006.

Labonté-Roset, C. (2004), 'Social Work Education and Training in Europe and the Bologna Process', *Social Work & Society*, 2:1, 98–103 <http://www.socwork.net/ labonté-roset2004pdf>, accessed 15 June 2006.

LaFrantiere, S. (2005), 'Cellphones Catapult Rural Africa to 21st century', *New York Times*, 25th August, <http://www.nytimes.com/2005/08/25/international/africa/ 25africa.html?%20ei=5088&en=cad54d043ab15f30&ex=1282622400&partner= rssny>.

Lang. P. (ed.) (2005), *Evidence-Based Social Work. Towards A New Professionalism?* (Bern: European Academic).

Larson, C. (1973), 'Heroic Ethnocentrism: The Idea of Universality in Literature', in Ashcroft et al. (eds).

Lauglo, J. (2000), 'Social Capital Trumping Class and Cultural Capital? Engagement with School among Immigrant Youth', in Baron, S., Field, J. and Schuller, T. (eds).

Lauvås, P. and Handal, G. (2000), *Veiledning og praktisk yrkesteori* (Oslo: Cappelen).

Lave, J. and Wenger, E. (1991), *Situated Learning: Legitimate Peripheral Participation* (Cambridge: Cambridge University Press).

Lave, J. (1997), 'Learning, Apprenticeship, Social Practice', *Nordisk Pedagogikk,* 17:3, 140–151.

Lea, M. R. and Nicoll, K. (2002), *Distributed Learning. Social and Cultural Approaches to Practice* (London: Routledge Falmer).

Lee, J. A. B. (2001), *The Empowerment Approach to Social Work Practice: Building the Beloved Community*, 2nd edition. New York: Columbia University Press.

Lee, P. R. (1929), 'Social Work: Cause and Function', in Lowry, F. (ed.).

Leonard, P. (1983), 'Sosialt arbeids teori og sosialdemokratiske ideologi. Historien om et symbiotisk forhold' in E. Vetvik (ed.).

Levin, I. and Trost, J. (1996), *Å forstå hverdagen* (Oslo: Tano-Aschehoug).

Ligon, J. et al. (1999), 'Comparing Student Evaluations of Distance Learning and Standard Classroom Courses in Graduate Social Work Education' *Journal of Teaching in Social Work Education* 19:1/2, 21–29.

Lindén, C. (2004), 'Empowerment eller evidens – spanningsfæltet inom socialt, *Nordisk Socialt Arbeid* 26: 3, 258–68.

Ljoså, E. (2001), 'Nettbasert læring – på markedets vilkår' in Alexandersen, J. et al.

Loizos, P. (2000), 'Are refugees social capitalists?' in Baron, S., Field, J. and Schuller, T. (eds).

Lorenz. W. (1994), Social Work in a Changing Europe (London: Routledge).

Lorenz, W. (2005a), 'Social Work and a New Social Order – Challenging Neo-liberalism's Erosion of Solidarity', *Social Work & Society* 3:1, 93–101, <http:// www.socwork.net/Lorenz2005.pdf>, accessed 15 June 2006.

Lorenz, W. (2005b), 'Social Work and the Bologna Process', *Social Work & Society* 3:2, 224–235 <http://www.socwork.net/Lorenz2005b.pdf>, accessed 15 June 2006.

Lowry, F. (ed.) (1939), *Readings in Social Case Work 1920–1938: Selected Reprints for the Practitioner* (New York: Columbia University Press).

Loxley, A. (1997), *Collaboration in Health and Welfare: Working with Difference* (London: Jessica Kingsley).

Ludvigsen, S.R. and Lundby, K. (2002), 'Forskning på nettbasert læring: Ny teknologi – ny social praksis'in *Apollon 1/02* <http://www.apollon.uio.no/2002_1/tema/nettbasert.shtml>, accessed 15 January 2003.

Lund, T.E. (2000), 'Den dresserte kroppens tale' *Prosa* 6:1, 26–31.

Lynn, R. (2001), 'Learning from a "Murry way"', *British Journal of Social Work* 31:6, 903–916.

Lyon, D. (1994), *Postmodernity* (Buckingham: Open University Press).

Lyons, K. (1999), *Social Work in Higher Education. Demise or Development?* (Aldershot: Ashgate).

Lyotard, J.-F. (1979), *The Postmodern Condition: A Report of Knowledge* (Manchester: Manchester University Press).

Lødemel, I. and Trickey, H. (eds) (2001), *An Offer You Can't Refuse: Workfare in International Perspective* (Bristol: Polity Press).

Løfsnæs, B. (2006), 'Hjelp din søster – kvinners styrke i et krigsherjet land', in Døhlie, E. and Askeland, G.A. (eds).

Macaulay, C. (2000), 'Transfer of Learning', in Cree, V. and Macaulay, C.

Macdonald, G. and Sheldon, B. with Gillespie, J. (1992), 'Contemporary Studies of the Effectiveness of Social Work', *British Journal of Social Work* 22:6, 615–643.

Madoc-Jones, I. and Parrot, L. (2005), 'Virtual Social Work Education – Theory and Experience', *Social Work Education* 24:7, 755–768.

Maidment, J. (2005), 'Teaching Social Work Online: Dilemmas and Debates, *Social Work Education* 24:2, 185–195.

Mandela, N. (1995), *Long Walk to Freedom* (London: Abacus).

Manthorpe, J. (2007), *Report of the International Social Care Workers' Seminar July 2006* (London: Kings College).

Mäntysaari, M. (2005), 'Propitious Omens? Finnish Social Work Research as a Laboratory of Change', *European Journal of Social Work* 8:3, 247–258.

Marsh, P. and Triseliotis, J. (1996), *Ready to Practise? Social Workers and Probation Officers: Their training and First Year in Work* (Aldershot: Gower).

Marsh, P. and Crow, G. (1997), *Family Group Conferences in Child Welfare* (Oxford: Blackwell).

Martin, E. P. and Martin, J.M. (1995), *Social Work and the Black Experience* (Washington DC: NASW Press).

Mattock, J. (ed.) (2003), *Cross-Cultural Communication: The Essential Guide to International Business* (London: Kogan Page).

Maxwell, J., Williams, L., Ring, K. and Cambridge, I. (2003), 'Caribbean Social Work Education. The University of the West Indies', *Caribbean Journal of Social Work* 2: July, 11–35.

Mayor, B. and Swann, J. (2002), 'The English Languages and 'Global' Teaching', in Lea and Nicoll (eds).

McCarty, D. and Clancy, C. (2002), 'Telehealth: Implications for Social Work Practice', *Social Work* 47:2, 153–160.

McFall, J.A. and Freddolino, P.P. (2000), 'Quality and Comparability in Distance Field Education: Lessons Learned from Comparing Three Program Sites', *Journal of Social Work Education* 36:2, 293–307.

McLaughlin, K. et al. (2002), *New Public Management: Current Trends and Future Prospects* (London: Routledge).

Meinert, R. et al. (2000), *Social Work. Seeking Relevance in the Twenty-First Century* (New York: Haworth Press).

Meland, P. (2001), 'Essaykunst fra Zygmunt Bauman' *Prosa* 7:2, 72–75.

Mendes, P. (2006), 'Welfare Lobby Groups Responding to Globalization: A Case Study of the Australian Council of Social Service (ACOSS)', *International Social Work* 49:6, 693–704.

Mesec, B. and Mesec, M. (2004), 'Conceptualization of the New Methods of Self-help Appearing on the Internet,' *European Journal of Social Work* 7:2, 195–209.

Messina, B.A. (2002), 'Distance Learning: An Option for your Future?' *Journal of PeriAnaesthesia Nursing* 17:5, 204–209.

Mezirow, J. and associates (2000), *Learning as Transformation: Critical Perspectives on a Theory in Progress* (San Francisco: Jossey-Bass).

Midgley, J. (1997), *Social Welfare in Global Context* (Thousand Oaks, CA: Sage).

Moll, P. (2003), 'Chaos Pilots for Training Social Entrepreneurs', *Institute for Social Inventions* www.globalideasbank.org/diyfut/DIY-229.HTML, accessed 5 January 2004.

Monroe, B. and Oliviere, D. (eds) (2007), *Resilience in Palliative Care* (Oxford: Oxford University Press).

Monzini, P. (2005), *Sex Traffic: Prostitution, Crime and Exploitation* (London: Zed Books).

Morgan, S. and Payne, M. (2002), 'Managerialism and State Social Work in Britain' *Hong Kong Journal of Social Work* 36:1/2, 27–44.

Moxnes, P. (1992), *Angst i individ, gruppe og organisasjon*, 2nd Edition, (Oslo: Forlaget Paul Moxnes).

Moxnes, P. (2000), *Læring og ressursutvikling i arbeidsmiljøet*, 2nd Edition. (Oslo: P. Moxnes).

Možina, M. (2002), 'Can we Remember Differently? A Case Study of the New Culture of memory in Voluntary Organisations', *International Journal of Social Welfare* 11:4, 310–20.

MRB Bedriftsutvikling (2001),'*Moderne ledelse og Innovasjonstrender – KaosPiloter og Jamming. Fra struktur mot frihet – fra gjenskaping mot nyskaping*' , *DeFacto* 2, 4.< http://www.sintefmrb.no/upload_images/18.pdf>, accessed 10 March 2007.

Muleya, W. (2006), 'A Comparative Study of Social Work Intervention in Context in Zambia and England', *International Social Work* 49:4, 445–457.

Mullen, E.J. and Dumpson, J.R. et al. (1972), *Evaluation of Social Intervention* (San Francisco: Jossey-Bass).

Mumm, A.M. and Kersting, R. (1997), 'Teaching Critical Thinking in Social Work Practice Courses', *Journal of Social Work Education* 33:1, 75–84.

Munn, P. (2000), 'Social Capital, Schools and Exclusions', in Baron, S., Field, J. and Schuller, T. (eds).

NASW (2007), *NASW Foundation National Programs Eileen Kelly International Social Work Program*, <http://www.naswfoundation.org/kelly.asp>, accessed 30 January 2007.

NCFGD (2006), *National Centre on Family Group Decisionmaking*, <http://www.americanhumane.org/site/PageServer?pagename=pc_fgdm>, accessed 26 August 2006.

Neuberger, J. (2004), *Dying Well: A Guide to Enabling a Good Death*, 2nd Edition. (Oxford: Radcliffe).

Newman, J. (2002), 'The New Public Management, Modernization and Institutional Change: Disruptions, Disjunctures and Dilemmas', in McLaughlin et al.

Ngoh-Tiong, T. and Rowland, A. (eds) (2004), *Social Work Around the World III* (Berne: IFSW Press).

Nickelsen, T. (2002), 'Hva skjer når læring flytter ut på nettet?' in *Apollon* 1–2, <http:/www.apollon.uio.no/2002_1/tema/ikt-pbl.shtml>, accessed 5 May 2003.

Niemi, H. and Tirri, K. (1997), 'Valmuedet opettajan ammattiin opettajien ja opettajien kouluttajien arvioimina', in Sinko, M. and Lehtinen, E.

Nimagadda, J. and Cowger, C. D. (1999), 'Cross-cultural Practice: Social Worker Ingenuity in the Indigenization of Practice Knowledge', *International Social Work* 42:3, 261–76.

Oduaran, A. (2006), 'Globalization and Lifelong Education: Reflection on some Challenges for Africa' in Jarvis, P.

Offer, J. (2006), *An Intellectual History of British Social Policy* (Bristol: Policy Press).

Ogden, T. (1998), 'Multisystemisk terapi', *Spesialpedagogen* 63: 5, 16–24.

Oravec, J.A. (2000), 'Online Counselling and the Internet: Perspectives for Mental Health Care Supervision and Education', *Journal of Mental Health* 9:2, 121–135.

Orcutt, B.A. (1990), *Science and Inquiry in Social Work Practice* (New York: Columbia University Press).

Osborne, A. (1985), *Distance Learning in Social Work Education* (London: CCETSW).

Osei-Hwedie, K. et al. (2006), 'Searching for Appropriateness in Social Work Education in Botswana: The Process of Developing a Master in Social Work (MSW) Programme in a 'Developing' Country', *Social Work Education* 25:6, 569–590.

Oterholm, I. (2005), 'Kritisk refleksjon på nett' (Copenhagen: Nordisk Socialhøjskole Committee's Conference 12th–14th August), <http://graphic.digicast.dk/graphic/dsh/doc/Inger_Oterholm.doc>, accessed 17 January 2006.

Owolabi, K.A. (2001), 'Globalization, Americanization and Western imperialism', *Journal of Social Development in Africa* 16:2, 71–92.

Page, R. (2004), 'Globalisation and Social Welfare', in George, V. and Page, R.M. (eds).

Pahl, J., Hasanbegovic, C. and Yu, M.-K. (2004),' Globalization and Family Violence', in George, V. and Page, R.M. (eds).

Palier, B. (1995), *Comparing Social Welfare Systems in Europe: Volume 1: Oxford Conference: France-United Kingdom* (Paris: Mission Recherche et Experimentation, Ministre des Affaires Socials, de la Sante et de la Ville).

Parton, N. (2006), *Safeguarding Childhood: Early Intervention and Surveillance in a Late Modern Society* (Basingstoke: Palgrave Macmillan).

Paulsen, M.F. (2000), *An International Analysis of Web-based Education and Strategic Recommendations for Future Development of Online Education* (Bærum: The NKI Internet College), <www.nettskolen.com/in-english/cisaer/abstract.htm>, accessed 5 January 2002.

Payne, M. (1995), 'Going Missing: Issues for Social Work and the Social Services', *British Journal of Social Work* 25:3, 333–48.

Payne, M. (1999), 'Social Construction in Social Work and Social Action', in Jokinen, I. et al. (eds).

Payne, M. (2005a), *The Origins of Social Work: Continuity and Change* (Basingstoke: Palgrave Macmillan).

Payne, M. (2005b), *Modern Social Work Theory*, 3rd Edition, (Basingstoke: Palgrave Macmillan).

Payne, M. (2006), *What is Professional Social Work?*, 2nd Edition, (Bristol: Policy Press).

Pearson, V. (1991), 'Western Theory, Eastern Practice: Social Group Work in Hong Kong', *Social Work with Groups* 14:2, 45–58.

Pearson, P. (1998), 'The Educational Orientation of Graduate Social Work Faculty', *Journal of Social Work Education*; 34: 3, 427–436.

Pease, B. and Fook, J. (eds) (1999), *Transforming Social Work Practice: Postmodern Critical Perspectives* (London: Routledge).

Perrons, D. (2004), *Globalization and Social Change: People and Places in a Divided World* (London: Routledge).

Petracchi, H. E. (2000), 'Distance Education: What do our Students tell us?' *Research on Social Work Practice* 10:3, 362–376.

Petracchi, H.E. and Patchner, M.E. (2001), 'A Comparison of Live Instruction and Interactive Televised Teaching: A 2-year Assessment of Teaching an MSW Research Methods Course', *Research on Social Work Practice* 11:1,108–117.

Phillipson, R. (1999), 'The Globalization of Dominant Languages', in Broch-Utne B. and Garbo, G. (eds).

Pine, B.A. and Healy, L.M. (2007), 'New Leadership for Human Services: Involving and Empowering Staff through Participatory Management', in Aldgate et al.

Polanyi, M. (1983), *The Tacit Dimension*, 2nd Edition, (Gloucester, MA.: Peter Smith).

Pollit, C. (2002), 'The New Public Management in International Perspective: An Analysis of Impacts and Effects', in McLaughlin et al.

Porter, R. (2000), *Enlightenment: Britain and the Creation of the Modern World* (London: Allen Lane).

Preston-Shoot, M. (2000), 'Stumbling Towards Oblivion or Discovering new Horizons? Observations on the Relationship between Social Work Education and Practice', *Journal of Social Work Practice* 14:2, 87–98.

Punie, Y. and Cabrera, M. (2006), 'The Future of ICT and Learning in the Knowledge Society, Report on a Joint DG JRC-DG EAC Workshop held in Seville, 20–21 October 2005', Brussels: *European Commission, Directorate-General: Joint Research Centre.*

Putnam, R.D. (2000), *Bowling Alone: The Collapse and Revival of American Community* (New York: Simon and Schuster).

Quinney, A. (2005), '"Placement Online": Student Experiences of a Website to Support Learning in Practice Settings', *Social Work Education* 24:4, 439-50.

Rafferty, J. et al. (2005), 'Towards eLearning: Opportunities and Challenges' in Burgess, H. and Taylor, I. (eds).

Rakhsh, S. (2003), 'MIRA counsellor from Iran', *Aftenposten 26 October 2003.*

Ramon, S. and S. Pathak (1997), 'Recent Trends in European Social Work', *International Perspectives* 8:1, 3–5.

Reamer, F.G. (1994), 'The Evolution of Social Work Knowledge', in Reamer, F.G. (ed.).

Reamer, F. G. (ed.) (1994), *The Foundations of Social Work Knowledge* (New York, Columbia University Press).

Redd Barna Nyheter (2006), <http://www.reddbarna.no/default.asp?V_ITEM_ID=11157>, *Gigantløft for barn i krig*, accessed 18 October 2006.

Reid, P.N. and Edwards, R.L. (2006), 'The Purpose of a School of Social Work – An American Perspective', *Social Work Education* 25:5, 461–484.

Reid, W.J. and Hanrahan, P. (1982), 'Recent Evaluations of Social Work: Grounds for Optimism', *Social Work* 27:328–40.

Reinoehl, R. and Shapiro, C.H. (1986), 'Interactive Videodiscs: A Linkage Tool for Social Work Education', *Journal of Social Work Education* 22:3, 61–67.

Rekkedal, T. (2001), 'Nettbasert undervisning og læring. Modeller og metoder for læring og undervisning på nettet – fra NKIs erfaringer' in Alexandersen, J. et al.

Rekkedal, T. and Møystad, E. (2002), 'Recruitment Barriers to Learning on the Internet II: Survey among Active Correspondence Students and Prospective Students at NKI', *Paper to the AECS Conference: Re-Thinking Distance Learning for the Next Millennium, Vienna, 24-26 June 1999*, <http://www.nettskolen.com/forskning/43(recruitment_barriers.html>, accessed 5 January 2003.

Ritzer, G. (2000), *The McDonaldization of Society,* 3rd Edition, (Thousand Oaks, CA: Pine Forge).

Roberts, R.W. and Nee, R.H. (eds) (1970), *Theories of Social Casework* (Chicago: University of Chicago Press).

Roberts-DeGennaro, M. et al. (2005), 'Using an Online Support Site to Extend the Learning to Graduate Field Practicum in the United States', *Social Work Education* 24:3, 327–342.

Roberts-DeGennaro, M. (2002), 'Constructing and Implementing a Web-based Graduate Social Policy Course: A Pilot Test in Cyberspace', *Social Policy Journal* 1:2, 73–90.

Robertson, R. (1992), *Globalization: Social Theory and Global Culture* (London: Sage).

Robinson, L. (1995), *Psychology for Social Workers: Black Perspectives* (London: Routledge).

Robinson, L. (1999), 'Racial Identity Attitudes and Interracial Communication: Implications for Social Work Practice in Britain', *European Journal of Social Work* 2:3, 315–326.

Rose, M.A. (1991), *The Post-modern and the Post-industrial* (Cambridge: Cambridge University Press).

Routh, R.V. (1941), *The Diffusion of English Culture Outside England: A Problem of Post-war Reconstruction*, in Phillipson, R. (1999).

Ruch, G. (2002), 'From Triangle to Spiral: Reflective Practice on Social Work Education, Practice and Research', *Social Work Education* 2:2, 199–216.

Ruch, G. (2005), 'Relationship-based Practice and Reflective Practice: Holistic Approaches to Contemporary Child Care Social Work', *Child and Family Social Work* 10:2, 111–123.

Said, E.W. (1978), *Orientalism* (New York: Random House).

Sainsbury, E. (1987), 'Client Studies: Their Contribution, and Limitations in Influencing Social Work Practice, *British Journal of Social Work* 17:6, 633–644.

Salomon, A. (1937), *Education for Social Work* (Zurich: International Committee of Schools of Social Work).

Satka, M. (1995), *Making Social Citizenship: Conceptual Practices from the Finnish Poor Law to Professional Social Work* (Jyväskylä: SoPhi).

Satka, M. and Karvinen, S. (1999) 'The Contemporary Reconstruction of Finnish Social Work Expertise', *European Journal of Social Work* 2:2, 119–129.

Satterwhite, R. and Schoech, D. (1995), 'Multimedia Training for Child Protective Social Workers: Results of Initial Development and Testing', *Computers in Human Services* 12:1/2, 81–97.

Schoech, D. and Helton, D. (2002), 'Qualitative and Quantitative Analysis of a Course Taught via Classroom and Internet Chatroom', *Qualitative Social Work* 1:1, 111–24.

Schön, D. (1987), *Educating the Reflective Practitioner* (San Francisco: Jossey-Bass Publishers).

Schön, D. (1991), *The Reflective Practitioner* (Aldershot: Arena).

Seden, J. and Ross, T. (2007), 'Active Service-User Involvement in Human Services: Lessons from Practice', in Aldgate et. al.

Seibel, F.W. and Lorenz, W. (eds) (1998), *Soziale Professionen für ein Soziales Europa* (Frankfurt: IKO).

Seim, S. (2007), 'Brukermedvirkning- et fremmedord for barn og ungdom i barnevernet' in Seim, S. and Slettebø, T. (eds).

Seim, S. and Slettebø, T. (eds) (2007), *Brukemedvirkning i barnevernet* (Oslo: Universitetsforlaget).

Sen, A. (1999), *Development as Freedom* (Oxford: Oxford University Press).

Setayesh, R. (2007), [untitled] <http://www.ipetitions.com/petition/CEDAW/signatures-16.html>, accessed 10 February 2007.

Sewpaul, V. (2003), 'The Caribbean-South African Diaspora: Towards Locally Specific Social Work Education and Practice', *Caribbean Journal of Social Work* 2: July, 123–42.

Sewpaul, V. (2005), 'Global Standards: Promise and Pitfalls for Re-inscribing Social Work into Civil Society', *International Journal of Social Welfare* 14:3, 210–217.

Sewpaul, V. and Hölscher, D. (2004), *Social Work in times of Neoliberalism: A Postmodern Discourse* (Pretoria: J.L. Van Schaik Publishers).

Sewpaul, V. and Jones, D. (2005), 'Policy Document: Global Standards for the Education and Training of the Social Work Profession', *International Journal of Social Welfare* 14:3, 218–230.

Shardlow, S.M. and Cooper, S. (2000), *A Bibliography of European Studies in Social Work* (Lyme Regis: Russell House).

Shardlow, S.M. and Walliss, J. (2003), 'Mapping Comparative Empirical Studies of European Social Work', *British Journal of Social Work* 33:7, 921–941.

Shipman, A. (2002), *The Globalization Myth* (Cambridge: Icon).

Shriver, J.M. (1987), 'Harry Lurie's Assessment and Prescription: An Early View of Social Workers' Roles and Responsibilities regarding Political Action', *Journal of Sociology and Social Welfare* 14:2, 111–127.

Shulman, L. (1999), *The Skills of Helping Individuals, Families, Groups, and Communities*, 4th Edition, (Itasca, Illinois: F.E. Peacock Publishers).

Siebert, D.C.and Spaulding-Givens, J. (2006), 'Teaching Clinical Social Work Skills Entirely Online: A Case Example', *Social Work Education* 25:1, 78–91.

Siegel, E. et al. (1998), 'Distance Learning in Social Work Education: Results and Implications of a National Survey', *Journal of Social Work Education* 34:1, 71–80.

Sim, S. (ed.) (1998), *The Icon Critical Dictionary of Postmodern Thought* (Cambridge: Icon).

Sinko, M. and Lehtinen, E. (1997), *The Challenges of ICT in Finish Education*, (Tampereen Yliopston opettajankoulutuslaitoksen jukaisuja 10) Juva: Atena, <www.sitra.fi/Julkaisut/sitra227.pdf>, accessed 5 January 2002.

Skjervheim, H. (1979), 'Kritikk', *PaxLeksikon* (Oslo: Pax Forlag).

Sklair, L. (2002), *Globalization: Capitalism and Its Alternative*, 3rd Edition (Oxford: Oxford University Press).

Skutnabb-Kangas, T. (1999), 'The Globalization of Language Rights' in Broch-Utne, B. and G. Garbo (eds).

Slettebø, T. (2007), 'Foreldres opplevelse av medvirkning i barnevernet', in Seim, S. and Slettebø, T. (eds).

Slettebø, T. and Seim, S. (2007), 'Brukermedvirkning i barnevernet' in Seim. S and Slettebø, T. (eds).

Slovic, P. (1999), 'Perceived Risk, Trust and Democracy' in Cvetkovich, G. and Löfstedt (eds).

Solomos, J. (2003), *Race and Racism in Britain*, 3rd Edition, (Basingstoke: Palgrave).

Solstad, D. (1997), 'Om meddelelsens problem', *3 essays. Skrift III* (Oslo: Forlaget).

Specht, H. and Courtney, M. (1994), *Unfaithful Angels: How Social Work Abandoned its Mission* (New York: Free Press).

St. meld. nr. 11 (2001–2002), *Kvalitetsreformen* ('the Quality Reform'). Oslo: Utdannings og torsknings departementet au 8 marc 2002.

Stiglitz, J. (2002), *Globalization and its Discontents* (New York: Norton).

Stjernø, S. (2005), *Solidarity in Europe. The History of an Idea* (Cambridge: Cambridge University Press).

Stocks, J.T. and Freddolino, P.P. (1998), 'Evaluation of a World Wide-Web-based Graduate Social Work Research Methods Course', *Computers in Human Services* 15:2/3, 51–69.

Stocks, J.T. and Freddolino, P.P. (2000), 'Enhancing Computer-mediated Teaching through Interactivity: The Second Iteration of a World Wide Web-based Graduate Social Work Course', *Research on Social Work Practice* 10:4, 505–18.

Stubbs, P. (2002), 'Globalisation, Memory and Welfare Regimes in Transition: Towards an Anthropology of Transnational Policy Transfers', *International Journal of Social Welfare*, 11:4, 321–330.

Szmagalski, J. (2004), 'Structural Problems in the Development of Social Work in Central Europe under Transformation. The Case of Poland', *Social Work & Society* 2:2, 243–49 <http://www.socwork.net/Szmagalski2004.pdf>, accessed 15 June 2006.

Taylor, B. (2000), *Reflective Practice: A Guide for Nurses and Midwives* (Buckingham: Open University Press).

Taylor, C. and White, S. (2000), *Practising Reflexivity in Health and Welfare: Making Knowledge* (Buckingham: Open University Press).

Taylor, I. (1996), 'Reflective Learning, Social Work Education and Practice in the 21st Century', in Gould, N. and Taylor, I.

Taylor, I., Sharland, E., Sebba, J. and Leriche, P. (2006), *The Learning, Teaching and Assessment of Partnership Work in Social Work Education* (London: Social Care Institute for Excellence).

Taylor, J.C. (2001), *Fifth Generation Distance Education,* (Higher education series Report No. 40 June, Australia Department of Education, Training and Youth Affaires, Higher Education Division). http://www.dest.gov.au/archive/highered/hes/hes40/hes40.pdf, accessed 20 March 2000.

Thurow, L.C. (1998), 'Economic Community and Social Investment', in Hesselbein, F. et al. (eds).

Thyer, B. (1994), 'Empiricists versus Social Constructionists: More Fuel to the Flames', *Families in Society* 75:5, 308–312.

Thyer, B.A. and Kazi, M.A.F. (eds) (2004), *International Perspectives on Evidence-Based Practice in Social Work* (Birmingham: Venture).

Tinto, V. (1997), 'Classrooms as Communities. Exploring the Educational Character of Student Persistence', *Journal of Higher Education* 68:6, 599–623.

Tranøy, K.E. (1988), 'Habermas, Jürgen', *Aschehoug og Gyldendal Store Norske Leksikon* (Oslo: Kunnskapsforlaget).

Trinder, L. (2000), 'Introduction: The Context of Evidence-based Practice' in Trinder, L. and Reynolds, S. (eds).

Trinder, L. and Reynolds, S. (eds) (2000), *Evidence-Based Practice: A Critical Appraisal* (Oxford: Blackwell).

Tronvoll, I.M. et al. (eds) (2004), *Hjelp i kontekst. Praksis, refleksjon og forskning* (Indre Billefjord: Idut).

Tronvoll, I.M. and Marthinsen, E. (eds) (2001), *Sosialt Arbeid - Refleksjoner og nyere forskning,* Trondheim, Tapir Akademisk Forlag.

Tutu, D. (2003), 'Chairperson's Forward' in Truth and Reconciliation Commission of South Africa', *Report* <http://www.info.gov.za/otherdocs/2003/trc/>, accessed 22 March 2007.

Twine, F. (1994), *Citizenship and Social Rights: The Interdependence of Self and Society* (London: Sage).

UddannelsesGuiden.dk (2006), *Uddannelses Guiden* http://www.ug.dk/Vejlednings-portal/Elementer/S%c3%b8gesider/Friteksts%c3%b8gning.aspx?FullTextSearch Str=kaospilot, accessed 10 March 2007.

Ulrich, D. (1998), 'Six Practices for Creating Communities of Value, not Proximity' in Hesselbein, F. et al. (eds).

Universities and Colleges Act, No 22 of 12 May 1995 (Norway).

Vetvik, E. (1983), *Synspunktet på sosialt arbeid* (Oslo: Diakonhjemmets sosialhøgskole).

Vince, R. (2002), 'Organizing Reflection', *Management Learning* 33:1, 63–78.

Walton, R. and el Nasr, M. (1988), 'Indigenization and authentization in terms of social work in Egypt', *International Social Work* 31:2, 135-44.

Ward, C. (2001), *The Impact of International Students on Domestic Students and Host Education: A literature Review. Prepared for the New Zealand Ministry of Education* (Wellington: Victoria University of Wellington) <http://www.vuw.ac.nz/cacr/reports/docs/Ward-2001.pdf>, accessed 29 January 2007.

Warren, J. (2007), *Service User and Carer Participation in Social Work* (Exeter: Learning Matters).

Washington, J. and Paylor, I. (1999), 'Europe, Social Exclusion and the Identity of Social Work', *European Journal of Social Work* 1:3, 327–338.

Webb, S. A. (2001), 'Some Considerations on the Validity of Evidence-based Practice in Social Work', *British Journal of Social Work* 31:1, 57–79.

Webb, S. (2003), 'Local Orders and Global Chaos in Social Work', *European Journal of Social Work* 6:2, 191–204.

Weiner, M.E. and Petrella, P. (2007), 'The Impact of New Technology: Implications for Social Work and Social Care Managers' in Aldgate et al.

White, S., Fook, J. and Gardener, F. (eds) (2006), *Critical Reflection in Health and Welfare* (Maidenhead: Open University Press).

Wilkinson, R. (1996), *Unhealthy Societies: The Afflictions of Inequality* (London: Routledge).

Williams, L. (2007), '"Home Alone" Childhood Migration and the Experience of Coming Home', in Dominelli, L. (ed.).

Wolf, M. (2005), *Why Globalization Works* (New Haven, CT: Yale University Press).

Wolfson, G.K. et al. (2005), 'Changing the Nature of the Discourse: Teaching Field Seminars Online,' *Journal of Social Work Education* 41:2, 355–361.

Wong, Y.C. (2004), 'Engaging Students in a Virtual Classroom: The Use of Bulletin Boards in Teaching and Learning for Chinese Learners', *Journal of Technology in Human Services* 22:3, 41–67.

Wong, Y.C. and Law, C.K. (1999), 'Learning Social Work Online: A WebCT Course on Policy Issues among Chinese Students', *New Technology in Human Services* 11:14, 18–24.

Yip, K.S. (2004), 'A Chinese Cultural Critique of the Global Qualifying Standards for Work Education', *Social Work Education* 23:5, 597–612.

Yu, N.G. (2006a), 'Ideological Roots of Philippine Social Welfare', *International Social Work* 49:5, 559–570.

Yu, N.G. (2006b), 'Interrogating Social Work: Philippine Social Work and Social Human Rights under Martial Law', *International Journal of Social Welfare* 15:3, 257–263.

Zahl, M. and Furman, L.D. (2005), 'Koblingen mellom sosialt arbeid og religion/ livssyn: et tilbakelagt stadium eller del av et helhetssyn?, *Nordisk Sosialt Arbeid* 25:2, 98–109.

Zaviršek, D. (1999), 'Civil Society, Memory and Social Work', in Lešnik, B.(ed.) *International Perspectives in Social Work: Social Work and the State* (Brighton: Pavilion).

Author Index

Aase, T. 74-5
Adams, J. 29
Agger, B. 37
Alexander, J. 28
Alexandersen, J.
Algie, J. 105
Argyis, C. 35
Ashcroft, 17, 59
Ashford, M. 112
Askeland, G. A. 27, 33, 36, 39, 41, 42, 43,
    80, 85, 100, 113, 126, 132-3
Askheim, O. 93
Atherton, C. 103

Baldwin, M. 39, 95
Barnes, J. 87
Barnett, R. 36
Bass, B. 98
Baudrillard, J. 26
Baumann, Z. 37, 115
Bernard, W. 119
Bgoya, W. 57-8
Biestek, F. 80
Black-Hughes, C. 39, 146
Bolland, K. 103
Bootle, K. 147
Bourn, D. 145, 147
Boyne, R. 22-3
Bradley, G. 41
Braye, S. 93, 96
Brechin, A. 64
Broch-Utne, B. 58
Brookfield, S. 36-8, 43, 44, 56, 90
Burr, V. 38

Cabrera, M. 99, 138, 143, 146, 147
Castles, S. 50
Clancy, C. 137, 148
Cox, D. 48
Craib, I. 29
Cree, V. 87, 92, 100
Crow, G. 15

Davidson, A. 50
Davis, A. 87, 92, 100
Derrida, J. 26, 38
Døhlie, E. 126, 132, 133
Dominelli, L. 85, 86, 87, 119
Dreyfus, H. 111, 147

Edwards, R. L. 83, 84, 88, 111
Edwards, R. 103, 110, 113
el Nasr, M. 5
Elkjær, B. 41, 43
Eraut, M. 35, 111

Faux, T. 139, 146
Firth, R. 34, 92
Fischer, J. 63, 64
Fisher, W. 19, 20-1
Fisher, M. 42-3, 93
Flanagan, J. 39, 42
Fook, J. 33, 34, 37, 39, 42, 43, 44, 115
Ford, P. 33, 36, 38
Freddolino, P. 139, 145
Furman, L. 97

Giddens, A. 11, 29, 109
Glans, K. 105, 110, 116
Gould, N. 35, 39, 95
Graham, M. 4, 17, 53, 97
Gray, M. 5
Gross, E. 91

Habermas, J. 35-6, 37
Hall, E. 132, 133
Hall, S. 22-3
Halmi, A. 104
Hanrahan, P. 64
Harris, J. 82, 85, 86, 89-90, 111
Hassan, I 26
Healy, K. 33, 35, 96, 98
Healy, L. 81, 82, 83, 87, 94
Hopkins, D. 16
How, A. 37

Subject Index